What Others Are Saying About
A Parent's Guide to Preventing Homosexuality

"Every concerned parent will benefit from this practical parenting advice on how to help a child develop a secure gender identity that leads to a normal heterosexual orientation in adulthood.

"Dr. Nicolosi is an internationally recognized professional expert on therapies that promote normal heterosexual adjustment. He is known for his long-standing leadership in a key professional association that applies scientific findings to psychosexual adjustment. But his breadth of technical scientific knowledge is combined with years of extensive clinical experience helping everyday people.

"This combination has enabled the authors to explain psychological research findings to parents in a very practical way. Their book provides clear guidance on what parents can do to promote their child's sexual adjustment."

George A. Rekers, Ph.D., Professor of Neuropsychiatry and Behavior Science, University of South Carolina School of Medicine

"Utilizing an eclectic form of psychotherapy based on psychoanalytic principles, Dr. Nicolosi has shown how homosexual impulses and enactments can be modified or, in some instances, removed. This gives hope to parents of gender-disturbed children who have previously succumbed to despair.

"There are numerous clinical vignettes throughout the book presented in a highly readable and scientific manner. I most heartily recommend it."

Charles W. Socarides, M.D., former Clinical Professor of Psychiatry, Albert Einstein College of Medicine/Montefiore Medical Center, New York, and Fellow, American Psychiatric Association

"To get to [the issue of sexual-identity disorder and what can be done to help], we will turn to the very best resource for parents and teachers I have found. It is provided in an outstanding book titled *A Parent's Guide to Preventing Homosexuality,* written by clinical psychologist Joseph Nicolosi, Ph.D., and Linda Ames Nicolosi.

"Dr. Nicolosi is, I believe, the foremost authority on the prevention and treatment of homosexuality today. This book offers practical advice and a clear-eyed perspective on the antecedents of homosexuality. I wish every parent would read it, especially those who have reason to be concerned about their sons. Its purpose is not to condemn but to educate and encourage moms and dads."

Dr. James Dobson, President, Focus on the Family, quoted in *Bringing Up Boys: Practical Advice and Encouragement for Those Shaping the Next Generation of Men*

"In *A Parent's Guide to Preventing Homosexuality,* based on his many years of specialization, Dr. Nicolosi has translated the vocabulary of research science into plain English, easily understandable to the lay public. Though the book is primarily oriented to the needs of dads and moms concerned about a child's gender development, it is also a guide for good parenting in general.

"In well-described, clear accounts of his clinical sessions and discussions of the theories he does and does not support, Dr. Nicolosi has contributed a most valuable addition to the sexuality literature. More important, it should prove invaluable to all those concerned with child rearing, development, and education."

Toby B. Bieber, Ph.D., clinical psychologist, and coauthor of *Homosexuality: A Psychoanalytic Study of Male Homosexuals*

"As a clinical professor of psychiatry, I heartily endorse Dr. Nicolosi's effort at the prevention of homosexuality. Parents should be aware of the warning signs and the possibility of modifying their child's gender identity, thus making the choice, should they desire it, to maximize the child's likelihood of growing up heterosexual.

"Making this choice is not 'homophobic.' It is a commonsense approach to parenting that fits the value systems of many families. In writing this book, the authors have broken important ground."

A. Dean Byrd, Ph.D., MBA, vice president of the National Association of Research and Therapy of Homosexuality (NARTH)

"Joseph and Linda Ames Nicolosi have written a wonderful, *accurate* book on homosexuality and the significance of the parental role.

"Human beings who are born with one type of sexual equipment do not attempt to change *unless* there are serious problems in their early experience, especially in relation to parents.

"I believe it is imperative that at the very first signs of deviance, parents take themselves to a psychiatrist knowledgeable about this problem and make every effort to become aware of what may be damaging in their relationships with the child in question.

"I conclude with a 'bravo.'"

Natalie Shainess, M.D., psychiatrist; psychoanalyst; author on sex and gender issues

"Dr. Nicolosi's principles on the prevention of homosexuality would benefit any parent of a young son to raise him with a healthy sense of gender identity. I wish my parents had had this material when I was in my formative years. The practical knowledge and timeless—but often unknown—principles would have saved me from years of heartache when, as an adult, I began the tough road to overcome my homosexual struggle. Joseph and Linda Nicolosi's book should be required reading for all education classes on child development."

John Paulk, Homosexuality and Gender Specialist, Focus on the Family, former chair of the North American Board of Exodus International, and author of *Love Won Out*

"*A Parent's Guide to Preventing Homosexuality* meets a great need of the hour for parents. It offers insights into the parent/child conflicts and personality mismatches that can set the stage for same-sex attractions. The authors' use of parents' diaries in describing successes, struggles, and even failure provides down-to-earth, practical advice for addressing prevention at the root level.

"The understanding that can be gained from this book will go a very long way toward eliminating pain and frustration in families, while defining the healthy nurturing that is so essential to reinforcing every child's unique personality and sexual identity."

Don Schmierer, author, *An Ounce of Prevention* and *What's a Father to Do: Facing Parents' Tough Issues*

"This book meets a great need. It is sound scientifically, countering the abundant misinformation on the subject of homosexuality with which the public is currently inundated.

"What it provides that no parent can find in any library, however, is what to do when one's own child seems to be developing in a homosexual direction. Dr. Nicolosi draws upon many years of clinical experience to offer parents clear guidelines on evaluating and then reacting constructively to the situation. The authors' points are practical and down-to-earth but always respectful of parents in their struggle to help their children.

"I believe this book will become a classic in the literature that parents will consult far into the future. It may be an eye-opener to many in the mental health professions as well."

Johanna Krout Tabin, Ph.D., ABPP, board and faculty member of the Chicago Center for Psychoanalysis, and former chief psychologist, Chicago Psychological Institute

"The Nicolosis have written a groundbreaking book. The authors challenge the American Psychological Association, rightly, on their narrow, totalitarian attitude about homosexuality.

"The authors make an excellent case that a significant number of homosexuals develop their identity from defective parenting, and that many such homosexuals later wish to change their orientation. They also lay out useful strategies to help parents both prevent, and in some instances reverse, homosexual development. For parents concerned with this issue, their book is a must."

Paul C. Vitz, Ph.D., Professor of Psychology, New York University, author of *Psychology as Religion: The Cult of Self-Worship*

"I am pleased to give my strong endorsement of the book *A Parent's Guide to Preventing Homosexuality*. Dr. Nicolosi is an experienced psychologist who is an expert in treatment of persons with gender-identity disorder, both children and youth, and also adults who seek to overcome unwanted feelings of same-sex attraction.

"He is the president of the National Association for Research and Therapy of Homosexuality, the leading national association of professional psychiatrists, psychologists and therapists devoted to providing professional help and treatment to individuals struggling with undesired same-sex attraction, gender-identity disorders and other homosexual behavioral issues. Thus highly respected by his peers, Dr. Nicolosi is eminently qualified to write this book.

"To help children and youth today cope with the tremendous stresses that create ambiguities and confusion regarding gender identity and sexual orientation, parents need to have more understanding of the process of gender development than earlier generations had. *A Parent's Guide to Preventing Homosexuality* by Joseph and Linda Nicolosi provides that kind of useful information for parents in the twenty-first century, not only for family and friends of children and adolescents who may be struggling with gender identity, but also for lawmakers, policymakers, schoolteachers, lawyers, and judges, who need to understand the complex processes of gender-identity development that are challenged today as they have never been in the past.

"I highly recommend this extremely interesting and very readable guide."

Lynn D. Wardle, Professor of Law, J. Reuben Clark Law School, Brigham Young University, and secretary-general, International Society of Family Law

"With such sagacity acquired over years and thousands of hours of working with gender-identity disorders, Dr. Nicolosi utilizes acumen with theory and practicality to present a most readable book explicit in its purpose in the prevention of gender-identity disorders. I commend it as a primer in infant and child rearing for all parents concerned with the appropriate sexual orientation of their growing children."

Benjamin Kaufman, M.D., Clinical Professor, Department of Psychiatry, University of California at Davis School of Medicine

A PARENT'S GUIDE TO
Preventing
HOMOSEXUALITY

Joseph Nicolosi, Ph.D., & Linda Ames Nicolosi

IVP Books
An imprint of InterVarsity Press
Downers Grove, Illinois

InterVarsity Press
P.O. Box 1400, Downers Grove, IL 60515-1426
World Wide Web: www.ivpress.com
E-mail: email@ivpress.com

InterVarsity Press® is the book-publishing division of InterVarsity Christian Fellowship/USA®, a student movement active on campus at hundreds of universities, colleges and schools of nursing in the United States of America, and a member movement of the International Fellowship of Evangelical Students. For information about local and regional activities, write Public Relations Dept., InterVarsity Christian Fellowship/USA, 6400 Schroeder Rd., P.O. Box 7895, Madison, WI 53707-7895, or visit the IVCF website at <www.intervarsity.org>.

Cover photograph: ImageState
ISBN-10: 0-8308-2379-4
ISBN-13: 978-0-8308-2379-6

Printed in the United States of America ∞

Library of Congress Cataloging-in-Publication Data

Nicolosi, Joseph.
 A parent's guide to preventing homosexuality / Joseph Nicolosi and
Linda Ames Nicolosi.
  p. cm.
Includes bibliographical references and index.
 ISBN 0-8308-2379-4 (pbk.: alk. paper)
 1. Sexual orientation. 2. Gender identity. 3. Homosexuality. I.
Nicolosi, Linda Ames, 1947- II. Title.
 HQ16 .N45 2002
 306.76—dc21

                                                                                    2002009337

P	24	23	22	21	20	19	18	17	16	15	14	13	12	11	10	9	8
Y	22	21	20	19	18	17	16	15	14	13	12	11	10	09	08	07	06

We are honored to have been given the joy

and responsibility of bringing up our son, Joseph Jr.,

to whom this book is affectionately dedicated.

Contents

ACKNOWLEDGMENTS

We wish to thank Lela Gilbert for her skill and patience in the preparation of the first draft of this book. Our heartfelt appreciation also goes out to Don Schmierer for his encouragement, support, and belief in the importance of a book for parents as well as his confidence that we could carry this work forward. And we are especially grateful to Richard Wyler, who permitted us to quote extensively from the insightful personal stories on his website, <www.peoplecanchange.com>.

INTRODUCTION
For Parents: Words to the Wise

Jacob, a twenty-five-year-old client, had been in treatment for several months because of depression about his unwanted homosexuality. One day—driven by feelings of both sadness and anger—he confronted his mother:

> I told her, "Mom, you saw me play with Barbie dolls. You allowed me to use makeup and to fix my hair in front of the mirror for hours. My brothers never did any of this. Why didn't you stop me? What were you thinking?"
>
> I have no doubt that Mom had wanted the best for me. But she had nothing to say. She just sat there and looked at me, stunned and tearful.

For many years, I[1] have worked with homosexual men who are profoundly dissatisfied by their same-sex attractions. Gay life did not work for them, and they all suspected, on some level, that events in their early lives had laid the foundation for their homosexual feelings. This book flows directly from what I have learned from my two decades of work with these men, as they attempted to grasp the causes of their same-sex attraction and achieve progressive freedom. Again and again, these men have taught me what was missing in their boyhoods.

The life stories I hear every day, told by men like Jacob who are struggling to heal their homosexuality, typically include painful memories of gender confusion. The fact is, there is a high correlation between gender nonconformity in boyhood and adult homosexuality. Most of the men I counsel were not as feminine in boyhood as Jacob—they did not play with dolls or dress like girls. But just the same, there were telltale signs of conflict and doubt about claiming their gender; particularly, there was a disturbing fear that they somehow did not fit in with other boys.

And yet their parents—the vast majority of whom loved their children very much and sought the best for them—often missed the early warning signs and waited too long to seek help for their children. One reason for this is that the mental health profession is not telling them the truth about their children's gender confusion. Parents have no idea what, if anything, to do about it.

Perpetuating Gender Stereotypes?

We cannot go along with people who—many of them within the mental health profession—say that each of us can "be whatever we want to be," in terms of gender identity or sexual orientation. They speak as if being gay or lesbian did not have the deepest consequences for us as individuals, for our culture, and for the human race. They speak as if our anatomy was in no way our destiny. They imply that when we help our children to grow more fully into the maleness or femaleness that is their created destiny, we are merely perpetuating outdated gender stereotypes.

But the human race was designed male and female; there is no third gender. Furthermore, civilization has shown us that the natural human family (father, mother and children), with all its faults, is the best possible environment for the nurturing of future generations. Have we really gotten it all wrong for so many hundreds of centuries? Are we going to cast all of history aside, in favor of the latest TV show about the glories of gender bending?

As one prominent psychoanalyst, Dr. Charles Socarides, says, "Nowhere do parents say, 'It makes no difference to me if my child is homosexual or heterosexual.' "[2] Given a choice, most parents would prefer that their children not find themselves involved in homosexual behavior.

It is fashionable in intellectual circles to believe that we human beings have no innate "human nature" and that the essence of being human is the freedom to redefine ourselves as we wish. But what good can freedom bring us, if it is used in defiance of who we are?

Some things, we would argue, are not redefinable. If indeed normality is "that which functions according to its design"—and we believe that to be true—then nature calls upon us to fulfill our destinies as male and female.

In this book we will use the following terms interchangeably: *prehomosexual, gender-conflicted, gender-confused,* and *gender-disturbed.* All of those conditions have the potential to lead to a homosexual outcome. *Gender-identity disorder* (GID) refers to a psychiatric condition that is an extreme example of this same problem of internal gender conflict. In GID the child is unhappy with his or her biological sex. Many of the children we describe—in the course of their development toward homosexuality—fell short of the strict criteria for a clinical diagnosis of GID, but the warning signs of gender conflict and homosexuality were there nonetheless.

At Odds with the Mental Health Profession

Today's mass media convey the message that men ought to be encouraged to discover a homosexual or bisexual identity. "Isn't sexual diversity wonderful?" they ask. A number of TV and movie producers (some of whom are gay themselves) try to persuade us with idealized coming-out-of-the-closet stories. We believe their efforts are misguided attempts to encourage what is actually the unfortunate situation in which too many of our young people find themselves.

Of course, in taking this view, I (Joseph) am often at odds with members of my own profession. Those who oppose me say the 1973 decision by the American Psychiatric Association (APA) to remove homosexuality from the *Diagnostic and Statistical Manual* (DSM) has settled the issue: homosexuality is normal. But that 1973 decision was made (as even some gay activists have noted) under heavy political pressure from gay activism.[3]

The removal of homosexuality from the DSM had the effect of discouraging treatment and research. When it became "common knowledge" that homosexuality was "not a problem," clinicians were discouraged—and in many cases, prevented—from expressing opinions to the contrary or presenting papers at professional meetings. Soon scientific journals became largely silent on homosexuality as a developmental problem.

In fact, as of this writing, the American Psychological Association refuses to cooperate in any way with the National Association of Research and Therapy of Homosexuality (NARTH) because they disagree with NARTH's view that the condition is a developmental disorder. Furthermore, they believe that a sci-

entific position of this sort "contributes to the climate of prejudice and discrimination to which gay, lesbian and bisexual people are subject."[4] In effect, the
APA has placed a moratorium on debate about this subject.

This silence among researchers was not brought about by new scientific evidence showing homosexuality to be a healthy variant of human sexuality.
Rather, it became fashionable simply not to discuss the condition anymore as
a problem. Homosexuality was reported and discussed the way one reports the
evening news—as something that "just is," like the next day's weather.

Ronald Bayer, a researcher from the Hastings Center for Ethics in New
York, summarized the entire process. "The American Psychiatric Association,"
wrote Bayer, "had fallen victim to the disorder of a tumultuous era, when disruptive elements threatened to politicize every aspect of American social life. A
furious egalitarianism . . . compelled psychiatric experts to negotiate the pathological status of homosexuality with homosexuals themselves."

The result—homosexuality's removal from the psychiatric manual of disorders—came about not through a rational process of scientific reasoning, "but
was instead an action demanded by the ideological temper of the times."[5]

Prevention: A Growing Need

Before the APA's decision in 1973, it was accepted practice to try to prevent
homosexuality. The condition was a disorder, and disordered sexual-identity
development should be avoided whenever possible. Today, we believe it is time
that this idea of prevention be revisited. It is for that purpose that we have written this book.

Few previous books have been written for parents other than the 1968 classic *Growing Up Straight* by Peter and Barbara Wyden. Since the removal of homosexuality from the diagnostic manual, the only book written by a clinician
on prevention has been Dr. George Rekers's *Growing Up Straight: What Every
Family Should Know About Homosexuality* (Chicago: Moody Press, 1982). Then
there was a recent book aimed at Christian families, *An Ounce of Prevention* by
Don Schmierer (Nashville: Word, 1998), which offers scientifically grounded
words of practical wisdom from a seasoned pastoral counselor.

Now, we hope that *Preventing Homosexuality* will continue to respond to this
growing need. Most of the parents of prehomosexual children who come to us
for help are people of religious faith—Catholic, Protestant, Mormon, Jewish—
but a few, too, are secularists who intuitively sense that humankind is designed

to be heterosexual. We can empathize with these parents' concern because we share their worldview.

Yet some gay activists (mostly within academic circles) will condemn us for taking this position. Who are we to call someone's sexual identity into question, much less help a child to avoid it, or an adult homosexual to change it? But we take our stand with history and with the majority of the population that thinks same-gender sex is something that hurts people.

We have included many clients' testimonies to illustrate the chapters in this book. Naturally, names, places and any identifying details have been changed to protect their privacy. But be assured that their stories are true.

This book's focus on the role of parents is not intended to *blame* but to *educate*. Not one of the parents I worked with had wished to influence his or her child—or even to *fail to intervene* where intervention was necessary—in a way that could lay the foundation for future homosexuality. But despite the best of intentions, many remained trapped in harmful family patterns. And indeed many were sadly misinformed, believing that nothing could be done to influence a child's sexual-identity development. The reasons for this truly shameful lack of accurate information from the mental health profession are discussed in chapter eight, "The Politics of Treatment."

Thankfully, we have found that once parents are given accurate advice, they quickly make changes and proceed enthusiastically toward helping their child develop a healthy gender identity. One father acknowledged that his "gut" told him something was wrong, and he indeed sensed what he needed to do, but he heard nothing but warnings from teachers and counselors not to "traumatize your son" but rather to accept him "for who he is."

But when parents consult with a psychotherapist who validates their desire for heterosexuality in their child, and who offers specific guidance to what they intuitively know they should do in response to his gender confusion, there is hope for a heterosexual outcome. Once they have found professional support for their parental intuition, these mothers and fathers immediately grasp their therapist's treatment plan. They are more than willing to begin applying the positive and affirming strategies that have been outlined for them. This book contains many of those same intervention strategies.

Dr. George Rekers, a nationally known expert on sexual disorders, writes that "gender nonconformity in childhood may be the single most common observable factor associated with homosexuality." And there is considerable evidence, he asserts, that the child with a gender-identity problem *can* resolve the difficulty—with or without psychiatric intervention. Rekers reports, "In a sizable number of cases . . . the gender-identity disorder resolves fully."

Although biological factors *do* have a predisposing effect in some children, Dr. Rekers believes change is possible because family and social influences appear to have the most powerful influence in the development of homosexuality. Most parents hope for heterosexuality for their children, he notes, and the therapist should not direct the course of treatment to work against the parents' values.[6]

In addition, Dr. Rekers believes that when the therapist is working with a teenager, he should clarify some important points:

- There are life-threatening health risks associated with a gay lifestyle.
- A gay lifestyle adjustment will be difficult and socially controversial.
- Premature sexual activity is psychologically risky.
- The client will be much better able to make wise choices in adulthood about his sexuality.

The bulk of research on gender identity has been with boys. Male homosexuality is, in fact, my own clinical specialty; therefore, most of the advice within this book is about boys. We hope that another writer will carry our work further to more fully investigate lesbianism and its prevention.

Perhaps you are concerned about your child and his or her sexual development. Maybe your son or daughter is saying things like "I must be gay" or "I'm bisexual." You have found same-sex porn in his room. You have found intimate journal entries about another girl in your daughter's diary. The most important message we can offer is that there is no such thing as a "gay child" or a "gay teen." We are all designed to be heterosexual. Confusion about gender is primarily a psychological condition, and to some extent, it can be modified.

We think you will find the information in the pages that follow to be both encouraging and affirming. In reading these stories, you may see something of your own son or daughter and be motivated to more strongly affirm that child's healthy, sex-appropriate gender development.

In closing, we wish to reiterate that we have strong philosophical differences with the American Psychological Association, of which I am a member. They have taken a one-sided, gay-affirming stance in recent years, supporting a political philosophy that actively promotes gay marriage, gay adoption and the normalization of homosexuality, while stigmatizing traditional values and eroding the nuclear family model. The APA's positions are not purely scientific stances, since none of these are strictly scientific matters; they represent the APA's political-philosophical opinions and its own sexual-liberationist values.

The APA's political control over the free flow of ideas has in fact grown so oppressive in recent years that we would call it less of a scientific group than a professional trade guild whose goal is to advance a liberal political agenda within our society. In fact, in a rare article of rebuke published in a major professional journal, one bold psychologist-critic charged that the APA's lack of respect for viewpoint diversity actually "biases research on social issues, damages psychology's credibility with policymakers and the public, impedes serving conservative clients, results in *de facto* discrimination against conservative students and scholars, and has a chilling effect on liberal education."[7]

In writing this book, we have made every effort to represent the scientific data in a fair and accurate manner. We do not wish to imply that the model of prehomosexuality described here is the only pathway to homosexuality. However, we believe this model is the most common one. Nor do we wish to imply that there is one easy answer that will prevent homosexual development. What you, as a parent, can do is provide the optimum environment that is within your ability to provide.

If you agree with us that normality is "that which functions according to its design," and that nature calls us to fulfill our gendered destinies as male and female, then we invite you to read on. As parents ourselves, our goal is to offer you hope, support, education, and encouragement.

Note: As you've probably already observed, this book sometimes uses "I" and sometimes "we" in expressing authorship. This alternation is not as random as it may appear. The "I" represents Joseph Nicolosi speaking; all other sections represent the contributions of both authors.

1

MASCULINITY
IS AN ACHIEVEMENT

A woman is, but a man must become. Masculinity is risky and elusive.
It is achieved by a revolt from a woman, and it is confirmed only by other men.

CAMILLE PAGLIA, LESBIAN ACTIVIST

At the very heart of the homosexual condition is conflict about gender. In the boy, we usually see a gender wound that traces back to childhood. He comes to see himself as different from other boys.

Gender woundedness usually exists as a silent, secret fear—one that the boy's parents and loved ones only vaguely suspect. The boy has felt this way for as long as he is able to remember. That differentness creates a feeling of inferiority and isolates him from other males.

For some little boys, the gender confusion is obvious. Let me begin with the stories of a few of my clients, starting with "Stevie," whose case is unusually dramatic.

As a clinical psychologist who has treated hundreds of dissatisfied adult homosexual men, I get phone calls from all over the world. But with increasing frequency, the request concerns a child. Most of the people who call me are dedicated parents who want the best for their child, and I strive to guide, educate and support them.

The particular caller one day, my secretary informed me, was from nearby

Pasadena, California. I picked up the receiver and heard a woman's voice on the other end of the line.

"Doctor, my name is Margaret Johnson," she began. Her voice quavered, and for one long moment, I thought we might have been disconnected.

"Are you there? Can I help you?"

"Well, I . . . I think I saw you a couple of weeks ago on television. That was you, wasn't it? You were debating a psychiatrist?"

"It's possible," I said. I had been on a national TV show two weeks before, jousting with a gay activist who had become a familiar figure on the talk show circuit.[1] "You probably mean the debate with Dr. Isay."

"Yes," she said. "You were on a show that talked about little boys who want to be little girls."

"That's right," I said. "We were doing a show about gender confusion and—"

This time Mrs. Johnson spoke up with determination and urgency. "Doctor, you were describing my son Stevie. He's a beautiful little boy, a special child. But . . ." She hesitated. "Stevie's fascinated with little-girl things. Even more so than my daughters. In fact, he just loves the colors pink and red. He even . . . well, plays with Barbie dolls and . . . dances around the house on tiptoes like a ballerina."

As I listened, Mrs. Johnson gave me a few more specifics. Her son was five. "I've been noticing this kind of behavior for almost two years," she explained.

To me, that length of time was significant. It is okay if a little boy wonders what he would look like wearing long blonde curls and so he tries on a wig, simply to be silly. There is nothing particularly alarming about that. But if he keeps on doing it and has little interest in "boy" things, there likely is a problem.[2]

"This has been going on for two years?" I asked.

I think Mrs. Johnson misinterpreted my question as a rebuke. She sounded a little defensive. "But his teacher said not to worry, it was just a passing phase. So did my mother-in-law. She even gives Stevie her scarves and jewelry to try on. 'Grandma,' she tells him, 'adores her little baby doll.'"

"And you've been hoping they were right, that this is just a childhood phase."

"Yes. But I really *do* think there's something wrong." By now, Mrs. Johnson's voice sounded sharp and determined. "Last week," she said, "Stevie insisted I get him a Pocahontas doll. And then I saw you on TV. You were describing my son to a T, Dr. Nicolosi. And if you're right, then Stevie will grow up—" Then she hesitated, as if afraid to say the word. "He'll be gay. That's what you said. And to be honest, that's why I called you." Her voice began to quaver. "Doctor, *will* my son grow up gay?"

I wanted to waffle on the word *gay*. That word is a political term that carries a lot of ideological baggage.[3] A more scientific term is *homosexual*. But this woman was not interested in science or in gay politics; she was worried about her son.

As gently as possible, I replied, "The odds are that, without intervention, a boy like Stevie has a 75 percent chance of growing up homosexual, bisexual, or transgender. Gender nonconformity is often an early sign of—"

"So that means he'll be a homosexual? Then there's no hope?"

"He may, but not necessarily. There's still time to help him feel more comfortable with his maleness."

"Okay. Okay. But what should I do?" She paused. I could almost feel her intensity.

As the president of NARTH, the National Association for Research and Therapy of Homosexuality, I often give lectures on homosexuality. For the past fifteen years, I have treated many adult men dissatisfied with their homosexuality at my office in Encino, outside Los Angeles.

Most of my adult homosexual clients had never played with dolls—Stevie's situation was extreme. But almost all of these clients did display a characteristic gender nonconformity from early childhood that had set them painfully apart from other boys.

Most of these men remembered themselves in boyhood as unathletic, somewhat passive, lonely (except for female friends), unaggressive, and uninterested in rough-and-tumble play, and fearful of other boys, whom they found both intimidating and attractive. Many of them also had traits that could be considered gifts: they were bright, precocious, social and relational, and artistically talented. Because most of these men had not been exactly feminine as boys, in contrast to Stevie, their parents had not suspected anything amiss. Thus they had made no efforts at seeking therapy.

But on the inside, these men had, as boys, been highly ambivalent about their own gender. Many had been born sensitive and gentle, and they just were not sure that maleness could be part of "who they were." Some writers have aptly referred to this condition as "gender emptiness." Gender emptiness arises from a combination of a sensitive inborn temperament and a social environment that does not meet this child's special needs. This temperamentally at-risk boy needs (but does not get) particular affirmation from parents and peers to develop a secure masculine identity.

Such a boy will then, for reasons of both temperament and family dynamics, retreat from the challenge of identifying with his dad and the masculinity he represents. So instead of incorporating a masculine sense of self, the prehomosexual boy is doing the opposite—rejecting his emerging maleness and thus developing a defensive position against it.

Later, though, he will fall in love with what he has lost by seeking out someone who seems to possess what is missing within himself. This is because what we fall in love with is not the familiar, but the "other than me."

It's an Identity Problem

At the root of almost every case of homosexuality is some distortion of the fundamental concept of gender. We see this distortion in the case of the lesbian activist who wants Scripture rewritten with God called "She." Or when someone says, with obvious pride, "I don't fall in love with any particular gender, because gender doesn't matter. I fall in love with the *person*—it can be either a man or a woman." Or when a psychologist says that bisexuality is a superior orientation because it opens up creative new possibilities for sexual expression. Or when a high school boy insists he be allowed to wear a dress and high heels to school— and a judge orders the school to support the boy's illusion that he is a female.

Self-deception about gender is at the heart of the homosexual condition. A child who imagines that he or she can be the opposite sex—or be both sexes— is holding on to a fantasy solution to his or her confusion. This is a revolt against reality and a rebellion against the limits built into our created human natures.

But it's time to get back to Stevie.

Gender Identity Is Established Within the Context of a Family

Dealing with the problem of prehomosexuality is a process that must involve every family member. Continuing with our telephone conversation, I asked Mrs. Johnson to tell me a little about Stevie's father. The father plays a pivotal role in a boy's normal development as a male.[4] The truth is, Dad is more important to the boy's gender-identity development than is Mom.

Stevie's mom said, "My husband, Bill, is right here. Do you want to talk to him?" She asked her husband to pick up the phone and quickly summarized for him what I had just told her. "Bill, this psychologist says Stevie could become gay."

"So, what can we do?" asked the father, his voice gruff. He sounded like a man of action. Then he immediately answered his own question. "We'll come to your office."

I told him that would be a good idea. I went on to say that, with some professional guidance, the two of them could learn to do some important things and change some family patterns in order to help Stevie. But first, they had to understand what was going on.

Growing Up Secure in One's Gender

The next day, it was not hard for me to see some typical family dynamics at work when Bill, Margaret and Stevie Johnson walked into my office on Ventura Boulevard. Five-year-old Stevie was a beautiful boy, with porcelain white skin.[5] He had remarkably large eyes fringed with long, black lashes. Margaret was charming and articulate. Bill, a successful banking executive, had little to say. For me, this was a familiar pattern.[6]

I talked to them as a family for a few minutes and then took Bill and Margaret aside. I explained to them some basics about what a boy needs in order to grow up straight. "Mothers make boys," I said; "fathers make men."

I told them how this happens. In infancy, both boys and girls are emotionally attached to the mother. In psychodynamic language, mother is the first love object. She meets all her child's primary needs.[7] Girls can continue to develop in their feminine identification through the relationship with their mothers. On the other hand, a boy has an additional developmental task—to disidentify from his mother and identify with his father.

While learning language ("he and she," "his and hers"), the child discovers that the world is divided into natural opposites of boys and girls, men and women. At this point, a little boy will not only begin to observe the difference, but also he must now decide where he himself fits in this gender-divided world. The girl has the easier task, I explained to Stevie's parents; her primary attachment is already to the mother, and thus she does not need to go through the additional developmental task of disidentifying from the person closest to her in the world—Mom—to identify with the father. But the boy is different: he must separate from the mother and grow in his differentness from his primary love object if he is ever to be a heterosexual man.

This may explain why there are fewer female homosexuals than there are male homosexuals. Some studies report a 2 to 1 ratio. Others say 5 to 1 or even 11 to 1. We do not really know for sure, except that it is clear that there are more male homosexuals than there are lesbians.

"The first order of business in being a man," according to psychoanalyst Robert Stoller, "is don't be a woman."[8]

In Search of Masculinity

Meanwhile, the boy's father has to do his part. He needs to mirror and affirm his son's maleness. He can play rough-and-tumble games with his son—games that are decidedly different from those he would play with a little girl. He can help his son learn to throw and catch a ball. He can teach the toddler how to pound a wooden peg into a hole in a pegboard, or he can take his son with him into the shower, where the boy cannot help noticing that Dad has a male body, just like he has.

As a result, the son will learn more of what it means to be a male. And he will accept his body as a representation of his maleness. *This,* he will think, *is the way boys—and men—are made. And it is the way I am made. I am a boy, and that means I have a penis.* Psychologists call this process "incorporating masculinity into a sense of self" (or "masculine introjection"), and it is an essential part of growing up straight.

The penis is the essential symbol of masculinity—the unmistakable difference between male and female. This undeniable anatomical difference should be emphasized to the boy in therapy. As psychoanalyst Richard Green has noted, the effeminate boy (whom he bluntly calls the "sissy boy") views his own penis as an alien, mysterious object.[9] If he does not succeed in "owning" his own penis, he will grow into an adult who will find continuing fascination in the penises of other men.

The boy who makes the unconscious decision to detach himself from his own male body is well on his way to developing a homosexual orientation. Such a boy will sometimes be obviously effeminate, but more often he—like most pre-homosexual boys—is what we call "gender-nonconforming." That is, he will be somewhat different, with no close male buddies at that developmental stage when other boys are breaking away from close friendships with little girls (about age six to eleven) in order to develop a secure masculine identity. Such a boy also usually has a poor or distant relationship with his father.

Listen to the words of Richard Wyler, who sponsors an online support group for strugglers. Wyler has assembled the stories of a group of ex-gay men and published them on his dynamic and insightful website <www.peoplecanchange .com>. He describes their shared feeling of alienation from their own masculine natures:

> Our fear and hurt at feeling rejected by the male world often led us to disassociate ourselves from the masculine—the very thing we desired most. . . . Some of us began to distance ourselves from other males, male interests and masculinity by consciously or subconsciously taking on more feminine traits, interests or mannerisms. (We often saw this in the gay community as deliberate effeminacy and "camp," where gays sometimes took it to such an extreme they even referred to each other as "she" or "girlfriend.")
>
> But where did that leave us, as males ourselves? It left us in a Never-Never Land of gender confusion, not fully masculine but not really feminine either. We had disassociated not just from individual men we feared would hurt us, but from the entire heterosexual male world. Some of us even detached from our very masculinity as something shameful and inferior. (<www.peoplecanchange.com>)

This means that homosexual men, as psychiatrist Charles Socarides explains, are still searching for the masculine sense of self that should have been established in early childhood and then solidified through adolescence.[10] But the dynamics involved are completely unconscious. And that is why Dr. Socarides uses psychoanalysis (and some of the tools of psychoanalysis, such as dream work) to help his adult homosexual patients understand and resolve their unconscious strivings.

I try to prevent a long and difficult therapy to change homosexuality in adulthood by encouraging early intervention in childhood. Parents, particularly fathers, can best affirm their sons' weak masculine gender identity while it is still in the formative stage. Parental intervention can lead to an increase in gender esteem, preventing the sense of male inferiority and alienation from the world of men that so many homosexual men describe.

The idea is to prevent the boy from detaching from his normal maleness and to encourage him to claim the masculine identity for which he was designed, not to somehow mold him into the caricature of a macho man (this may not be who he is, and that is okay), but to help him develop his own maleness within the context of the personality characteristics with which he was born.

Richard Wyler explains the needs he and the other strugglers felt as children—particularly, longings and loneliness like so many other gender-disidentified boys:

> Unknowingly, unintentionally, we had constructed a psychological gulf between ourselves and the heterosexual male world. Yet, as males, we needed to belong to the world of men. To be mentored by them. To be affirmed by other men. To love and be loved by them. Although we feared men, we pined for their acceptance. We envied the confidence and masculinity that appeared to come so easily to them. And as we grew, envy turned to lust. Watching men from afar, wanting to be like them, wanting to be included, they became the objects of our desire.
>
> From the far side of the gulf we had constructed, we could never grow out of homosexuality. Gay activists and gay-affirmative therapists would tell us that our true place was in fact on this side of the gulf, that it was a good place to be. If that is true for others, it certainly wasn't for us. We wanted something more. We wanted to face our fears, heal our underlying problems, and become the men we felt God wanted us to be. We didn't want to be affirmed as gay. We wanted to be affirmed as men. . . . We wanted to heal the hidden problems that our inner voice was calling us to heal. (<www.peoplecanchange.com>)

As Wyler explains, the normal process of gender identification has gone awry. Instead of identifying with their gender, such boys have defensively detached themselves from the world of men. To protect themselves from hurt, they have closed themselves off from male bonding and identification.

Much of this detachment began with a weak relationship with the father. Some fathers find a way to get involved in everything *but* their sons. They lose themselves in their careers, in travel, in golf, or in any number of activities that become so all-important to them that they have no time for their boys. Or they fail to see that this particular son interprets criticism as personal rejection.

Or the problem may be rooted in a temperamental mismatch—that "one particular son" was much harder for Dad to reach because of the child's own sensitive temperament. His father found him hard to relate to, because they did not share common interests (perhaps the activities this particular son enjoys are more social and artistic and less typically masculine). And in the busyness and rush of life, this harder-to-reach boy was somehow put aside and neglected.

A few fathers take this scenario to the extreme. I saw one father (an immature and inadequate man who warned his wife, before their son was born, that he did not want a boy) completely reject and ignore their son, while doting on their older daughter. Apparently threatened by the idea of having another "man in the house," this man made his displeasure so clear that their son, by the age of two, was wearing dresses like his sister and playing with her Barbie doll collection. Not surprisingly, this little boy felt much safer renouncing his masculine identity.

For a variety of reasons, some mothers also have a tendency to prolong their sons' dependence. A mother's intimacy with her son is primal, complete, exclusive, and this powerful bond can easily deepen into what psychiatrist Robert Stoller calls a "blissful symbiosis."[11] But the mother may be inclined to hold on to her son in what becomes an unhealthy mutual dependency, especially if she does not have a satisfying, intimate relationship with the boy's father. In such cases she can put too much energy into the boy, using him to fulfill her needs for love and companionship in a way that is not good for him.[12]

A "salient" (that is, strong and benevolent) father will interrupt the mother-son "blissful symbiosis," which he instinctively senses is unhealthy. If a father wants his son to grow up straight, he has to break the mother-son bond that is proper to infancy but not in the boy's best interest afterward. In this way, the father has to be a model, demonstrating that it is possible for his son to maintain a loving relationship with this woman, his mom, while still maintaining his own independence. In this sense, the father should function as a healthy buffer between mother and son.[13]

Sometimes Mom might work against the father-son bond by keeping her husband away from the boy ("It's too cold out for him," "That might hurt him," "He's busy doing things with me today") in order to satisfy her own needs for male intimacy. Her son is a "safe" male with whom she can have an intimate emotional relationship without the conflicts she may have to confront in her relationship with her husband. She might be too quick to "rescue" her son from Dad. She may cuddle and console the boy when his father disciplines or ignores him. Her excessive sympathy can discourage the little boy from making the all-important maternal separation.

Furthermore, exaggerated maternal sympathy fosters self-pity—a feature that is often observed in both prehomosexual boys and homosexual men.[14] Such exaggerated sympathy from the mother may encourage the boy to stay isolated from his male peers when he is hurt by their teasing or their excluding him. As Richard Wyler tells us:

Almost all of us had an innate sensitivity and emotional intensity that we learned could be both a blessing and a cure. (To whatever extent biology may contribute to homosexuality, this is probably where biology most affected our homosexual struggle.)

On the one hand, our sensitivity caused us to be more loving, gentle, kind and oftentimes spiritually inclined than average. On the other hand, these were some of the very traits that caused girls to welcome us into their inner circles, Moms to hold onto us more protectively, Dads to distance themselves from us, and our rough-and-tumble peers to reject us.

Perhaps even more problematic, it created within us a thin-skinned suscepti-bility to feeling hurt and rejected, thus magnifying many times over whatever ac-tual rejection and offense we might have received at the hands of others. Our perception became our reality. (<www.peoplecanchange.com>)

Gender Nonconformity: Just a Myth?

Could the stories of childhood gender nonconformity told us by so many ex-gay men hold true for only a small, stereotyped subgroup of homosexuals? Are such stories, in fact, not typical?

One highly regarded study of homosexuality offers some revealing answers to this question. The book *Sexual Preference: Its Development in Men and Women* is often cited as a reference work by gay activists. The study was funded by the Na-tional Institute of Mental Health and was designed by the Kinsey Institute for Sex Research. It found that men who became homosexual are far less likely than most men to report having "very much" enjoyed traditional boys' activities, such as baseball and football. In fact, only 11 percent of homosexual men had enjoyed those traditional boys' activities, in contrast to 70 percent of heterosexuals.

Twice as many homosexual men reported having enjoyed solitary activities "very much," particularly drawing, music, and reading. Typical girl activities (such as playing house, hopscotch, and jacks) were enjoyed by about half of the homosexual men, versus only 11 percent of heterosexual men.[15] More than one-third (37 percent) of the homosexual men had dressed up as girls or pre-tended to be a girl during their grade school years, while only 10 percent of the heterosexual men had ever done so.

The family factors associated with the boys' gender nonconformity in this study were "mother-dominated father," "closeness to mother," "strong mother," and "low level of identification with father." The authors of the study conclud-ed, "Childhood gender nonconformity turns out to be a very strong predictor of adult sexual preference among the males in our sample."[16]

This finding of childhood gender nonconformity is not just true for people who are unhappy with their homosexuality; it has also been found to hold true in studies of other homosexuals who were not patients in psychotherapy.[17]

A Commitment to a Healthy Future

Recalling the words of psychologist Robert Stoller, I reminded Margaret and Bill that "masculinity is an achievement." What I meant was that growing up straight is not something that just happens. It requires good parenting. It requires family support. And it takes time.

Margaret got the idea. She said, "You mean it's a process?"

"Yes."

"How long a process?" she asked.

I knew what she was asking. How long before she would know whether Stevie was going to be homosexual? I explained that the crucial period is from one and a half to three years old, but the optimal time is before age twelve. "If we do nothing, then with the onset of puberty, when he begins to feel deep sexual stirrings and romantic longings, this search for gender will become eroticized."

"Eroticized?" asked the father, a worried frown creasing his brow.

"He may start experimenting with other boys," I explained. "Or even start coming into contact with older homosexuals."

He groaned. "That's got to be every father's worst nightmare."

I heard the anxiety in his voice. Like most parents, he hoped that when his son grew up, he would marry and have children.

"The fact is," I said to Bill, "a boy who is confused about his sexual identity may experiment with same-sex intimacy, sometimes with an older man. Of course, that is likely to reinforce a homosexual identity."[18]

Bill sat back in his chair and frowned. He told me, "Doc, we'll do whatever we gotta do. We'll sell the farm." In that moment, I think, Bill really meant that he would "do anything" to help Stevie, no matter how drastic the action was.

I could understand Bill's fears, but I assured him, "You don't have to sell the farm. Most of the work you can do yourself. Just be there for Stevie emotionally. Maintain a warm, loving relationship with him and don't let him pull away."

At that point, I recalled the many session hours I have spent listening to my adult homosexual clients telling me about their search for partners and their deep longing for male love and erotic intimacy. There was a great void in their lives, tracing back to their earliest years, for a man's attention, affection, and affirmation—a need to be hugged and held, and later to feel special to that one "best buddy" who "must certainly be out there somewhere." Many were still searching for the love of their fathers. "Be a salient father," I said to Bill.

He frowned. " 'Salient'? What do you mean by that?"

" 'Salient' means two things: strong and also benevolent. Stevie needs to see you as confident, self-assured, and decisive. But he also needs to see you as supportive, sensitive, and caring. In other words, Bill, give Stevie reasons for wanting to be like you." I gave Bill a long, searching look.

To Margaret, I said, "And you're going to have to back off."

She looked shocked. "I'm not sure I understand. Of course I have to take care of him and—"

I said, "What I mean is, don't baby Stevie. Let him do more things for himself. Don't try to be both Mom and Dad for him. If he has questions, tell him to ask his dad."

"Questions about what?"

"About anything. About sex, sure. But other questions, too. Why is the sky blue? Why does the wind blow? Defer to your husband any question, any task that will give him a chance to demonstrate that he is deeply interested in Stevie, that Stevie is very special to him. He's got to prove that Dad has something to offer him."

Many of my homosexual patients tell me that their fathers had nothing to give them. One of my homosexual clients, who was twenty-six, told me recently, "My Dad was there but not there. I mean, he was in the house, but I can't remember anything memorable or significant about him."[19]

Bill said, "So you're saying that Stevie doesn't need therapy?"

I told Bill that Stevie did not really need therapy. "He needs his dad."

He needs his dad. That was easy for me to say.

The following week, when Margaret drove in from Pasadena, this time she was alone. And, sadly, I was not the least bit surprised that Bill did not show up. This, I am sorry to say, is a familiar pattern. Moms often sense what needs to be done. And, as is often the case, many dads just don't seem to get the importance of it. ("Your mother," they say, "will handle it.")

"Bill hasn't been paying much attention to Stevie," Margaret told me rather apologetically. "Even when we were driving home after our session with you," she said, "Bill hardly even talked to Stevie. And, as far as I know, they haven't had any one-on-one moments since then."

I asked, "What happens when Bill comes home from work?"

"He doesn't talk to Stevie, that's for sure. He barely talks to me. He makes himself a martini and turns on the TV."

Uh-huh, I thought, *it's the same old story.*

It had not been more than a week since Bill had said he would "sell the farm" to save his boy. I did not doubt that this father loved his son and that, in his mind, he truly wanted to do the "big" thing. But he could not do the little things—the everyday, caring, and loving things that were necessary if his son was to resolve his gender confusion. As it was, Bill could not even talk to his son. Tragically, it is an all-too-familiar pattern. In fifteen years, I have spoken with hundreds of homosexual men. Perhaps there are exceptions, but I have never met a single homosexual man who said he had a close, loving, and respectful relationship with his father.[20]

I have found this to be a good test of the early father-son bond: who does the little boy run to when he is happy, proud of something he has done, looking for encouragement, or seeking fun and excitement? If it is always Mom, then something is wrong with the father-son relationship.

In our own clinical work, and from the experience of the many men we have known, it seems very rare for a man who struggles with homosexuality to feel that he was sufficiently loved, affirmed, and mentored by his father while growing up or to feel that he identified with his father as a male role model. In fact, often the son remembers the relationship as characterized by a feeling of neglect, mutual hostility, and paternal lack of interest (a form of psychological abandonment).

But like all human experience, this is not universal. Sometimes the father-son relationship does seem reasonably adequate. In such cases, there may be a problem with aggressive and hostile (usually older) brothers or other male peers or abusers who have created a deep wounding. Still, the same essential problem remains: the boy has a deep sense of gender inadequacy, of not measuring up in the company of men, of not being good enough within the world of males. Call it a problem in gender esteem.

As Richard Wyler explains, speaking for a group of ex-gay men including himself, "We have never known a single case where a man who struggles with unwanted homosexual feelings was not emotionally estranged from or wounded in his relationships with other men or the male world" (<www.peoplecanchange .com>).

Every boy has a deep longing to be held, to be loved by a father figure, to be mentored into the world of men, and to have his masculine nature affirmed and declared good enough by his male peers, his male elders, and mentors. If none of these relationships is strong enough to welcome the boy into the world of men, then he will yearn after other men from a distance. Like Richard Wyler, I have never known a single case of a homosexual man who was not wounded in his relationships within the male world.

I was not quite ready to give up on Stevie's father. Still, I advised Margaret, as a stopgap, that she ought to start looking for other male role models for her son. An uncle who could take Stevie fishing. A cousin who could teach the boy baseball. Other trustworthy adult males who would spend time with this boy and make him feel special.

Of course, no intervention can guarantee that a child will grow up heterosexual. All Margaret and Bill could do was to maximize Stevie's chances by creating the best possible environment. I trusted that Margaret and Bill would still love their son if those efforts were not successful.

But there was a great deal that *could* be done to lay a healthy foundation, and it was time to get started.

2

THE PREHOMOSEXUAL BOY
Why Should Parents Intervene?

The road to manhood is a long one.

It is a road of learning, trying, failing, trying again. . . .

Some boys, however, do not reach this destination.

At some point the striving became too much, the defeats and failures too painful,

so they opted out. . . . [T]hey took a detour. . . . I was one of those boys.

My detour took me into the world of homosexuality.

ALAN MEDINGER

What are the odds? That is the question in the forefront of parents' minds when they begin to worry about the implications of their children's gender confusion. And the odds are not good. As I told Stevie's parents, little boys who have a fascination and preoccupation with feminine activities have at least a 75 percent chance of growing up to be homosexual, bisexual, or transsexual.[1]

Of course, Stevie's story does represent an extreme example. Most gender-confused boys exhibit somewhat less obvious signs of prehomosexuality than did Stevie—they are alienated from Dad, lacking male friends, and secretly nursing a "male wound" buried deep in their psyche; because their symptoms are more subtle, they would not be diagnosed with gender-identity disorder of childhood. But these boys, too, are at risk to grow up homosexual.

Gender nonconformity in childhood, most researchers agree, is the single most common factor associated with homosexuality. This is accompanied by the feeling, when these men look back, of having been different from other children. Unfortunately, many members of the mental health profession—psychiatrists, psychologists, and social workers—think it is unnecessary to inform parents of the possibility of a homosexual outcome.

For too long, many professionals have maintained a patronizing disregard for parents who express concern about their children's sexual orientation. These professionals would rather ignore the child's symptoms, it seems, and focus on the parents' problem with "unenlightened homophobia" or "heterosexism." But when clinicians take this approach, they are replacing genuine helpfulness with a social agenda that conflicts with the values and concerns of most families. This is because one undeniable fact remains: most parents do not want their children to grow up homosexual.

A couple came to my office recently to tell me about their son, Aaron, a very effeminate four-year-old. Both parents proudly identified themselves as broad-minded and quite tolerant of cross-gender behavior. But when I told them of the statistical probabilities that their son would eventually involve himself in homosexual behavior if we did not intervene, they were shocked.

Despite their self-proclaimed broad-mindedness, these parents decided to give away the little boy's dolls. And under my direction, they resolved to do their own "reparative therapy." That meant they began to address some of their son's natural "boy needs," which had previously remained unmet. As is always the case, their son needed to get closer to his father. He needed to experience some separation from his mother. And both mother and father had to learn to work together as a parental team in order to figure out ways of bringing out the boy's natural, gender-appropriate masculinity. (More about how this is done in the following chapters.)

"If we start now," I told the parents, "early enough in Aaron's development, he'll learn to get comfortable with his own maleness. And that means it's a lot more likely that he'll grow up straight."

Many clients describe their homosexual problem as a "gender emptiness" or lack of "gender esteem." And without this esteem, as Richard Wyler warns, life will be full of problems:

> Usually, the pain had to do with our feeling unloved or unwanted—or at least, not loved or wanted enough. The pain often included "father hunger," "mother enmeshment," peer rejection, poor "gender esteem" and, with disproportionate frequency (compared to the general population), childhood sexual abuse or premature exposure to sexual experience. When this occurred, it was inevitably at the hands of other males, causing untold confusion between love and abuse, and male and female. Time alone could never really heal these kinds of deep wounds

without our going back to face them, acknowledge them, grieve them, release our legitimate anger over them, take steps to repair the damage they had caused us (to the extent we could), and finally, to forgive and move on. (<www.peoplecanchange.com>)

Drs. Kenneth Zucker and Susan Bradley, experts in gender-identity problems in children, believe that treatment of the gender-disturbed child should begin as early as possible:

> In general we concur with those who believe that the earlier treatment begins, the better. . . .
>
> It has been our experience that a sizable number of children and their families can achieve a great deal of change. In these cases, the gender identity disorder resolves fully, and nothing in the children's behavior or fantasy suggest that gender identity issues remain problematic. . . .
>
> All things considered . . . we take the position that in such cases clinicians should be optimistic, not nihilistic, about the possibility of helping the children to become more secure in their gender identity.[2]

Is Homosexual "Who Some People Are"?

"But maybe my son was *born* gay?" some parents ask me. "Is it possible that homosexual is just 'who he is'?"

Science is often said to have "proved" that a homosexual orientation is a natural, inborn part of who a person really is.[3] (In the next chapter, we'll get into the biological theories of homosexuality in depth.) According to the "born that way" argument, a sexual orientation is a part of a person's core identity, so such a homosexually oriented person must be accepted as expressing his or her own true, created nature.

But there are problems that undermine this argument *even if a "gay gene" were discovered tomorrow.* Science—in spite of what many people assume—is inherently limited in what it can tell us. Science describes the world and tells us "what is," but it cannot tell us "what ought to be." Let me illustrate with an example.

Your son Jack is born with a gene that makes it likely he will gain weight. You really love to cook for him, and so he grows up loving desserts and fried foods. At school he is teased, excluded, and called names, and so he goes home and comforts himself the way he knows best—by eating. *(Maybe they're right,* Jack decides. *Maybe this is who I am.)* Pretty soon Jack is so overweight that his doctor gives him a note excluding him from physical education class.

Is fat "who he really is"? He got that way through a combination of biolog-ical factors, parental influence, social influence from peers, and behavioral choice. (Just as with homosexuality.)

Yet as much as overeating may be understandable for Jack (and indeed feel perfectly normal to him), we still recognize that obesity is not normal and healthy—for Jack or for anyone else. This is because human beings simply were not designed to burden their bodies with obesity.

Your son's teacher sees Jack's unhappiness and the teasing and exclusion he suffers. Her heart breaks. Naturally, she wants to protect him. As part of our program to "make schools safe" for children who are teased and ostracized, should we—prompted by understandable feelings of compassion—teach that "obesity is normal for some people"? Furthermore, should the teacher say that the only problem with obesity is society's discrimination against it?

The truly compassionate answer is no. This may be a painful course to take in the short run, but the farsighted response—taking these kids' future lives into account—will require an accurate understanding of obesity. We are not de-signed to be seriously overweight. School administrators should affirm such a child as a person, and should have great sympathy for his struggle, yet they should not affirm his problem as an integral part of his identity.

The same goes for a sexually confused teenager.

Alan Medinger, who has counseled hundreds of men coming out of homo-sexuality and who was himself homosexually active for seventeen years, ex-plains that true freedom is not to be found in coming out as gay but in choosing to live according to one's true nature—as he says, "resuming the journey" to manhood from which "some men have gone AWOL":[4]

> The road to manhood is a long one. It is a road of learning, trying, failing, trying again, a journey of victories and defeats. Most boys are not even conscious that they are on the road, and few realize when they have reached its primary desti-nation, but the great majority do reach it. . . .
>
> Some boys, however, do not reach this destination. At some point the striving became too much, the defeats and failures too painful, so they opted out. They got off the main road; they took a detour. . . . I was one of those boys. . . . As with so many boys, my detour took me into the world of homosexuality. . . . I came to see that my homosexual problem was largely a problem of undeveloped manhood.

What Are the Disadvantages for the Gender-Disturbed Boy?

Looking at this issue from a strictly practical standpoint, there are many serious disadvantages to a gay lifestyle. Psychiatrist Richard Fitzgibbons warns parents not to dismiss childhood cross-gender behavior and its accompanying problems as "just a passing phase."

> Gender identity problems, including cross-dressing, exclusive cross-gender play, and a lack of same-sex friends should be treated as a symptom that something may be very wrong. Boys who exhibit such symptoms before they enter school are more likely to be unhappy, lonely and isolated in elementary school; to suffer from separation anxiety, depression, and behavior problems; to be victimized by bullies and targeted by pedophiles; and to experience same-sex attraction in adolescence.
>
> If they engage in homosexual activity as adolescents, they are more likely than most boys to be involved in drug and alcohol abuse or prostitution; to attempt suicide; to contract a sexually transmitted disease, such as HIV/AIDS; or to develop a serious psychological problem as an adult. A small number of these boys will become transvestites or transsexuals.[5]

In spite of the politically sensitive issues involved, there remain clinicians who are well aware that treatment of gender confusion is both important and appropriate. Zucker and Bradley believe that treatment of childhood gender-identity disturbance (GID) can be both "therapeutic and ethical." Treatment of GID offers the child several key benefits, they say, including

- the opportunity for the child to overcome cross-gender behavior and the negative intrapsychic factors associated with it
- a major reduction in social rejection by peers
- less likelihood of transsexualism (the belief that one is the opposite sex, often with the conviction that one must have sex-change surgery to feel normal)
- less likelihood of homosexuality in adulthood[6]

Maybe My Child Was Born with a Gender Problem

A number of intriguing studies suggest that for a few men and women, gender-identity development may have been distorted before birth by a "biological accident."

A few years ago, a prescription drug taken by expectant mothers to reduce the likelihood of miscarriage was found to have the side effect of masculinizing the brains of girl fetuses. A higher than average proportion of those girls eventually grew up to be lesbian.

Then in the year 2000, three Canadian scientists found a connection between left-handedness and homosexuality.[7] Their paper concludes that male homosexuals are about one-third more likely than heterosexuals to be left-handed, while lesbians are almost twice as likely to be left-handed as heterosexual women.

Some people's brains may have undergone a disruptive event in the womb. That is what happened to the girls whose mothers took the prescription drug; an abnormal flood of hormones distorted the fetuses' gender development. The Canadian researchers believe that both left-handedness and homosexuality (in cases where homosexuality is biologically influenced) may result from a "biological developmental error."

But as scientist Neil Whitehead explains, "There is possibly some link between left-handedness and homosexuality, but not a highly significant one. The fact remains that most left-handed persons are not homosexual, and most homosexual people are not left-handed."[8]

GID Children Can Change

In fact, experts have reported that GID children who were assumed to have a biological problem may in fact respond surprisingly well to therapeutic intervention. Researchers Rekers, Lovaas, and Low describe one of their young clients:

> When we first saw him, the extent of his feminine identification was so profound (his mannerisms, gestures, fantasies, flirtations, etc., as shown in his "swishing" around the home and the clinic, fully dressed as a woman with a long dress, wig, nail polish, high screechy voice, slatternly, seductive eyes) that it suggested irreversible neurological and biochemical determinants.
>
> After 26 months follow-up, he looked and acted like any other boy. People who viewed the video taped recordings of him before and after treatment talk of him as "two different boys."[9]

Of course, the GID child should not be forced into a predetermined mold that will cause him to deny his fundamental nature—his natural gifts of creativity, sensitivity, kindness, gentleness, sociability, intuitiveness, or high intellect. Dr. Lawrence Newman clarifies this important distinction:

> Treatment should be directed not at turning the feminine boy into an athlete or

suppressing his aesthetic yearnings, *but rather at developing his pride in being male.* . . .

These boys are remarkably responsive to treatment given between the ages of 5 and 12, becoming more masculine in behavior and more comfortable with their identity as males.[10]

Researcher Kenneth Zucker agrees that treatment can be effective in many ways: "Based on my experience assessing over 300 children for gender-identity conflict . . . many of these youngsters (and their families) benefit from therapeutic intervention. These youngsters feel better about themselves as boys or girls, develop close friendships with children of their own gender, and experience improved interactions within the family matrix."[11]

Are Overweight People "Born That Way"?

As we mentioned previously, we see a good analogy to homosexuality in the problem of obesity. Researchers know that a gene predisposes some people to put on weight. But it would make no sense to say that being overweight is normal and healthy, just "because fat people are (sometimes) born that way." Our genes provide only one influence—a predisposition, in some people, to gain weight. There is also family influence ("Did Mom put Coca-Cola instead of milk in your baby bottle?"), cultural influence ("Did your extended family celebrate get-togethers with marathons of fried sausage and pasta?"), situational stressors ("Are you under a lot of pressure at work, causing you to drink beer and snack in front of the TV all night?"), and, of course, your own choice to exercise self-control ("Do you choose to diet, or do you simply give in to the comfort and pleasure of eating?").

Many people who are overweight undoubtedly have little or no genetic tendency to be fat. Their obesity is due to some combination of the above-mentioned environmental factors.

The situation with homosexuality is very much the same. As Dr. Whitehead has said, biological factors do not force us into particular behaviors; they only make those responses more likely.

The "Gay Gene"

We have already discussed the possibility of a prenatal hormonal problem in some gender-atypical children, due to a prenatal accident that caused a flood of hormones to alter the unborn child's brain development in his or her mother's womb. Now, what about the possibility of a "gay gene" that has been passed on through your family and that your child has inherited? (Genes do not make people homosexual, as we have already explained, but they do lay the foundation for us to react to our environment in certain ways.) What might that genetic contribution be?

One recent study of the biological factors suggests that the genetic component contributing to homosexuality might be some inherited tendency toward gender nonconformity.[12] Many clinicians, over the years, have suggested the same scenario. The gender-nonconforming boy feels less masculine in relation to his peers, so he romanticizes the masculinity he sees in them, which he himself lacks. The gender-nonconforming boy retreats to the safety of Mom and rejects the challenge of the masculine represented in his more aggressive, rough-and-tumble male peers. (More about this in the next chapter.)

Supporting a Masculine Gender Identity: Rites of Passage

Primitive cultures exhibit an intuitive understanding that boys need special help and encouragement to grow into their masculine identity. These cultures do not allow their young men to grow up without putting them through an elaborate set of male initiation rites. For them, becoming a man is understood to require a struggle; true manhood does not come automatically.

Young tribal men often go through a series of trials that help them "prove" or "discover" their masculinity. They hunt and kill prey and tribal enemies. They go through painful and exhausting physical regimens. They are subjected to rituals, in the company of male elders, that disavow their boyhood and declare them to be adult males. And when they come out the other side of the gauntlet they have to run, the tribe is there to celebrate their victory. Now they are men. Now they will no longer play around their mothers' campfires in the company of their grandmothers and sisters. Now, instead, they will go out hunting and fishing with the other men.[13]

Today, in our society, it is not quite so easy to help young men solidify their male identity. Young boys are not generally expected to go through initiation rites. Instead, with today's confused approach to gender issues, their teachers may tell them to embrace their "feminine side" or "androgynous nature," or, worse, their school counselors may encourage them to identify themselves as "gay." Students of all grade levels may be encouraged by public school educators to try on various sexual identities. Some school gay-affirming programs even encourage them to experiment with same-sex relationships or to consider bisexuality as an option.

In fact, some psychologists now believe that limiting ourselves to heterosexuality places an unnecessary constriction on human potential: when we overcome our fears of bisexuality, it is said, we will discover rich, creative new possibilities.[14] When a psychologist made this statement of scientific *fact* (that people are capable of a wide range of sexual responsiveness) in a scientific journal recently, she then slipped directly into an area that is within the realm of *ethics* (implying that sexual diversity is good). Science cannot, of course, tell us whether limiting ourselves to heterosexuality—or celebrating all forms of sexual diversity—is right or wrong.

Ironically, had this psychologist instead called for celebrating a monogamous, heterosexual ethic, she would have been dismissed as a "heterosexist" whose opinions should be limited to Sunday sermons. But when a psychologist's moral prescription calls for celebration of sexual diversity, her work is considered uncontroversial and is assumed to be a pronouncement of science! One cannot help but be taken by the irony.

School Programs at Their Worst

A parents' rights activist, Brian Camenker, describes school programs in Massachusetts that require children to role-play as if they were members of homosexual couples. Junior high students are required to attend workshops during "Homophobia Week" that condemn traditional values, extol the normality of transgenderism, and effectively shame any children who disagree. Camenker describes one program in which children were asked to wear pink triangles at school to show their solidarity with the gay movement—and very few children, naturally, had the courage to *refuse* to wear the gay symbols.

In one such high school, he says, the ninth grade textbook teaches that "sexuality is a matter of trial and error and personal choice." Among its lessons is this provocative statement encouraging early sexual experimentation: "Testing your ability to function sexually and give pleasure to another person may be less threatening in the early teens with people of your own sex." The textbook also advises children that they may, in fact, "come to the conclusion that growing up means rejecting the values of your parents."[15]

Sex-Change Operations: Two Views

Mixed messages about sexuality come from many different directions. I know one psychotherapist whose advice to an effeminate boy was the assurance "When you get older, you can have a sex-change operation. But, in the meantime, you'd get along best if you just try to act like a boy." This kind of advice will only reinforce the boy's feminine fantasies. Why should he seek to develop his masculinity when, in a few years, his fantasy of actually *being* a female can come true, through surgery? Never mind that many transsexuals, after surgery, find that nothing has changed inside. Many remain conflicted and unhappy people.[16]

Traditionalists (including most people of faith) believe that a natural order written into our bodies tells us who we are. For this reason, traditionalists cannot accept the view that a man who "feels like a woman inside" is justified in having his genitals amputated, breast implants inserted, and female hormones pumped into his bloodstream so that he can make his body conform to his interior sense of who he is. Traditionalists shiver with horror at the sight of this person, born a man, gesticulating in a caricatured femalelike manner, having artificial breasts that contrast with the faintest shadow of a beard and the telltale angularity of a man's jaw. What that person did to force his body to conform to his desired biological sex does not in fact look noble; it looks like raw butchery. Reflecting on the same scenario, sexual liberationists applaud—this person exercised *choice* (the highest human good!) and made himself conform to who he believed he could be, with the help of modern medicine.

There is a vast, possibly irreconcilable difference between liberationists and traditionalists. While sexual liberationists applaud the married man who leaves his wife in order to come out as gay (they call this man brave, honest, and noble), traditionalists shudder. In spite of themselves, traditionalists wince at the mental images conjured up by the thought of what homosexuals do in the act of intercourse. Almost feeling guilty about their visceral reaction, they still cannot help but see such acts as perverse and, in fact, unnatural.

Making the Decision: *Who Am I?*

Along with many of my colleagues, I am concerned that young men who involve themselves in same-sex experimentation may be too quick to label themselves as gay. Such a gravely significant decision should be made only in adulthood. Not all of these young people will necessarily *continue* to desire homosexual relationships. But with a school counselor cheering them on, they could become habituated into same-sex experiences and become hopelessly enmeshed in gay life.

For a young man experiencing painful peer-group rejection, immediate embrace by a countercultural group is intoxicating. A new (young) face will initiate welcome and celebration within the gay community, and along with flattering approval will come immediate sex. Sex can be found anonymously with very little effort in gay bars, bathhouses, and bookstores and through contacts made on the Internet in gay chat rooms.

Such experiences can quickly become addictive, as Richard Wyler explains:

> Idolization of men turned easily to eroticism. Unable to feel "man enough" on the inside, we craved another male to "complete" us from the outside. Looking at or touching another male's body allowed us to literally "feel" masculinity in a way we could never seem to feel on our own, inside ourselves.
>
> But indulging the lust through pornography, fantasy or voyeurism only intensified it. It further de-humanized the men we lusted after and isolated us from them, widening the growing gulf between us and "real men" that made them seem like the "opposite" sex. Lust also opened the door for us to the quicksand of sexual addiction. (<www.peoplecanchange.com>)

There is, of course, the possibility of a better outcome. With counseling, both the gender-identity confusion and the accompanying same-sex fantasies may diminish when the sexually confused teenager recognizes the importance of growing fully into his own gender.

Dr. Elaine Siegel discovered that gender-confused girls in therapy with her "knew they were girls, but were not at all certain that being a girl was desirable, possible, or useful to them." When successfully treated, not only were these girls' gender-identity problems significantly resolved, but previous educational blocks at school were overcome, and they were able to make a healthier general adjustment.[17]

"Indifference" or "Deficiency"?

It has been said by some gay activists that the homosexually oriented person is born with an "indifference to gender," and the reason for his suffering is that we live in a gender-polarized world—a world that must change.[18] But if gays really consider gender unimportant, then why are gay men not bisexual? Why is masculinity so highly valued in the gay world? Why do gay "Personals" ads commonly seek a partner who is "straight acting"? And why do we see such compulsive and dangerous sexual behavior in a quest for the masculine?

We think this is because homosexuality represents not an *indifference* to gender but a *deficit* in gender. Deficit-based behavior comes from a heightened sensitivity to what one feels one lacks, and it is characterized by compulsivity and drivenness—where the person will persist in the behavior despite social disadvantage and grave medical risk. Deficit-based behaviors also have a quality of caricature, seen vividly in "leather" bars, where men are dressed up as soldiers and policemen, wearing studded belts and carrying instruments of torture. Such exaggerated behavior actually represents a heightened awareness and pursuit of the internally deficient gender—that is, maleness—but in caricatured ways.

Identifying Gender-Identity Disorder (GID)

I believe in a reparative approach to gender-identity conflict. Something is lacking in the GID or gender-empty child's sense of himself as truly male (or her sense of being female). Along with other like-minded psychotherapists, I hope to offer a choice that could change the course of lives *before* these young people are so deeply entangled in unwanted homosexual behavior that it is almost impossible for them to find their way out.

Are you concerned about your child's behavior? Are you wondering if he or she may be displaying symptoms of gender confusion?

First, remember that *most* boys who become homosexual were never obviously feminine. The effeminate boy is an exaggerated case of the general syndrome of gender nonconformity that leads to homosexuality. However, both the GID (effeminate) and gender-nonconforming boy (when same-sex peer problems are also present) are in conflict about claiming their appropriate gender. And both conditions lay the groundwork for a homosexual outcome.

Certain signs of prehomosexuality are easy to recognize, and these signs usually come early in the child's life. Indicators of childhood GID, described by the American Psychiatric Association (APA), are listed below. Clinicians are told to use the following five markers to help them determine whether a child has this disorder:

1. Repeatedly stated desire to be, or insistence that he or she is, the other sex.

2. In boys, preference for cross dressing, or simulating female attire. In girls, insistence on wearing only stereotypical masculine clothing.

3. Strong and persistent preference for cross-sexual roles in make-believe play, or persistent fantasies of being the other sex.

4. Intense desire to participate in the stereotypical games and pastimes of the other sex.

5. Strong preference for playmates of the other sex.[19]

The onset of most cross-gender behavior occurs during the preschool years, between the ages of two and four. Cross-dressing, as Dr. Richard Green's research indicates, is one of the first signs.[20]

Of course, for most gender-conflicted boys, the signs of early homosexual development will be more subtle—a reluctance to play with other boys, fear of rough-and-tumble play, shyness about being naked in the presence of other males (but not when in the presence of females), lack of comfort with and attachment to the father, and perhaps an overattachment to the mother.

The story Richard Wyler tells us on his website is typical of the gender-non-conforming prehomosexual boy. He describes the common, early feelings of "genderlessness." None of the men whose stories he tells had ever dressed or acted like a girl, but there remained a deep sense of male inadequacy:

Initially, at least, we didn't feel homosexual so much as we felt genderless and, lacking sufficient maleness within ourselves, attracted to that which we felt would make us feel masculine and whole.

As long as we felt that men were the opposite from us, while we identified with women as our sisters, we remained attracted to our opposite—the mysterious, unknown masculine. To us, it often felt like men were the opposite sex, so being sexually attracted to them felt natural. (<www.peoplecanchange.com>)

Differentiate between games and obsessions if your child shows an interest in opposite-sex clothing and activities. You need not worry about rare occasions of cross-dressing. You should become concerned, though, when your little boy continues doing so and, at the same time, begins to acquire some other alarming habits. He may start using his mother's makeup. He may avoid other boys in the neighborhood and their play activities, and prefer being with their sisters instead, regularly joining them in their play with dolls and dollhouses. Later, he may start speaking in a high-pitched voice. He may affect the exaggerated gestures and even the walk of a girl or become fascinated with long hair, earrings, and scarves. Feminine things may take on a special interest for him, even to the point of obsession. In fact, he may actually act more girlish than his own sister and mother.

When asked to draw a person, the gender-confused boy will almost always draw a female first, and only after that, perhaps, will he draw a male. His drawing of a girl or woman will usually be rendered in bright colors, particularly pinks and red, with great detail and in a large size. In his drawings of males, the subjects are small, drab, thin, and often stick figures. These drawings represent the boy's perception of reality. Women are exciting, powerful, and alluring, while males (this usually includes Dad) are weak, uninteresting, and even negative figures.

The prehomosexual boy may display a precocious curiosity about female genitalia. Some clinicians have found that GID boys have a particular interest in the vagina, unlike normal boys under the age of twelve. At the same time, the boy may deny his own maleness and feel a disconnection (or even revulsion) toward his own male genitalia, pushing his penis back into his body and perhaps sitting down to urinate in imitation of his sister. These behaviors suggest that the boy considers *that* part of his body "not me." Some GID boys actually insist they are girls.

One mother of a GID boy bought her son Barbie dolls because, as a self-avowed liberal-minded mother, she refused to bow to society's gender stereotypes. She says her son would "obsess" about the Little Mermaid and Cinderella and mimic their gestures and songs, while pointedly ignoring the Ken doll she bought him. The mother describes that searing moment of truth when she realized that her four-year-old son was *not* just going through a stage—it occurred when the boy stood up in a shopping cart he was riding in and started bawling when she told him that he could never be a mother.[21]

In one study of sixty-six effeminate boys aged four to twelve, 98 percent of them engaged in cross-dressing, and 85 percent said they wished they had been born girls.[22] I have found that it is usually the very young boy who will confide this desire, and almost always to his mother. One parent reported to me that her three-year-old son told her repeatedly that he wanted to cut off his penis. As these boys get older, their growing sensitivity to parental disapproval makes them less likely to explicitly verbalize the wish to be a girl.

Social and Psychological Problems in the Gender-Confused Boy

In spite of the claim by some psychologists and most gay advocates that this blatant distortion of reality is "normal for some people," cross-gender behavior remains a symptom of a deeper problem—a problem of distorted identity and "not belonging." Boys suffering gender-identity confusion will suffer many related psychological and social problems. They are more likely to be anxious, depressed, and lonely.[23] Many parents recognize that their GID children are not happy. These children are moody and easily upset and often lament that they do not fit in.

Eventually the prehomosexual child usually becomes the "kitchen window boy" who looks out longingly at the other boys in the neighborhood, wishing he could play with the children who reject and tease him. Instead, he ends up staying inside with Mom to clean the house with her and bake cookies.[24] Parents of these children are quite right to be concerned, because this pattern, seen as early as preschool and first grade, portends many other adjustment problems later in life.

Some GID boys defy the usual stereotype of timidity and passivity and, instead, are superior-acting or extremely egocentric. Such boys "insist on their own rules in games . . . and when they do not get their way, they either withdraw or have temper tantrums."[25]

Others are excessively worried about getting hurt and bruised, with a sense of fragility about their bodies. Some of these boys have an almost phobic reaction to aggressive language. They often complain about other children's rough language, and they seem genuinely frightened by aggressive behavior.[26]

As Dr. Richard Fitzgibbons notes, fear of sports and other boys' aggression sets the stage for a weak masculine identity:

> Weak masculine identity is easily identified and, in my clinical experience, is the major cause of [homosexuality] in men. Surprisingly, it can be an outgrowth of weak eye-hand coordination which results in an inability to play sports well. This condition is usually accompanied by severe peer rejection. In a sports-oriented culture such as our own, if a young boy is unable to throw, catch, or kick a ball, he is likely to be excluded, isolated, and ridiculed.
>
> Continued rejection can be a major source of conflict for a child and teenager. In an attempt to overcome feelings of loneliness and inadequacy, he may spend more time on academic studies or fostering comfortable friendships with girls. The "sports wound" will negatively affect the boy's image of himself, his relationships with peers, his gender identity, and his body image. His negative view of his masculinity and his loneliness can lead him to crave the masculinity of his male peers.[27]

Other studies found poor coordination and difficulties in playing contact sports to be common among prehomosexual boys.[28] Similarly, a number of studies show that such boys appear to have trouble distinguishing between normal rough-and-tumble play and the deliberate intent by other boys to hurt them.[29]

Dutch psychologist Dr. Gerard van Aardweg agrees with Dr. Fitzgibbons's observations regarding fear of aggressive play. The tendency of boys to be cautious and unaggressive and to not participate in team sports is a universal finding recollected in samples of clinical as well as nonclinical homosexuals and is also true in other cultures.[30]

In elementary school, other children will begin to call these gender-confused boys "sissies," "faggots," "queers," or "gays." Most mistakenly and tragically, their teachers may even identify them as "gay children," and, thus labeled by their own teachers, the children may even come to think of themselves as "born gay." They may not be sure what being "gay" means, but they begin to suspect that they are very different indeed. Before long, their emotional estrangement from their own sex will begin to surface in same-sex romantic longings.

My former client "Alex" writes of his secret, early longing, but from afar, for male attention. We also see, in his writings, the failure to bond with members of the same sex and the early development of defensive detachment from males (shown by fear and excitement):

> The first gay feelings that I can remember having occurred back in the fourth grade when I was nine years old. I started to notice a boy with dark brown hair, wearing a dark blue jacket. I remember liking his smile at first. As I kept looking at him, I started to become attracted to him and to think how cute he was. Whenever I would be on the playground, I immediately started to look around for him. Once I had him in my sight, it was hard not to look at him.
>
> Being only a fourth grader, I didn't know what was happening to me. All I knew was that I liked this new kid a lot. I remember being so scared of him—not because he was a bully or anything, but because I liked him so much.

But make no mistake about this: A gender-nonconforming boy *can* be sensitive, kind, social, artistic, gentle—and heterosexual. He can be an artist, an actor, a dancer, a cook, a musician—and a heterosexual. These innate artistic skills are "who he is," part of the wonderful range of human abilities. No one should try to discourage those abilities and traits. With appropriate masculine affirmation and support, however, they can all be developed within the context of normal heterosexual manhood.

Parental Reactions

Mothers of gender-confused boys may become overprotective, and, sometimes, in a playground situation, they may even interfere with the normal rough-and-tumble aggression and competition that is so common among little boys. In the eyes of those other boys, the sons of interfering mothers get marked as sissies, and there is a natural tendency for boys to be especially rough on sissies.

"Oh, come on, sweetheart," Mom may say. "You don't need to play with those troublemakers. You're too good for those bullies." Indeed, many adult homosexual clients have reported to me their mothers' well-meaning attempts to console them in just this manner.

Many of us who work with adult homosexuals have found that, when they were young, these men disliked roughhousing with the other little boys and mostly avoided their company. They much preferred the company of little girls, who were gentler and more social, like they were. But later, by midadolescence, these gender-disidentified boys suddenly did a switch: by then, other boys had become far *more* important—even fascinating and mysterious—in their eyes, while girls became unimportant.

Gender Rigidity in Children:
A Normal and Healthy Developmental Stage

Exactly the opposite process occurs with their heterosexual classmates: while solidifying his male gender identity, the normally developing boy spurns the company of little girls. From about age six to age eleven, boys, especially, give up their close, opposite-sex pals. "I hate girls," the boys will say. "They're dumb. We don't want them in our club." "Boys are so sickening!" the girls insist. Such children will, for a time, become very rigid and stereotypical in their gender roles. The idea of a *girl* joining the guys' *Boy* Scout troop is outrageous. Boys' tree houses bear signs saying, "No Girls Allowed." This is not sexism; in fact, it is part of the healthy and normal gender-identification process!

What is happening is that these healthy boys and girls are solidifying their gender identity, and in order to do that, they need to surround themselves with same-sex close friends. In this way, they will firmly establish their newly acquired sense of "boyness" or "girlness." This is an important prerequisite before they can reach out later, in adolescence, to the opposite sex.

During this important developmental period, the opposite sex becomes mysterious, and this lays the foundation for the opposite sex's future erotic and romantic attractiveness. (We become romantically attracted to the "other than me.") Therefore, a period of exaggerated same-sex associations seems to be a necessary phase in the developmental process of deepening and clarifying our normal gender identity.

Remember, as Richard Wyler said, isolation from the same-sex world is at the root of homosexuality:

> Our fear and hurt at feeling rejected by the male world often led us to disassociate ourselves from the masculine—the very thing we desired most. . . .
>
> But where did that leave us, as males ourselves? It left us in a Never-Never Land of gender confusion, not fully masculine but not really feminine either. We had disassociated not just from individual men we feared would hurt us, but from the entire heterosexual male world. (<www.peoplecanchange.com>)

A child's sense of being a boy or girl, especially for little children, is more than just a vague idea. Gender holds deep emotional significance. When boys are asked if they are girls, and when girls are asked if they are boys, researchers find that many children have "quite a strong reaction, some finding it quite hilarious, while others seemed offended and irritated. Children who *don't* do this are far less typical and healthy than children who *do.*"[31]

Then, by the teenage years, the tables turn. By now, the normally developing boy has begun to be attracted to the girls. They are not so unimportant now—they are suddenly much more interesting, difficult to understand, and even romantically mysterious.

A gay psychologist says that "individuals become erotically or romantically attracted to those who were dissimilar or unfamiliar to them in childhood." Thus, he says, the "exotic becomes erotic."[32] That is, the prehomosexual boy or girl experiences arousal in response to the perceived strangeness of his *same sex.* However, this feeling of strangeness around same-sex childhood peers seems to this gay psychologist to be perfectly normal!

The Fallout: After the Boy Distances Himself from the Father

Effeminate boys, even more than gender-normal boys, need from their dads what we reparative therapists call "the three A's": affection, attention, and approval. When they fail to get what they need, they interpret their father's behavior as personal disinterest in and rejection of them. They feel a deep and powerfully hurtful affront to their sense of self. In defense against further hurt, they diminish Dad in their minds, rendering him unimportant or even nonexistent. Their actions say, "If he doesn't want me, then I don't want him either."

From that point on, they want little or nothing to do with their father. Most of all, they do not want to be like him. In effect, they are surrendering their natural masculine strivings. Then, when other boys shun the gender-confused boy (as indeed they will), they become more deeply mired in loneliness, and this loneliness and rejection only confirm their belief in their not being "good enough." This leads to the problem of idolizing other boys' maleness. As Richard Wyler explains:

> Feeling deficient as males, we pined to be accepted and affirmed by others, especially those whose masculinity we admired most. We began to idolize the qualities in other males we judged to be lacking in ourselves. Idolizing them widened the gulf we imagined between ourselves and so-called "real men," the Adonis-gods of our fantasies.
>
> In idolizing them, we increased our sense of our own masculine deficiency. It also de-humanized the men we idolized, putting them on a pedestal that deified them and made them unapproachable. (<www.peoplecanchange.com>)

Normal boys actively and aggressively play with one another, while prehomosexual boys feel intimidated, so they sit on the curb and watch them. They wish they could join in, but they are held back by the sense that they are different and even "less than" other boys. They feel inadequate and ill equipped to join in.

All too often, the next step is a depressive reaction. Consequently, they often become loners and dreamers and withdraw into a world of fantasy. Quite a few become enthralled with theater and acting and the chance to play a role as someone else. Some overcompensate by pushing themselves to excel in academics; others find it hard to pay attention in class and do poorly despite their above-average aptitude.[33]

Understandably, parents of such children are concerned when they see these signs. Simply using their own common sense, they know something is wrong. As I have said before, for parents these days, if they are unlucky enough to fall into the hands of psychologists who have accepted the premises of gay activism, they may find the experts telling them that what these boys are experiencing is inevitable and derives strictly from their "gay genes" or "gay brains."

The bad news is that so many well-educated people in positions of influence do not understand the facts about gender-identity confusion in children. The good news is that you, as the parent of a boy or girl, can have an influence on your child's future sexual orientation.

Don't care if your child is straight or gay? There are no doubt thousands of other mental health practitioners who will support you in affirming your child's prehomosexuality if you choose this path.

One such practitioner is psychiatrist Justin Richardson. There is nothing wrong or problematic as such with a boy's effeminacy, Richardson says, and it is only society's disapproval that causes the boy's problems.

Dr. Richardson is an openly gay man. He believes a sensitive and artistic temperament is pivotal in laying the foundation for male homosexuality, but he also acknowledges (as does the American Psychological Association) that there are psychological and social influences that ultimately will solidify such a boy's gender identity and future sexual orientation. How this boy becomes a "sissy" and a homosexual, Richardson acknowledges, also goes back to the personalities of the boy's parents and how these personalities mesh or contrast with the boy's own, thus influencing the depth and quality (or lack thereof) of the parent-child emotional bond. Another factor Richardson identifies is how the boy and his parents react to his developing male body. Still another factor is the ongoing influence of the boy's playmates. All these are factors that Dr. Richardson identifies—*just as we do*—as influential in confirming or weakening the boy's developing sense of masculine gender identification. But significantly, Richardson does not consider any of these influences pathological, because he does not view a homosexual outcome as pathological. In essence, he believes homosexuality "just is."

Is feeling unmasculine and being detached from one's same-sex parent and boyhood peers problematic? Not so to Richardson, because gender itself, he believes, is a matter of indifference. He suggests that parents should consider not only not discouraging their son's effeminacy but also actually communicating that they admire the boy's effeminacy as a mark of healthy nonconformity. In fact, Richardson goes so far as to say that an indifference to gender distinctions is a mark of intellectual superiority![34]

We, on the other hand, are rather backward. We are stuck in "concrete" notions of gender—we believe that a boy who likes to wear dresses does indeed have a problem.

There are other therapists, in contrast to Dr. Richardson, who believe that healthy development requires that a person's interior sense of gender identity and his biology must correspond. Mind, body, and spirit must work together in harmony. The gender-nonconforming boy might be artistic, creative, and relational, but in order to grow into his potential, he must also be confident that he belongs to the world of men.

Once mothers and fathers recognize the real problems their gender-confused children face, agree to work together to help resolve them, and seek the guidance and expertise of a psychotherapist who believes that change is possible, there is hope. Growth into a heterosexual identity is indeed possible.

3

Born This Way?

It's important to stress what I didn't find.

I did not prove that homosexuality is genetic. . . .

I didn't show that gay men are born that way,

the most common mistake people make in interpreting my work.

Dr. Simon LeVay, Author of the "Gay Brain" Study

People often say, "Gays are born, not made." Advice columnist Ann Landers is one of many public figures who misled millions of Americans when she repeated that unsubstantiated theory.[1]

The myth first took hold when the media described a few scientific studies in sound bites, while omitting the most important qualifiers. Unfortunately, millions of people worldwide then began to see homosexuality as a given, part of a person's core identity. They discarded the understanding that homosexuality develops during an individual's formative years through an interaction of parenting, peer, social, and biological influences.

But a closer examination of the evidence offers this striking revelation: the scientists whose research supposedly proved the "born that way" theory now agree it is a myth. They say that genetic and biological influences open the door to homosexuality in some people, but they admit that it is the addition of environmental (that is, parental, social, and experiential) influences that beckon the individual through that door to be confirmed as homosexual.

The author of *My Genes Made Me Do It!* explains how the biological research has been misinterpreted:

A constant stream of media articles—several per year—assures us that there is a link between homosexuality and biological features. These articles mention genes, brain structure, hormone levels in the womb, ear characteristics, fingerprint styles, finger lengths, verbal skills . . . and by the time you read this, some others may have appeared.

Genes are responsible for an indirect influence, but on average, they do not force people into homosexuality. This conclusion has been well known in the scientific community for a few decades, but has not reached the general public.[2]

The Evidence

The "born that way" research has proven to be an enormous political boon for gay activism. The myth that homosexuals are born with their orientation first exploded into public consciousness in 1991, when researcher Simon LeVay studied the brains of thirty-five cadavers presumed to be of homosexual men. LeVay is himself a gay man and an outspoken gay activist, although the media did not question his social-political allegiances and the possibility that these could pose a conflict of interest.

LeVay examined a tiny cluster of neurons, called the hypothalamus, in the men's brains.[3] He could not say whether the small differences he found there were a result of homosexual behavior or the cause of it. Neither could he know whether those differences were caused by brain damage from the gay men's active HIV infections. His small study was never repeated by another researcher, but it fortified gay activists' claims that homosexuals are "a people," born different. Because the LeVay study fulfilled the media's desire for news that supports sexual liberationism and gay activism, it made headlines around the world.

However, since that time, LeVay has quietly admitted that he has *not* proven that homosexuals are "born that way." He stated: "It's important to stress what I didn't find. I did not prove that homosexuality is genetic, or find a genetic cause for being gay. I didn't show that gay men are born that way, the most common mistake people make in interpreting my work."[4]

Ten years after his study was first reported, LeVay admitted to a gay magazine that research such as his has, in fact, been politicized—which means, of course, that it was exaggerated, misused, and distorted for a political purpose. But from the perspective of gay activism, he says, it has served a useful goal:

The question of whether or not gayness is immutable is rather crucial in the political arena. The American public will have a different attitude toward gay rights depending on whether they believe being gay is a matter of choice or not. . . .

If science can show sexual orientation is a deep aspect of a person's being, there is potential for immense good.[5]

Soon after the LeVay study, in 1993, geneticist Dean Hamer of the National Cancer Institute released a study that claimed to have found a gene that appeared to be the foundation for male homosexuality.[6] Hamer—like LeVay, a gay man—is also an activist for gay causes. The press announced his study as further evidence that homosexuals are "born that way." However, when two other researchers tried to reproduce Hamer's results in an even larger and more extensive study of their own, their findings were quite different.[7] In fact, they concluded, "It is unclear why our results are so discrepant from Hamer's original study. Because our study was larger than that of Hamer et al., we certainly had adequate power to detect a genetic effect as large as was reported in that study." Later, to his credit, when asked if homosexuality was rooted solely in biology, Hamer did admit: "Absolutely not. From twin studies, we already know that half or more of the variability in sexual orientation is not inherited."[8]

But the media headlines of Hamer's study had conveyed a quite different message to the public than Hamer's own words—they conveyed, incorrectly, the message that homosexuality *is* inborn. And as for female homosexuality, Hamer later wrote that lesbians seem even *less* influenced than male homosexuals by biology. "The best recent study," Hamer said, "suggests that female sexual identification is more a matter of environment than heredity."[9]

What the Twin Studies Show

The public was also bombarded with politicized news about the "gay twin studies." A much-publicized study of identical twins made headlines worldwide as further evidence for a genetic basis for homosexuality.[10] But as scientist Neil Whitehead explains, the studies of identical twins actually showed the powerfully shaping influence of environment, because if genes *make* someone homosexual, one would expect to find every pair of identical twins to be either uniformly homosexual or uniformly heterosexual.

Dr. Whitehead, the author of the book *My Genes Made Me Do It,* explains that in about half of the cases one twin was homosexual while the other was not. "Identical twins have identical genes," Dr. Whitehead notes. "If homosexuality was a biological condition produced inescapably by the genes (such as eye color), then if one identical twin was homosexual, in 100% of the cases his brother would be too. *But we know that only about 38% of the time is the identical twin brother homosexual. . . .* If one [twin] is homosexual, the other usually is not."[11]

Furthermore, the subjects used in that twin study were not a random sample but were self-selected (volunteers who had responded to an advertisement). Members of the gay community would be well aware of the political importance of "proving" homosexuality to be inborn, and thus twin pairs in which both brothers were homosexual would be those pairs most likely to volunteer. As Dr. Whitehead says:

> During the last decade, twin studies have come up with figures that suggest a genetic contribution of about 50% for homosexuality—much higher than the estimated contribution suggested by other disciplines.
>
> But increasing refinement of twin study methodology—particularly that relating to the use of twin registers, rather than twin volunteers—has brought that figure down to something consistent with 10% both for male and female homosexuality.[12]

Intriguingly, Dr. Whitehead says that these same twin studies also highlight the different ways brothers and sisters perceive the same set of parents. This would support the common observation that many families with several children will produce only one homosexual child, while the child's other brothers and sisters grow up heterosexual. "[The researcher's] team asked identical twins—one was homosexual, one not—about their early family environment, and found that the same family environment was perceived by the twins in quite different ways. These differences led later to homosexuality in one twin, but not in the other." Dr. Whitehead concludes: "The scientific truth is—our genes don't force us into anything. But we can support or suppress our genetic tendencies. . . . We can foster them or foil them."[13]

Remember, as we have said, it is true that there does seem to be a temperamental predisposition that sets some children up for homosexuality. Boys are particularly vulnerable; for example, there are five times more boys than girls diagnosed with gender-identity disorder of childhood. But that does not mean that it should be said of any particular child, "We know this is a gay child. We should identify him right away and get him into a gay club or community sup-

port center." A person's self-identity and behavior will be shaped by too many
other factors over the formative years—including peer and family influences
that mold a person's sense of self, society's approval or disapproval of a gay lifestyle, choice whether or not to act on one's feelings, sexual abuse in childhood,
religious beliefs and mentoring influences—to conclude that any child is "destined" to be homosexual.

Researcher Bias in the Social Sciences

Besides the "gay gene" studies, we see an increasing number of studies that
seem to prove that lesbians and gay men are as good *or better* parents than a
married, opposite-sex couple. Political allegiance of the investigators is, as
with "born that way" studies, a serious problem in the research on gay
parenting.[14] This does not mean these researchers' work should be discount-
ed out of hand. But their studies should be given an especially stringent process of review before they are accepted for publication. Instead, we are
seeing sweeping conclusions based on the studies that defy common sense,
such as "Children with two parents of the same gender are as well-adjusted
as children with one of each kind," and—from the American Psychological
Association itself—"Not a single study has found children of gay and lesbian
parents to be disadvantaged in any significant respect relative to children of
heterosexual parents."[15]

Ironically, we actually see a weaker review process screening gay and lesbian
studies before publication, while research that contradicts the aims of gay activism (that is, studies showing that homosexuals can change) is discouraged or actively excluded from professional journals.

A case in point: *The Journal of Pastoral Care* published an article on the possibility of sexual-orientation change titled "Conversion Therapy Revisited: Parameters and Rationale for Ethical Care."[16] But at the journal's next board
meeting, an angry protest erupted from a segment of the religious journal's
leadership. They said they were "highly concerned" about the article on sexual-
orientation change, which they called "highly questionable in its premises, and
highly offensive to our constituency."[17] The board labeled the article—whose
tone was thoroughly scholarly and scientific—"disrespectful of the worth and
dignity of gay and lesbian persons."

At the same time this article appeared, the National Association of Research
and Therapy (NARTH) was scheduled to run an advertisement in the same

journal's fall issue. The ad encouraged pastors who shared NARTH's vision of homosexuality as changeable to contact them for membership information. Abruptly, however, NARTH was informed that the scheduling of the advertising insert had been suspended indefinitely.

And all of this uproar came from the board of a *religious* journal!

Behind the Media Filter

Whenever a study comes out declaring a discovery about a "gay gene," as we have explained, gay activists have the help of the major media to promote the story to headline status. But we have yet to see a media discussion of the subtleties (psychological, biological, and social) that are actually considered within scientific circles to produce a homosexual orientation.

The following model described within the scientific literature offers a helpful way to envision the relationship between the biological and the environmental factors, particularly in boys.[18] The authors of this model consider it to be a likely framework fostering the development of homosexuality.

- The first level is a temperamental predisposition. A boy is born with a tendency to be sensitive and easily hurt and to avoid the rough-and-tumble play through which most males compete and develop a sense of themselves.

- Such a child is particularly sensitive to parental moods due to a "constitutional vulnerability to high arousal in stressful or challenging situations." (This is probably the same temperamental variable that makes the boy avoid rough-and-tumble play.) This child has difficulty in bouncing back from physical and emotional hurts and in persevering against aggression.

- Take a boy with that particular type of temperament (or with a physical problem, like asthma, that similarly handicaps him) and put him in an environment where the father is unavailable or unattractive as an identification object, and where the mother is very emotionally attractive or too available, and you have a strong potential for a homosexual outcome.

This is why, in a large family, just one child may become homosexual. He is usually the sensitive, relational son who suffers deeply from his father's disinterest or criticism and who easily becomes enmeshed in a mother's protection.

How Biological Factors Could Open the Door to Homosexuality

Dr. Judd Marmor is a former president of the American Psychiatric Association and an outspoken supporter of gay activism. He says biologically induced gender nonconformity is a "facilitating factor" that can lay the foundation for homosexuality because it makes the gender-nonconforming child think differently about himself and also causes him to be labeled by others as different. But does that mean the child was born homosexual? No, he says; homosexuality is "by no means inevitable . . . for, as has often been noted, constitutionally 'effeminate' boys or 'masculine' girls *can* develop normal heterosexual object relationships when their family environments and their opportunities for appropriate gender-role identification are favorable."[19]

In other words, a biological predisposition to gender nonconformity need not be destiny. In fact, when we break through the media filter and go back to the academic community and the scientists, we invariably hear that homosexuality is due to a combination of psychological, social, and biological factors working in concert.[20]

- The American Psychological Association (which has many gay activists in leadership positions) gives some credence to the "born that way" theory, but then it adds that "many scientists share the view that sexual orientation is shaped for most people at an early age through complex interactions of biological, psychological and social factors."[21]
- "Gay brain researcher" Simon LeVay says, "At this point, the most widely held opinion [on the causation of homosexuality] is that multiple factors play a role."
- The gay support group P-FLAG's booklet "Why Ask Why? Addressing the Research on Homosexuality and Biology" states: "To date, no researcher has claimed that genes can determine sexual orientation. At best, researchers believe that there may be a genetic component . . . sexuality, like every other behavior, is undoubtedly influenced by both biological and societal factors."[22]
- Sociologist Steven Goldberg says, "I know of no one in the field who argues that homosexuality can be explained *without* reference to environmental factors."[23]

But one question remains oddly unaddressed: if the researchers themselves admit no one is "born gay," then why is the American Psychological Association not interested in studying the family and social influences that lead to a homosexual identity? I believe the answer is clear: gay activists in the association do not want them to. In fact, whenever the National Association of Research and

Therapy of Homosexuality (of which I am president) addresses a letter to the president of the American Psychological Association, it is routed to the Office of Gay and Lesbian Concerns—a group of gay activists. They are determined *not* to address that vitally important issue of causation.

The Greg Louganis Story: Born Gay?

The social and family factors leading to homosexuality are amply illustrated in Olympic diver Greg Louganis's autobiography, *Breaking the Surface*. In spite of the obvious predisposing factors in Louganis's background, the media followed passively along with the "born that way" assumption. Louganis's heartbreaking biography was widely publicized.

In a *20/20* television interview in 1995 with Barbara Walters, Louganis described his abusive relationship with the father who adopted him when he was an infant. As Louganis's mother lamented, "He [his father] had nothing to do with Greg until Greg took first place [in diving]. He never played with him, he never took him any place, he wasn't a role model for my son."

Then in a *People* magazine interview, Louganis described a particularly painful memory: one day his father struck him with a belt to make him practice a dive he had been reluctant to do in the freezing weather. Louganis says, "He hit me across my backside and legs until it burned. That I can't forget. He made me do four or five back one-and-a-half pikes. To punish him, I would land flat, trying to hurt myself. . . . The best way to deal with my father was to steer clear." Louganis did not get support from his boyhood peers; he was labeled "nigger" for his Samoan complexion, and he was teased for being a sissy and because of his stuttering.

Louganis's mother proved to be the lonely boy's only ally, and not surprisingly, they developed a close attunement to each other. She told Walters, "He'd come home from school and I could tell you the way he felt when he walked in the door. I knew exactly what he was feeling, I knew exactly what he was going to do."

"My mom loves me no matter what," Louganis told *People*. Both he and his mother became socially withdrawn because his father was reportedly so abusive.

When his schoolmates discovered Louganis was athletically gifted, their attitudes toward him changed. Louganis had finally found an antidote to his deep sense of inferiority. But in spite of his athletic successes, he attempted suicide once at twelve years old and twice again before he graduated from high school.

Louganis describes his first homosexual contact with an older man he met on a beach. Like many such young men, he reports, "I kept going back for the affection, the holding, the cuddling—more than the sex. I was starved for affection." Before long, he identified himself as gay.

What was interesting about the Barbara Walters interview was what was missing. Walters refrained from pointing out the obvious about his background. Nor did she ask him why he stayed in physically and emotionally abusive relationships with his lovers, one of whom eventually infected him with AIDS. It seems we are to assume that Louganis was "born homosexual."

Genes Can Be a Facilitating Factor

In summary, then, psychiatrist Jeffrey Satinover says that we should not be looking for a "gay gene" that makes people homosexual, because none exists.

> The real genetic question is—what is it in the background of people who become homosexual that *opens that door* for them, whereas the door is essentially closed for other people?
>
> In a nutshell, *every* behavioral trait in human nature has a genetic component. For example, basketball playing is clearly genetic. . . . But if you ask yourself what that's about, it's clear that it's NOT that there is a gene for basketball playing. . . .
>
> The reason there's a genetic association is that there's an *intermediate* trait which allows people who carry these traits to become basketball players in greater numbers than those who do *not* have those traits—namely, height, athleticism, and so on.
>
> So, it's not surprising that there is a growing number of studies that show a genetic association to homosexuality. But that is a far cry from saying that homosexuality is genetic in the way that eye color is genetic.[24]

So, is it true that homosexuality really *is* an inborn and normal variant of human nature? For some people, there are no doubt genetic or prenatal hormonal influences that "open the door" to homosexuality, and those influences are likely those that induce a child to see himself or herself as gender-atypical.[25]

The answer to the question of inevitability, according to psychiatrist Jeffrey Satinover, is no—no one is "born gay." There is no evidence demonstrating that homosexuality is genetically or prenatal-hormonally set in stone simply because that child has gender-atypical interests. In fact, none of the research claims that homosexuality is mandated by biology. Only the press and certain researchers do, when speaking in sound bites to the public.[26]

Still, even as we were writing this book, columnist Ann Landers had just written another column that furthers this old myth. She informed her millions of readers, "If your daughter is a lesbian . . . she was born to be attracted to members of her own sex."[27] Much work remains to be done to accurately inform our culture's opinion makers!

In the next chapter, we'll take a close look at family roles, parental dynamics, and a number of ways you can take action to help overcome your own child's gender-identity confusion.

4

ALL IN THE FAMILY

I had a very close relationship with my mother

and a somewhat distant one with my father. . . .

In my adolescence I warred with my father

and sided with my mother in the family fights . . .

and in all this, I suppose, I followed a typical pattern of homosexual development.

ANDREW SULLIVAN, AUTHOR AND GAY ACTIVIST

Danny was just six when his mother, Jenny, bought him a matching apron and told him he was going to be "my little chef" while she prepared dinner. Jenny had watched for years as her husband and their two older sons made fun of the little boy for not being good at sports. In fact, they made fun of him for just about anything you could think of. Jenny felt terrible about Danny's hurt feelings, and she decided that rather than trying to talk to her husband—Steve—once more, she would step in and help the boy herself.

A slight, frail child, Danny struggled with both nearsightedness and a lack of coordination. Above all else, he was very emotional and, as Jenny put it, "he feels things very deeply." In her view, his macho dad and rough-and-ready brothers were the crux of his problem. Why couldn't they just be nice instead of hassling him?

Besides, if the truth were known, Jenny really enjoyed having her youngest son's company. She herself often felt overpowered by the houseful of males, who always seemed to be rushing out the door to play ball together or go off somewhere with their guy friends. Danny was a quiet, sweet ally who really liked to stay home and be with her. Together, they shared many hours of talking about their dreams, their hurts, their hopes, or the books they had read. "Danny," Jenny said, "is the only member of this family who understands me."

By the time Danny reached adolescence and became my client, he was struggling with same-sex attractions at school and found himself completely uninterested in girls, except occasionally as friends. He admitted to me that he was fascinated by the world of men but felt like an outsider in relation to it. Instead of hanging out with the guys, he watched them from a distance and fantasized about what it would be like to be the best buddy of the star athlete of his junior high school's baseball team. Steve and Jenny had become conscious of Danny's gender confusion (Steve was infuriated by it), but they had no idea what to do about it.

How Parents Respond

Despite parents' key roles in forming the gender identity of their sons and daughters, many of them are astonishingly unaware not only of their own behavior with an emotionally vulnerable son but also of their child's resulting deficits. They say, "Our son sometimes acts girlish. The other boys tease and exclude him. Is this just a phase?" Or they say, "Our daughter dresses like a boy and has no close female friends. Should we ignore it? Does this behavior mean our girl will turn out gay? What should we do?"

Confronted with signs of their children's prehomosexual tendencies, most parents are surprised and confused. The vast majority of the mothers and fathers who consult me are the parents of effeminate sons (we'll talk more about girls in chapter seven). These parents have been aware that there was a problem for quite some time—sometimes for years—before seeking professional advice.

In reacting to their sons' effeminacy, most parents demonstrate three predictable phases:

1. Denial. "It's just a phase; he'll probably outgrow it," they say. Or they claim, "It's no big deal. He looks so cute—he's just trying to get attention when he dresses up like a little girl."

Of course this denial stems, in part, from the fact that our culture has made it increasingly hard for parents to determine what gender development is normal and what is abnormal, what is worth worrying about and what is not. To make matters worse (as we'll soon see), many parents, by their lack of action, inadvertently reinforce the way their son is behaving. This, in turn, creates even more denial.

The question is, does a normal little boy sometimes act like a little girl? The answer is, a certain amount of cross-gender play is tolerable. However, if your son does not give it up quickly, you will need to take a look not only at his behavior but also at yours.

2. Confusion. Parents often say, "Oh, this is part of the culture; there are cultural reasons for his confusion."

One mother who was highly educated consulted me regarding her son Shawn. The boy's effeminate behavior included wrapping himself in pink towels and spending hours trying on makeup. Worried, she spoke to his teacher, who assured her: "Don't worry; it's perfectly healthy—he's getting in touch with his feminine side."

But Shawn continued to draw pictures of fairy princesses, Snow White, and other feminine characters. He seemed obsessed with them and spent hours alone drawing and dressing up his sister's doll collection.

His mom then spoke to the school guidance counselor, who warned her, "Don't intervene. What he's doing is in no way a problem. You don't want your son to be a stereotyped macho man, do you?" *Of course not,* she thought. But her basic maternal intuitions told her something was wrong.

Next, she went to the school psychologist, who reiterated what the teacher and the counselor had said. "Don't worry about it," they told her. "There is absolutely nothing amiss."

Finally, she heard about my work and came to see me. After listening to her story, I said, "The indicators are very clear. And if we don't make decisive interventions, your son will not have a normal gender identity and will probably become a homosexual."

3. Avoidance. Many parents who do finally consult a psychologist have been worried about their sons for months, and many of them for years, but have done nothing about it. They just postpone. "We thought it was an attention-getting device and that we should ignore it."

To the contrary, Dr. Richard Green has found that parents typically did notice the behavior but did not interfere or discourage it, thus implying that the child had their approval.[1] Some parents do, in fact, wonder if, by trying to intervene, they would be disrupting something that is normal for this particular boy, which would mean they were infringing on their son's personality or individuality.

A troubled child may either intimidate his parents or evoke sympathy from them. One mother was quite pleased to see her son so happy dressing up and "playing pretend." "I don't want to hurt his feelings," she explained to me. "He seems so crushed when I ask him to give away his Barbie dolls. I just can't do it."

Some Boys Are More Girlish Than a Girl

The typical prehomosexual boy displays telltale signs of gender nonconformity and discomfort with males, of not fitting in. But the GID boy's nonconformity is even more extreme—in fact, it is so caricatured that it is actually more girlish than a girl's. There is an intense, obsessive quality to the boy's fascination with female characters that marks it as more than a natural affinity or playful curiosity.

One mother of a GID son explained, "It's so scary! He gets almost hypnotized with this female stuff." And it's true. Some boys can become entranced and enter an almost altered state when watching female characters on television, or they sit transfixed in front of movies such as *Pocahontas* or *The Little Mermaid*. Another mother reported to me, "When I get dressed, my son sits on the bed and watches me in fascination. 'Oh, Mom,' he says, 'you're so beautiful!' I've got to admit, it feels a little creepy."

I have also seen this same intense fascination with neutered or genderless cartoon characters. One father told me that his son, who is now involved in homosexuality and is refusing to consider change, had a boyhood obsession with Bozo the clown. At the time the parents thought it was cute, even if a little strange. But he held on to the obsession until the age of twelve. The truth is, these obsessive interests are boys' attempts to lose themselves in a fantasy world where they can imagine themselves as something other than male and where the challenges of gender do not exist.

Gender Is Not Just a Construct

The first step in intervention is for parents to educate themselves. This often means correcting false information. Gender—our sense of maleness and femaleness—is not merely an arbitrary social construct. It is, rather, a basic and essential way in which we humans participate in society and express ourselves within the real world.

Reparative therapists see a secure gender identity as a primary avenue through which we grow to maturity. In contrast, a defining characteristic of the gay movement is the drive to destabilize the categories of sex and gender. A child psychiatrist at Emory University advised parents in a workshop that they should help their children break down gender stereotypes; when their children ask if a particular person is male or female, parents should respond that "there is no way to know unless they look under that person's clothes."[2]

We see this gender confusion played out in the gay world's fascination with entertainment that involves cross-dressing, in the idea that a man who feels like a woman should be obliged by being addressed as "she," in the idea that gay men can "mother" their children as well as a woman can, and in the drive to purge all language of gender-specific terminology.

We also see this attitude in gay theology. The Reverend Mel White—pastor of a large gay church and the leader of Soulforce, a group that pickets religious denominational conventions to push for gay marriage—has repeatedly referred to the Christian God as "She."

The popular media's preoccupation with gender bending has caused many parents to question their own intuitive perception of what constitutes a healthy gender role. Of course, there is nothing wrong with asking a boy to help Mom around the house, but we should be aware that for him to act and pretend to *be* Mom or to be a little girl helper is quite another matter and should be seen as clearly suggestive of a gender-identity problem.

To be of help to concerned parents, the therapist must not only be informed about childhood indicators of future homosexuality, but must also be sensitive and respectful toward those parents who desire to maximize the possibility of their child growing up straight. If the parents share the therapist's view of what is healthy and normal, they can establish a trusting and successful therapeutic alliance. But whenever the parents think that gender is just a social construct, I tell them that they would be better served by seeking counseling with a different therapist—one who supports their perspective.

Marital Problems and the Prehomosexual Child

Rather often, couples who come to a therapist looking for help with their child are experiencing disharmony in their marital relationships.

The wife will complain, "My husband is so hard to reach. He's just not emotionally connected to me or the kids."

The husband will respond, "The truth is that she's a major control freak! If she would just back off, I'd get more involved."

"And how am I supposed to not get involved if you're not doing anything!" she'll retort. "You do nothing, and that forces me to take the initiative."

All too often, a bad marriage contributes to a son's confusion. A boy's concept of masculinity suffers when Mom conveys a negative perception of the male world ("Men are worthless. Who needs them? They can't be trusted"). In families where there is a child with gender confusion, the mother may not have made it clear that she values masculinity—particularly, her husband's masculinity.

The late Irving Bieber, a prominent researcher, observed that some boys become the victims of their parents' unhappy marital relationship. In a scenario in which Mom and Dad are battling, one way Dad can get even with Mom is by emotionally abandoning their son.[3]

Reading literature written by gay men and lesbians, we often see an expressed disillusionment with marriage as an institution, along with cynicism about the possibility of a benevolent male acting as head of a family. Gay men are often cheerleaders for the radical feminist movement, with its theme that men cannot be trusted with power. This is understandable; the family system and the father, in many cases, have personally disappointed them.

The Traditional Family Is "Not Good for Society"?

One prominent gay leader describes the cynicism about family life that is a common theme in gay literature. His words reveal his own cynicism about fathers and his disillusionment with the nuclear family:

> Not surprisingly, statistics about the state of the nuclear family show that children fare better in day-care centers than at home. . . .
>
> When Dan Quayle trumpeted the need for fathers in each home, he ignored the findings of the National Committee for the Prevention of Child Abuse, according to which most sexual assaults in the home are the work of fathers or stepfathers. . . .
>
> The time has come to reject nostalgia for traditional family groupings and to seek new ways to realize the satisfaction they once brought. . . . [We must create] fresh new kinds of relationships, bearing no resemblance to past rituals, but opening doors to greater measures of individual happiness.

This writer, like most other gay activists, demands an end to the repressive expectations of what gay activists call "the gender system." He looks forward to a brave new world where there would be a maximizing of "consensual physical contact" outside of marriage and people would find joy in lives that are not centered around parenthood and the "reproduction of one's gene pool." He scorns the Judeo-Christian ideal of the nuclear family in favor of unrestricted eroticism. He says, "None but the narrowest approach to love would insist, as fundamentalists and their ilk do, that monogamy is [a relationship's] only virtuous, fulfilling, and loving expression."[4]

Yet beyond this insistence by gay activists that fathers and traditional families do not matter, we hear the wise words of psychiatrist Richard Fitzgibbons:

> When fatherless boys grow up, there's often a tremendous hunger for male embrace because they weren't getting it at home. The gay hotlines get a lot of calls from men just hungry for another man to hold them.
>
> Some of them are married, and they're not all necessarily homosexual. I think we're going to see more and more homosexual experimentation by young people, gay and straight, who are still looking for the fatherly love that they didn't get when they were growing up.[5]

A Closer Look at Mom

Back in the 1960s, when my client "Dan" was thirteen, he had been a misfit at school for as long as he could remember, and so he desperately wanted to be cool. One Saturday, when he went to get a haircut, he told the barber, "Square it off in the back and leave it a little long in the front."

In his imagination, Dan must have envisioned himself as James Dean or Elvis Presley. However, when he got home, his mother was less than impressed. She took one look, murmured, "Oh my goodness!" and then said, "Danny, that's disgusting! *You* are disgusting! Who do you think you are?"

With that, she marched Dan right back to the barber, and pushing him ahead of a crowd of men, she demanded, "Taper it in back, and trim the front! I won't have my son looking like some kind of a hood!"

The barber winked at the men in his shop and changed Danny's haircut with a twinkle in his eye. The other men's responses varied from smirks to outright laughter. Dan was mortified and refused ever to return to that particular barbershop again. This incident of shaming in front of other males remained in his memory and was recounted to me, his therapist, as one of the most humiliating experiences of his life. It deepened his suspicion that in the world of males, he was an outsider.

Without realizing it, mothers can become overinvolved in their sons' lives. In some cases, this behavior may have arisen because of a mother's need to attend to her son's childhood illnesses. In fact, a number of studies have shown a higher than average correlation between adult homosexuality and early childhood medical problems. Many of my own clients have told me of childhood struggles with asthma, a heart condition, obesity, or poor eyesight that prevented them from joining the other boys in sports. All of these conditions set the boy up to see himself as different from—and inferior to—other boys.

Mothers of homosexual men tend, in our experience, to be expressive, extroverted, emotionally accessible, engaging, and highly involved in the boy's life. The mother's problem might be that she is too invested; the boundaries between her and her son are not clear.

Sometimes mothers overinvest in their sons for their own needs, because they have not found emotional intimacy in their marriage. Unlike the boys' fathers, who rarely notice, these mothers do see the boy's effeminacy, but they postpone intervention because they do not want to upset their sons. Nonetheless, most of the parents who seek professional help are far healthier and more psychologically attuned than those who do not.

The Classic Triadic Relationship

It can be painful for parents to hear from their counselor that one of them might be an "overinvolved mother" or a "distant father." While reading the following descriptions of parental personalities, you should remember, first, that we all make mistakes as parents. Second, our own personality limitations may have had little in the way of ill effects on one child in the family and yet, to our shock and dismay, they can prove seriously detrimental to our next child. Third, how we relate to our children typically reflects the types of relationships we had with our own parents. So we hope you will not feel blamed but will instead focus on opening up your heart and mind to considering how you might (or perhaps might not) fit to some degree into this parental model. Remember that we acknowledge that the vast majority of parents are well-intentioned and loving and want the best for their children.

Repeatedly, researchers have found the classic triadic (three-way) relationship in the family backgrounds of homosexual men.[6] In this situation, the mother often has a poor or limited relationship with her husband, so she shifts her emotional needs to her son. The father is usually nonexpressive and detached and often is critical as well. So in the triadic family pattern we have the detached father, the overinvolved mother, and the temperamentally sensitive, emotionally attuned boy who fills in for the father where the father falls short.

The close emotional bond is between mother and son. She feels bad for her son: "I'm his only safe haven, and everyone else makes fun of him. His peers reject him; his father seems to have forgotten him; so I'm the only one who understands and accepts him exactly as he is." That last is the killer phrase: "as he is." It is as if "who the boy is" could include his androgynous fantasies, fear of other males, rejection of his own body, and discomfort with his masculine nature.

At this point, education is necessary. Mothers need to understand that they can actively discourage distortions about gender without rejecting the boy himself. In fact, it is not a matter of rejection at all, but instead of offering adult guidance to prepare the boy for life in a gendered world—the world to which his anatomy has destined him—and of refusing to participate in his distortions about males and masculinity.

On the other hand, many of the mothers who come to our counseling office are very concerned about their sons' poor gender esteem or effeminacy, and they want to help them reach normal gender maturity, no matter how challenging that work may become. They intuitively understand the problem their sons are having, and they are at a loss to know how to help their child and to enlist their husbands in the process. They are grateful for whatever direction and advice I am able to provide for them.

A few mothers (particularly, narcissistic mothers) establish a relationship with such a profound blurring of boundaries that the boy is not able to clarify his own individual identity. Mothers who create such an intimate, symbiotic relationship will allow nothing to interrupt the mother-son bond. The longer the profound symbiotic relationship continues, the more feminine the boy. Of course, a mother who is upset by a boy's normal, rowdy behavior—and who reacts by encouraging him to be more passive and dependent (even though the boy's real need is for independence)—is putting her own needs before those of her son.

The authors of *Someone I Love Is Gay* describe this maternal pattern:

> Sometimes the relationship is so close that it becomes unhealthy, even bordering on a state of "emotional adultery." Typically, the son is his mother's confidante. She talks about her marital problems with him, rather than working them out with her husband. She looks to her son for emotional support and comfort when things go wrong.

In some cases, the mother's behavior crosses the line into sensuality. . . . Single
mothers and women with abusive or emotionally distant husbands are particularly
vulnerable to becoming overly dependent on their son.[7]

In some rare cases, mothers of homosexual boys wanted to be men themselves, and they sabotaged their sons' masculinity by putting themselves in competition with them.[8]

All in all, there is considerable research showing that families of gender-disturbed boys tend to be in turmoil. One study of 610 GID boys found a high
level of family conflicts.[9] Many clinicians have observed a higher rate of parental
divorce, separation, and marital unhappiness in their homosexual clients' families,[10] and many parents of GID children had undergone counseling before
their child's gender-identity disorder came to clinical attention.[11]

Psychologist Gregory Dickson points out a paradox regarding the intense mother-son relationship. The gender-conflicted boy usually feels an ongoing need for
mothering, but because the mother-son relationship represents a barrier between
himself and the male world, the boy feels both *angry* and *appreciative* toward her. He
also feels both *misunderstood* and *most understood* by her. His mother knows him very
deeply on one level, but there is another level where she can never go and which
she has not fully acknowledged as an integral part of who he is as a male.[12] So there
results a paradoxical love-hate, approach-avoidance conflict.

Hasn't This Research About Parenting Influences Been Disproved?

In spite of what you hear from gay activists, no literature disproves the classical
theories describing the way homosexuality develops. In fact, a 1996 book,
Freud Scientifically Reappraised: Testing the Theories and Therapy, evaluated the
prominent psychoanalytic theories in the light of the data now available
through modern research. The authors did find conflicting results on the maternal relationship, but the research on fathers was clear:

> The reports concerning the male homosexual's view of his father are overwhelm-
> ingly supportive of Freud's hypothesis. With only a few exceptions, the male ho-
> mosexual declares that father has been a negative influence in his life. . . .
>
> There is not a single even moderately well-controlled study that we have been
> able to locate in which male homosexuals refer to father positively or affection-
> ately. On the contrary, they consistently regard him as an antagonist. He easily
> fills the unusually intense, competitive Oedipal role Freud ascribed to him.[13]

It is important to emphasize here that the overinvolved mother is used repeatedly by us here in this book as *the* example of *the* mother of a gender-confused boy. Because the deeply involved mother is almost always the type to bring a child in for a consultation—and to actively work for change—she is the type of mother we have used to illustrate case scenarios. Indeed, the intimately involved mother is most likely to unwittingly encourage a son's gender nonconformity. But not all mothers are overinvolved. In fact, among adult homosexual clients, a smaller percentage of their mothers were actually disengaged.

This observation fits with the findings of *Freud Scientifically Reappraised,* in which the researchers analyzed the available studies and found that there is some inconsistency in findings about mothers. But—as those researchers agree—the one virtually unchanging variable is the poor relationship with fathers.

Quite a wake-up call, we would say, for fathers who hope for heterosexuality for their sons!

Other Routes to Homosexuality?

Of course, the common syndrome of the triadic family, combined with temperamental boyhood gender nonconformity, should not be considered the only route to homosexuality. There are other pathways, which no doubt involve somewhat different parenting styles, the problem of early sexual seduction and the sexual habituation that can result from it, and the influence of cultural messages.

Another, less common type of homosexuality (actually, this would be described as bisexuality) would involve the choice to seek out sexual and ego gratification in every form. The latter type of person is rarely described in the clinical literature because he or she would be unlikely to seek therapy to change.

And remember, outward gender appearances can be deceptive. It is often said, "So-and-so can't possibly have a problem with gender esteem, he's so masculine," but then we look under the surface and see the same, familiar dynamics. An example is the movie star Rock Hudson, who died of AIDS in the 1980s.

Hudson was a tall, handsome man who always played the quintessential romantic leading role. During the peak of his career, the public knew nothing of his homosexuality. But Hudson's autobiography reveals that he hated his father, who deserted the family, and did not get along any better with his stepfather, who beat him. When his mother worked as a live-in housekeeper, Rock and his mother shared a bed in the servant's quarters. Then, at the age of nine, Hudson was sexually molested by an older man (he says he encouraged and enjoyed the encounter). Throughout his life, Hudson became close and very comfortable with many of the women he starred with, but with almost none of the men, while he idealized and fell in love with some of his male directors.

This masculine-appearing screen idol once told his lover, "There's a little girl in me that I just trample to death. . . . '*You will not come out!*' "[14]

Gay Public Figure Describes His Boyhood

Noted writer and gay activist Andrew Sullivan also reports a childhood pattern that fits the triadic model. His closest friends in school were girls, who were "sometimes soulmates" with whom he had "countless, endless conversations." And like many gay men, he became interested in acting and the theater.

Sullivan describes the classic overinvolved mother and uninterested father: "I had a very close relationship with my mother and a somewhat distant one with my father." His father was undemonstrative, while it was his mother who, as he said, "filled my head with the possibilities of the world, who conversed with me as an adult, who helped me believe in my ability to do things in the wider world. It was her values that shaped and encouraged me. . . . In my adolescence I warred with my father and sided in my mother in the family fights . . . and in all of this, I suppose, I followed a typical pattern of homosexual development."[15]

Judy Shepard, the mother of Matthew Shepard (the young gay man who was the victim of an infamous hate crime), tells the same, classic story. She described her son Matthew as "my friend, my soulmate, my confidant."[16]

Advice for Single Moms

In today's complex world, the growing problem of single mothers (really, the problem of absent dads) poses a unique challenge for a boy's gender-identity development. Whenever I speak to audiences of parents around the country, a mother will inevitably ask how she, as a single parent, can raise a healthy boy. The single mother can proceed in three ways:

1. She can monitor the mother-son relationship. Single mothers should be mindful not to develop an excessively close relationship with their sons. If a single mother has no emotionally secure relationship with a man, she may unconsciously seek to satisfy her emotional needs with her son, maintaining an unhealthy, overly intimate connection that may seemingly meet her own needs but that will not be in the best interests of her son.

The gender-fragile boy, in particular, is typically bright and very verbal. Such a boy seems to be able to read his mother well, and sensing his mother's codependency with him, he may learn to manipulate her emotions and consequently grow up as an undisciplined, overindulged, and (ultimately) immature and self-absorbed young man who is ill equipped to face the demands of the world.

2. She can encourage masculine identification. The single mother has to go the extra mile in affirming her son's masculinity. From day one, she has to make him feel that his maleness is different from her femaleness and that that differentness is good, healthy, and a part of who he is.

This masculine affirmation is especially important in cases where the father is permanently absent. A single mother can respect and maintain the memory of the father in a positive way, even though the father may never return, thus promoting the positive image of the "good father." On the other hand, when men are often spoken of in a negative way in the home, a young boy may unconsciously adopt a feminine identity and effeminate mannerisms to make sure he remains safe from his mother's rejection.

Such efforts are admirable and helpful, but at the same time, in my opinion, a mother cannot do it by herself. In spite of her best efforts, she cannot model being a man, although she can do the next best thing. And that leads us to the third action a single mother can take:

3. She can find a father figure. Children can find a substitute for the absent father with an older brother, grandfather, or other male. It is important that the single mother support the boy's masculine interests and that she encourage and endorse them. It is detrimental if the mother conveys the message that she and her son can "just as well go it alone" because men are unnecessary elements within family life.

Finding a father figure does not (as I am sure the vast majority of mothers well know) mean coming home from some singles' watering hole every once in a while with a new male friend, allowing the man to spend the night, and then trying to get him to connect with the boy. This will be more confusing than beneficial. It is the consistent and reliable—and therefore long-term—relationship with a stable father figure that makes the difference.

For this reason, I suggest a family member: an older brother, an uncle, a grandfather. Do not be ashamed to express your concerns and ask for help. If a family member is not available, consider groups and organizations that can help. Big Brothers of America offers these kinds of opportunities. Churches usually have youth groups with leaders who make time for kids who have challenges at home. YMCA, Boy Scouts, athletic teams with male coaches, and school advisers or counselors all provide possibilities for good male relationships. A devoted Sunday school teacher could make a powerful difference as a role model in your child's life. Whenever possible, it is wise for single moms to request male teachers and mature, manly male tutors for their sons.

As an adult client working to overcome his homosexuality recalled:

> Whenever I felt rejected by my friends, my mother tried to console me. But that just didn't help. She was never a young guy, so nothing she could say could ever make me feel better. She'd say, "Oh, you don't want to play with those bad kids anyway." It would have been great if my father could have talked to me.

Rather than the mother being the source of solace and consolation when the boy experiences rejection from peers, other males should provide the necessary consolation.

Fathers—Key Players in the Gender Game

"Danny," one of my adult homosexually oriented clients, felt rejected by his father as soon as he began to grow into young manhood. His mother fussed over him continually, worrying about his health, his appearance, his proper behavior, and his safety. But when his father was not ignoring Danny, he was verbally abusing him. Dan told me about one incident that clearly illustrates the kind of family dynamics he grew up with. He described this scene to me:

"Be sure you take a sweatshirt and a change of socks in your backpack, Danny," his mom told him one school-day morning. "It's cold and rainy today, and you know how I worry about you."

"Leave the kid alone, Mary, for goodness' sake!" Danny's dad shouted from the bedroom. "If he doesn't have enough sense to stay warm and dry, the kid isn't worth worrying about!"

"Dad," Danny retorted, "stop yelling at Mom."

Danny's dad came roaring out of the bedroom. "Don't think you can stand up to me, young man. You are a nothing!"

Danny told me that his dad's words caused him to begin to tremble, and when the older man saw that Dan was frightened, he bellowed again, "You are a nobody!"

Gesturing at his son with his little finger pointed in the boy's face, he continued, "You are *this* big. Don't you *ever* think you can fight me!"

Danny's father belongs to that small minority of fathers who are explicitly punitive, even cruel. He needs a little boy around to be the weaker masculine figure—somebody he can intimidate to enhance his own sense of power. Boys like Danny have a hard time getting hold of what it means to be a male, because their mothers—the benevolent parents—protect them, but their fathers fight them off, put them down, and will not let them enter the masculine world. Danny was kept at bay as if he were growing up to be a competitor to his father. But his sad situation is, fortunately, not typical. The majority of fathers of pre-homosexual boys I have known are simply uninvolved, emotionally distant and disconnected, especially from their sons.[17]

Psychoanalysts have long recognized the importance of the father in the boy's development and in his separation from his mother. Some analysts have referred to the father as a "breath of fresh air" from overinvolvement with the mother. Dad can be the knight in shining armor with whom the child can play, while being distinctively different from his mother.

A Dad's Love and Devotion

When they become aware of their sons' conflicts, many wonderful fathers translate their heartbreak into an all-out effort to do everything they can. Listen to this dad's devotion, expressed to me in a letter written to NARTH:

> My son Ben disclosed his sexuality to me just a few weeks ago. The two of us immediately told his mother. That was clearly the most painful event of my life. It has dominated my thinking almost every waking moment. Ben made it clear he had resolved himself to the situation, and he offered me no encouragement of any desire to change. My life was in total disarray and I simply could not believe it. Thank God I did not lose my temper and reject him. My state of mind was one of total shock, as prior to that date I had no idea or suspicions whatsoever. His mother had none as well.
>
> I was intensely motivated to research the subject of homosexuality and went to a university library for that purpose. I found very little on the subject that was not advocating the condition. Thankfully, through the Internet I discovered NARTH and the good books and articles of your organization.
>
> A short profile on my son: white, age twenty-seven; brother, age sixteen. Ben was not athletic in grade and high school; has always been closer to his mother; and friends in school were mostly girls. He was meticulous, artistic, and a good

student. He was, and is, especially caring and considerate—the "perfect child."

In recalling my son's childhood and adolescence, I can look back and see the void that was always there. I never realized it or even thought about it before. My son did not have the same interests as me, and after about age ten, I aborted efforts to direct him to areas of my interest. I realize now how much in error this was. That was the time I should have done whatever necessary to enhance my relationship with him. I abdicated his rearing to his mother, while I spent more time and effort with his younger brother.

We do have a close family. I know my son loves me, and I feel he looks to me with envy. My feelings are that he has a feeling of inadequacy. Since studying the material dealing with homosexuality, I have devoted my time with him toward improving our relationship.

Last week I had a one-on-one talk with him. During that conversation I tried to recall my many failures and shortcomings with him. I sincerely and humbly asked for his forgiveness. I told him I wanted to spend as much time with him as he would give me, and I told him I wanted to make up for my past failures. I hoped and prayed he would allow me to do so. After the conversation, my feeling was of relief, as I believe my request was meaningful to him. My objective is to fill the void I created.

At the appropriate time, I will have another talk with him, give him some reading materials, and ask him to try therapy as a means to seek change. I pray every day he will be receptive.

I have personally learned a great deal about the condition of homosexuality. It is easier for me to deal with this devastating situation with the knowledge I now have of the condition. My mission in life will never change: *freedom for my son.*

The Salient Father

When father and son come into the consultation room together, I consistently see misunderstanding, distance, avoidance, hurt—the attitudes of two strangers who somehow never understood each other.

So that the boy can disidentify with his mother and identify with his father, the boy must perceive the father as worthy of emulation. He needs to see his father as salient (which is, remember, being benevolent and strong). Indeed, in my work with homosexual adults, the kinds of male figures my clients become infatuated with and emotionally dependent upon usually represent that ideal of the "good father"—benevolent, strong, confident men.

The void created by the passivity of a father who is not seen by the son as salient will predispose the temperamentally sensitive, relational, timid boy to falling into a close-binding mother-son relationship to fill the vacuum. Subsequently, the father may observe something odd about his son, but he takes no steps to interfere with his son's overidentification with the mother.

Dads, Do Not Let Your Sons Reject *You*

Many fathers of gender-confused sons simply give up and leave the boy to his mother. This is a big mistake. *Dad, do not let your son reject you and turn you away.* Your task is to pursue your son, push through his defensive detachment, and with steady and consistent efforts, to become an important person in his life. Make it your goal to heal the hurt he may have received from you at one time or another without your knowing how or understanding why. Rebuild the trust that was broken, even if you are not sure when, how, or why the relationship failed.

The primary measure of your son's healing will be his level of responsiveness to you. When parents report that their son now runs up to Daddy when he comes home from work, then I know that the basic goal of treatment has been accomplished. Now we simply need to reinforce and build upon that good relationship.

Parents' Responses to Gender Nonconformity

Parents' first response to their small son's cross-gender behavior is typically neutral, and some are even affirming of it.[18] In fact, some researchers have found that parents are unlikely to discourage their sons' effeminate behavior.[19] Because the parental response was either neutral or positive, some parents may be in unspoken collaboration with the child's cross-gender behavior.[20] In fact, some writers suspect that on some conscious or unconscious level, some mothers of small boys may actually communicate an expectation for effeminate behavior.[21]

Fathers of these boys typically have mixed feelings about therapy. My impression has been that they usually come to therapy simply because the wife has brought them along. In fact, it has been repeatedly found, and most certainly in my own practice, that mothers are more likely to bring their children for treatment.[22] Fathers, while they will give a verbal expression of concern about the boy, usually take a back seat to the wife's involvement.

Dr. Richard Green has noted a lack of parental concern—what he called parental "neutrality"—as the initial attitude toward effeminacy in about 80 percent of the cases of boys diagnosed with an overt problem of gender-identity disorder (GID). And when the parents' concern did develop, mothers became more concerned than fathers in about 80 percent of the cases.[23] Parents frequently do not know how to take their concern and translate it into systematic attempts to encourage gender-appropriate behavior.

Many fathers are at a loss as to what is happening inside their more sensitive sons. Generally, such a father tends not to be well attuned to the emotions of others, and when he is attuned, it is to another, more masculine-behaving son, who is easier to relate to and with whom he has more in common. The son who is gentle, passive, and relational—all characteristics of prehomosexuality—is a mystery to many fathers.

Here is a case example from a psychiatrist of a young homosexual man with serious problems. His parents were well meaning and loving but out of touch with his struggles and unaware of the childhood ridicule he had suffered. Neither did they suspect their son's secret homosexuality. The psychiatrist reports:

> I had a new patient today, a college student, who had a fairly good, although not close, relationship with his father. But he never told his parents about the ridicule he experienced. Most kids who get ridiculed by their peers don't tell their parents, because they are so terribly embarrassed. This patient's parents were waiting outside to join in the session, but the fellow wouldn't even let me mention the degree of ridicule and isolation he had experienced, or the fear he now has of straight males.
>
> It's weak masculine identity and a tremendous sadness, and a tremendous fear of rejection, that makes these fellows very, very discouraged and hopeless and makes them very vulnerable to highly self-destructive behavior.
>
> Like what this young man said to me—because I had just asked him about unprotected sex—he said, "Yeah, I engage in it, I don't care."[24]

We do find fathers who are perfectly capable of being in tune with their sons—*once they recognize there is a problem*—and are willing to participate and take an active role in the healing process. This requires a father to recognize the problem, honestly reevaluate his parental role, and actively and consistently participate in his son's healthy future development. Needless to say, for boys with cooperative, concerned dads, healthy change is much more likely.

Dads Must Remain Committed

Maintaining the parental team is very important, but generally the most challenging problem is keeping the father involved on a consistent basis. In fact, the difficulty of maintaining Dad's active, daily participation is the most common obstacle to successful therapy.

Remember, your son's effeminate behavior is a defense against identifying with the male role. You cannot take away the boy's security (his effeminacy) unless you provide something to take its place. Therefore, the treatment strategy is to draw the boy toward the masculine through a warm relationship with the father or father figure, rather than to simply rid him of the external markers of femininity.

Listen for Feelings

While we have been placing much of the focus of intervention on gender-appropriate *behavioral* change, we must not forget the true task, which is *emotional* bonding with the same-sex parent. And in this focus on achieving behavioral change, the child's feelings can easily be overlooked.

This is a difficult time, and not just for Mom and Dad. The child is under pressure from parental efforts to modify habits and behavior which by now likely feel like a part of who he is. Understandably he will express negative feelings. He may even feel unloved or misunderstood. And he may, if parental intervention is too harsh, go into withdrawal and isolation, becoming emotionally detached from the rest of the family.

Thus it is vitally important that Mom and Dad express their concern and respect for his emotional reactions to this challenging new expectation of "being a boy." Mother and father should encourage expression of whatever the child may feel, even when those feelings are negative or blaming. Encouragement to express hurt, anger, sadness, and disappointment is essential to keep him connected to you during this difficult transition time.

Some fathers think they can get rid of the effeminacy through militant monitoring of external behaviors, but that is not the right approach. It is through bonding with the father and finding emotional security in the father-son relationship that the boy will feel capable of giving up his cross-gender fantasy.

A weak father-son relationship typically poses the most serious obstacle to successful intervention. Here is an example:

A six-year-old boy was brought in by his parents; we'll call him "Joey." The father seemed very concerned, telling me that he did not want his son to be gay but did not know what to do about it.

At the beginning of our second session, I asked the parents, "How was the week?"

The mother was on the edge of her seat and began to talk. Interrupting her, I said, "Actually, let's hear from Dad first. How was the week with Joey?"

"Fine . . . I guess" was his reply.

The mother prompted, "No, it wasn't! Honey, tell him what happened."

He said, "What?"

She said, "Don't you remember?"

"Oh, yeah . . . right," he finally responded. "I don't know . . . I'm watching TV and my son walks by me and gives me a look like, 'Who do you think *you* are?' "

With that, the dad looked at the floor and fell silent. I prodded, "So what did you do about it?"

"Nothing. What *could* I do?" He shrugged.

The wife was staring at me, waiting for my response. "If Joey were my son," I began, "and he walked by and gave me a look like that, I'd engage him. I'd say, 'Come over here! What do you mean by that look?' I'd reach out to him, grab him, and pull him over, maybe a little roughly but still affectionately, and let him know that the look was unacceptable. And I'd push for a connection. 'Hey, kid,' I'd say. 'What's wrong? Mad at me? What'd I do? C'mon, Joey, tell me what's going on with you.' "

At that, the mother exclaimed, "That's *exactly* what I told him to do."

Like so many moms of prehomosexual boys, Joey's mom knew intuitively what was needed, but *she* was not the one who needed to do it. It had to be Dad.

As I have written elsewhere describing the fathers I have seen in therapy:

As a whole, these fathers could be characterized as emotionally avoidant. Exploration of their histories revealed that they had typically had poor relationships with their own fathers. They tended to defer to their wives in emotional matters and appeared particularly dependent on them to be their guides, interpreters and spokespersons.

While these men expressed sincere hope that their sons would transition to heterosexuality, nevertheless failed to live up to a long-term commitment to help them toward that goal.

In his first conjoint session, one father cried openly as his 15-year-old son expressed his deep disappointment with him; yet for months afterward, he would drive his son to his appointment without saying a word to him in the car.

Further, while these fathers often appeared to be gregarious and popular, they tended not to have significant male friendships. The extent to which they lacked the ability for male emotional encounter was too consistent and pronounced to be dismissed as simply "typical of the American male." Rather, my clinical impression of these fathers as a group was that there existed some significant limitation in their ability to engage emotionally with males.

The trait common to fathers of homosexuals seemed to be an incapacity to summon the ability to correct relational problems with their sons. Rather than actively extending themselves, they seemed characteristically inclined to retreat, avoid and feel hurt.[25]

The Pain of Missed Opportunities

In "Not Crying for Dad," an autobiographical story published in a gay anthology, we hear the sadness of a gay son who knows that on some level he is responsible for rejecting his own father—a man who wanted closeness with his son but, sadly, never found it.

Author Philip Gambone describes the strange experience of being unable to cry at his father's funeral. "I did not have much of a relationship with my father," he says. "Gay friends tell me that this is simply the way it is with gay sons and their dads."

Gambone goes on to describe a popular gay psychiatrist's explanation for this commonly seen estrangement, which relies on the "born gay" assumption: "A father intuitively senses his son is homosexual and distances himself, rather than directly confronting the discomfort and shame he feels about this queer presence in the family."

Gambone admits his father was a good man. He seems puzzled that he could never feel love for his father or even cry at his funeral. "In his own quiet way," Gambone says, "he never gave up on me. Through all the years that I remained silent about my homosexuality, he never wavered in the willing affability with which he greeted the guys—'my roommates'—whom I brought home."

"I have scoured the memories of our relationship, looking for clues as to why I never totally felt at ease with my father," he says. Sometimes Gambone wonders if the problem was his father's unconscious homophobia (referring to the "born that way" theory in which the father is thought to reject the gender-nonconforming son, thus causing the estrangement), while at other times Gambone blames his mother's and grandmother's deliberate efforts to cause a father-son estrangement—"They were telling me to stay away from him."

Still, Gambone admits, "none of these generalizations feels adequate." Looking back, he realizes that his father was really a kind and caring man who reached out to him and wanted the best for him, challenging his son to take more risks and to tackle the problems of life more aggressively. "In retrospect," Gambone laments, "I wonder if I just wasn't ready for the kind of intimacy my father had always been willing to have with me."[26]

As in the story written by the above author, many fathers feel rejected by their sons. However, we could say that at one time or another *all* fathers have felt rejected by their sons. The difference is that the father of the prehomosexual boy is likely the kind of man who accepts that rejection, who throws up his hands and fails to reach out to try to understand and break through the child's resistance. (Or, as in Gambone's case, the maternal relatives actively sabotage the father-son connection.) For whatever reason, the father fails to get past that block and instead settles for the alienation, the silence, and the rejection.

In the years that follow, such inaction could cost both father and son dearly. "Dan," a thirty-two-year-old client, describes this sadness about a lost opportunity:

> My father is like the Lincoln Monument: sitting up there rigid and aloof. I don't want to give myself to him. There is a fear, but also an aversion to what he represents. I sound like such a kid when I say I am afraid of this "Big Bad Wolf" thing. But he doesn't really know me, and I don't know him.
>
> All I ever really wanted was my daddy. That's all it is, and yet how mournfully I recognize that for all the years I've wasted, I can't go back into my childhood.
>
> Neither will he ever be a different man. At seventy years old, he'll never change. It's like, "Why should I bother to try to have a relationship with him?" I don't know him; he doesn't know me.

Three Types of Fathers

In my work with homosexually oriented men, I have observed that the majority of fathers appear to be—for the most part—within the psychologically normal range. That being said, it is necessary to repeat that, as a group, these fathers are characterized by one serious limitation: the inability or unwillingness to counter their sons' defensive detachment and to reengage them back into the masculine sphere.

Beyond that categorization, fathers appear to fall into three broad personality categories:

Immature. Such men are basically normal and healthy. However, during the critical developmental period (gender-identity phase) of their sons' lives, they were overextended and failed to see the consequences. Often, these were young men who had become fathers too soon and found themselves overwhelmed with marital, family, or financial burdens. As a result, their temperamentally vulnerable sons, if they had such sons, paid a price.

Narcissistic. Even a basically healthy man may have narcissistic personality features. But in the most extreme case of narcissism, a man sees his son as an extension of himself (as a "narcissistic self-object"), and he uses the boy to fulfill his own needs. The father acknowledges the boy only when he exhibits an attractive trait, appearance, skill, or personality type that the father personally values. If the boy has such traits, the father will put him up on a pedestal and treat the boy like he can do no wrong. If he lacks these traits, the boy, in effect, does not exist within the family. Such a father typically denies any responsibility for his son's problems. This is the most resistant type of father when confronted, and he is unlikely to cooperate in any kind of therapy.

Inadequate. These fathers may be great providers and thoroughly competent in the working world, but they generally are emotionally limited on an intimate social level and have little to give another person. They do not have the emotional resources to reach beyond themselves. Unlike narcissistic fathers who deny responsibility, these men may readily admit their failures and express remorse, but then no improvement takes place in the father-son relationship on a consistent basis. After a brief and often well-intentioned effort on the part of this father to comply, the relationship remains essentially unchanged.

One client told me, "My father was a nothing, a zero. My mother made all the decisions. She had the personality, and my father had very little to say. I don't even remember my father being home. If he was home, he was there physically, but that was about all."

Emotionally limited fathers are generally dependent upon others, particularly their wives, to interpret social situations and tell them the right way to respond. On their own, they are unable to sustain a long-term commitment to remain involved and help their sons change.

Alex's Story

The following is an excerpt from the journal of "Alex," a forty-two-year-old man in therapy with me for homosexuality. His father was a strong and forceful but negative figure, while his mother was apparently a codependent and fragile individual, with whom Alex became defensively aligned.

> My father taught us to be very, very respectful of him. He would not allow disrespect. And if he said to do something, you had better do it for your own good. He would punish us and make us afraid of him if we didn't do what we were supposed to do. Sometimes he would hit us, and although it wasn't very often, it was something that terrified me. He would also punish us by taking away privileges and making us go to bed without dinner. He had a way of making us all feel like we were no good.
>
> My dad was far from perfect, and as I grew older, I saw his imperfections. Still, he would push an image of himself as proud and righteous that would make us feel worthless in his sight.
>
> My mother practically worshiped the ground Dad walked on and loved him very much. And although she loved all us children very, very much, she loved my dad even more. And being very, very emotional, my mother couldn't stand to be on bad terms with my dad. My mom wouldn't stand up to my dad for us directly. She would try to make us do what was right so he wouldn't get after us. But when my dad let go his anger, my mom wouldn't do anything that I can remember to protect us from him. She was just as afraid of him as we kids were.

In summary, the most important person in the successful treatment of the gender-confused boy is the father. The early psychoanalysts looked to the influence of smothering mothers on their homosexual sons; Mom's excessive emotional closeness to her boy seemed to be the cause of the boy's homosexuality. Today, however, the most significant figure in the formation of male homosexuality is thought by most reparative therapists to be the father. Why? Because mother-son closeness is not a problem *as long as the father models for the boy how to be in relationship with a woman.* The father supports the boy's masculine identification so that the son can be close to, but not get lost in, the feminine. He shows the boy how to be close to a woman without sacrificing his masculine independence.

What Other Researchers Say

There is clinical evidence that in both boys and girls, clear cases of gender-identity disorder (GID) often result from intense frustration and stress within the family—either from some outside event, or from frustrating interactions between the child and his or her parents—that occurred during the early developmental period when the child should have been developing a coherent sense of self as male or female. Evidence is offered by the authors of *Gender Identity Disorder and Psychosexual Problems in Children and Adolescents.*

The authors, Kenneth Zucker and Susan Bradley, describe the most common characteristics of GID boys: an avoidance of rough-and-tumble play, parents who failed to discourage cross-gender behaviors, and a detached father. Temperamentally, these authors say, the gender-disturbed child is likely to be particularly sensitive to his parents' moods because he was born with a reactive and sensitive nature that does not handle stressful and challenging situations well. This probably is the same temperamental factor that makes gender-disturbed boys avoid rough-and-tumble play. Such boys generally feel inadequate as males, have problems interacting with their male peers, and tend to interpret any criticism as rejection. Other specific factors within this group of boys may be that they are unusually attractive, Zucker and Bradley say, and have highly developed sensory sensitivities.[27]

Mothers of such boys, the authors say, sometimes feel particularly threatened by male aggression, and so they discourage boisterous behavior and normal aggression. Out of their own intense need to nurture and be nurtured, many of the mothers encouraged feminine-type, reciprocal nurturance behaviors in their sons.

Fathers, the authors note, tend to go along with their wives' tolerance of cross-gender behavior, despite their own inner uneasiness about what they see happening. This type of father, they say, has difficulty expressing feelings and feels emotionally inadequate himself. These inadequacies make it difficult for him to connect with and to actively help a troubled son. Such a father deals with family problems by withdrawing, working long hours and distancing himself.

In such cases, the authors believe that "the parents' valuing of their son as a male and discouragement of cross-gender behaviors allows a gradual relinquishing of the defensive solution, and a building of confidence in a same-sex identity."[28]

Father and Son—A Hands-On Relationship

I recommend four examples of activities for fathers wanting to develop closer relations with their sons.

1. Physical aggression with Dad is a good way of breaking through the timidity and shyness associated with gender-disturbed boys. More important, it is an effective means through which dads can bond with their sons. This can be done on a living room rug or in a family room. The aim is to encourage a little of the "wild boy" to break through. By "playing weak" the dad allows the son to feel tough, strong, and aggressive.

2. Showering with Dad is good for small boys and can sometimes include brothers. This is best begun when the child is small, because boys approaching puberty will be shy about being naked with Dad for the first time. (Some fathers, too, may feel uncomfortable with this activity, depending on the attitude toward nudity in their childhood home.) Showering with Dad and other males in the house fosters a common, relaxed, anatomically based identity and breaks down the fascination and sense of mystery around male anatomy which will fuel male eroticism when puberty arrives.

3. Trips out of the house with just father and son are very helpful; even routine errands to the store or, say, fueling up the car (letting the son pump the gas). These quick trips can communicate a feeling of special togetherness. Buying the son ice cream and engaging him in discussion of something he enjoys makes the errand fun.

4. At bedtime, Dad should be the last person to tuck the son into bed. While Mom may participate, Dad should be the last one to say good night and turn out the lights. Especially for younger children, bedtime can bring feelings of vulnerability and anxiety that show themselves in dependence and even clinginess. The father should be the one to provide emotional comfort and reassurance after a period of quiet bedside prayer, Bible-reading, or conversation.

Some gender-disturbed boys may be hesitant to take part in such father-son activities at first, but they remain important. My adult homosexual clients rarely report having shared these activities with their fathers.

Fathers should be encouraged to have physical contact and to engage in physical activity with their sons. I place a great deal of emphasis on roughhousing, because the normal childhood connection with men is what usually was so lacking in my adult homosexual clients. Men and boys connect best through doing any sort of physical competition or shared activity, and if it is experienced as fun, it will facilitate father-son bonding. Rough-and-tumble play, like wrestling, is very important between father and son.

If there is a physical disability affecting the father, this should not be detrimental to the son's development. If the father can display physical affection but cannot participate in rough-and-tumble play, perhaps that kind of activity can come from a brother or someone else.

A lot of the men I counsel, when entering therapy as adults, describe getting sexually aroused by wrestling. They are unable to participate in that normal masculine sport without the intrusion of eroticism. In fact, many "Personals" ads in gay papers will solicit a "guy to wrestle with." What should be a normal, healthy, nonerotic competitive activity is twisted by gay men into an eroticized behavior. And the origin of this distortion is the unmet need for healthy masculine contact. As Richard Wyler tells us:

> The cultural message is clear: Real men don't touch. Unfortunately, this taboo often carries over to fathers and sons, even when boys are still very young, and to brothers and close friends. Men in our culture seem afraid of being perceived as homosexual, or even of "making" themselves or someone else homosexual by hugging, holding or touching them. But the very thing they fear is the thing they are creating—a society of touch-deprived boys who grow up longing to be held by a man.
>
> If the need to be touched and held isn't met in childhood, it doesn't just go away because a boy grows into a man. For us, the desire was so primal, and so long denied, that some of us sought sex with a man at times when all we really wanted was to be held. We just didn't know how else to receive the non-sexual touch we craved.(<www.peoplecanchange.com>)

A boy's need for physical contact with his father cannot be overstated. One of my homosexual patients shared with me a childhood memory of longing for his father's loving touch:

> We'd visit my father during summer vacations in Appalachia. On those hot, sultry nights, he'd lie on the couch with his shirt off, reading those paperback adventure novels. I remember lying there next to him, touching his hairy stomach. I remember trying to get his attention without angering him, but he was engrossed in his reading. I am coming to realize that my homosexual activities have been all about my wanting to get in that kind of contact with my dad.

Sometimes, in attempting to establish greater physical intimacy, these boys try to make physical contact with their fathers, but their dads say, "It doesn't feel quite right." A father may tell me that when his effeminate son hugs him, it feels a little uncomfortable—almost romantic or seductive. "It feels the way a daughter would hug her father." I advise them to model a different kind of hugging and connection that is warm and real but also manly and respectful of gender and generational boundaries.

A child's strongly negative reaction to attempts by you to affirm his authentic gender is an indication that professional counseling is called for. Signs that you should seek professional guidance and assistance include prolonged sadness, anger, hurt, resentment, anxiety, and fearful preoccupation.

Beyond Mom and Dad

Parents need not feel alone and unsupported in their efforts to assist their gender-disturbed child. Too often, shame or embarrassment will prevent them from soliciting the help of other significant people to become involved in their son's life. Let's take a moment to consider who, besides the mother and father, can help the boy.

Younger siblings usually do not have much of an influence, but older ones do. Typically, a GID boy is very close to his older sister; he may even idolize her. If the sister is mature enough, she can be encouraged to support the parents' efforts. The older girl's strong influence on the boy can greatly assist his masculine confidence.

Older brothers are also very important. In the course of his career, Freud worked with only a small group of homosexuals. But he did say that if a homosexual has an older brother, he will usually fear the older brother, and their relationship will be hostile. I have seen this confirmed over and over again. The homosexual usually perceives his older brother, like his father, with resentment and dread. Fear of other males can, in fact, become a strong preoccupation.

Many of my clients recall, "I was Mom's son, but my brother was Dad's son." It is an unspoken division: "Dad and my brother were together over *there,* and me and Mom and my sister were over *here.*" Therefore, it is important to get the older brother involved. I have been surprised at the cooperation of brothers as young as thirteen years old. Without explaining all your concerns, you can enlist an older brother's involvement, and he can be a powerful support in building the gender-confused boy's masculine confidence. "Your brother will make it hard for you to connect with him," you can say, "because he's shy and he's having trouble feeling comfortable with other guys. We need your help to get him over that."

Bringing relatives, friends, and neighbors into the intervention for a boy with weak gender esteem will broaden the field of players and keeps the parents from trying to do everything themselves. A few honest but discreet words about the situation (the boy is "having trouble feeling like one of the guys"), along with a request for male role-modeling and help in sports involvement, can make a big difference.

An athletic coach can play an important, even pivotal role in the healing process. Parents will need to explain their particular concerns to the coach. A cooperative and sympathetic coach, whether for karate, swimming, soccer, Little League, or any other kind of sport, can add an extra positive dimension to the team effort that parents are trying to create. Boys need masculine figures in their lives who are strong but gentle, and patient and encouraging.

Teachers also play key roles in the effort. Usually, when the school refers a boy to a psychologist for treatment, it is because the boy's behavior has created a class disruption. However, most gender-disturbed boys are the "good little boys" who never draw negative attention. Unfortunately, teachers are not trained to identify the subtle signs of gender confusion. Nonetheless, I think it is important for you to tell teachers about your concerns. It is not necessary to use the word "homosexual"; the phrase "gender issues" or even "low gender esteem" is sufficient.

Even if she has some politically correct notions, the teacher's best instincts and common sense will often overrule, and she will work with you. It is amazing how many teachers will readily cooperate with concerned parents.

Begin by explaining, "We want our son to be better connected with boys. We are consulting with a counselor right now, and our treatment plan includes your assistance. Can you encourage our son to play with boys and help diminish his female activities?"

This network of support is the key to the prevention of homosexuality. In fact, the need for friendships with other boys cannot be overemphasized. Apart from the obvious importance of Dad, followed by Mom and the family, other boys may well prove to be the people most indispensable to his healing process.

In the next chapter, we will take a look at the importance of male friends in the life of the gender-disturbed boy.

5

FRIENDS AND FEELINGS

I looked at the outside world of boys my own age

like a prisoner looking through a barred cell window.

I felt locked in the cell of myself, and I longed to get out.

MALCOLM BOYD, AUTHOR

As the gender-confused boy approaches puberty, he typically experiences a few life-altering events that convince him he must be gay. One such moment was described to me by one of my clients, as follows: "I recall the exact moment I knew I was gay. I was twelve years old and we were taking a shortcut to class. We were walking across the gym and we went through the boys' locker room. An older guy was coming out of the shower. He was wet and naked, and I thought, *Wow!*" I asked the client to tell me exactly what his experience was. He became quiet and thoughtful. Then he answered, "The feeling was, *Wow, I wish I was him.*"

Unmet normal developmental needs predispose a boy to the "Wow!" experience, and later, through the influences of an increasingly gay-affirming culture, these feelings of male admiration are interpreted to mean, *Then I must be gay.* As a little boy, this particular client had been asthmatic and physically frail. Clearly, the "older guy" coming out of the shower was his idealized self. Years of feeling not like other boys predispose the ten-, eleven-, and twelve-year-old to this "Wow!" experience. This shift marks the critical "erotic transitional phase," when the boy's same-sex-attachment needs transform into erotic attraction.

Gay activist Andrew Sullivan describes of his own feelings of not belonging and the fears they aroused. To this day, he can still feel the sting of his classmates' words: "I remember the first time it dawned on me that I might be a homosexual. I was around the age of ten and had succeeded in avoiding the weekly soccer practice in my elementary school. . . . I loathed soccer, partly because I wasn't very good at it and partly because I felt I didn't belong in the communal milieu in which it unfolded." Seeing his reluctance to join the other boys, a female classmate teased him, suggesting that maybe he was really "a girl under there." Her words, Sullivan says, "resonated so much with my own internal fears that I remember it vividly two decades later."[1]

Breaking Down the Isolation

Much of the challenge to grow in gender esteem involves relationships with other boys. The following entries come from the private journal of a mother, shortly after she became convinced that her four-year-old son, "Will," was defensively shutting himself off from the challenge to connect with other boys.

> *February 10.* My husband and I consulted with Dr. N. today. It was incredible and terribly depressing. Will's behavior is exactly the same as other young pre-homosexual boys. When in a sandbox, he's always pretending he is cooking something, and he never builds roads, as more masculine boys would. He cries when he has to play with the other boys, and he avoids them.

> *March 15.* I've tried hard to find some little boys that aren't so intimidating. Recently, Will has been more willing to stay with the boys in his class at preschool. However, he still feels insecure, and he took ten giant steps backwards today because he did not want to go back outside to play during recess with the other kids after one boy teased him.

> Recently, he's really been making an effort not to run so femininely. He used to run with his arms flying around. I told him he can run much faster if he pumps his arms at his sides when he runs, and it worked. I am also trying to encourage him to speak in a less high-pitched voice, because he does have a tendency to stop using his normal voice a lot of the time and imitate baby tones. Today we practiced sentences using his "real voice," the one I told him that God gave him.

He is still afraid of playing rough, but every day is an improvement. Since he seems to be more enthusiastic about being like Uncle Bob than being like his father, I told my brother about Will's problems and asked him if he would give my son a little extra attention when he came over. My brother makes sure that he holds him and plays with him now when they see each other.

March 18. Will's ball playing is improving, and he even enjoys it for a short time. My brother Bob spent a lot of time with him, and he said he's going to take him and Will's eight-year-old cousin, Sammy, along to miniature golf. Sammy is a kind, patient kid, and I'm hoping he'll take Will under his wing a bit.

March 22. Will asked to go and play with his cousin Brenton today, and we were more than happy to let him. Brenton's "all boy," really tough, really good in sports, and two years older. When Will came home, I asked him if he wanted to go and play with Brenton again soon, and he was not enthusiastic. But after I encouraged him, he finally said he would go, but only if his sister went with him. At least that's a start.

Like Will's mother, you should always remember that besides your immediate family, same-sex peers are among the most important influences in your son's life. Male friends are key factors in masculine gender formation and future heterosexual development. The influence of male friendships is illustrated by a particularly intriguing study that found that even for nursery school boys, their male classmates had a stronger influence on them than did their adult teachers.[2] Clinician Richard Friedman also found male friendships to be frequently painfully distorted during the juvenile phase of childhood in homosexual males.[3] Dr. Friedman believes this isolation from other boys plays a central role in homosexual development.

The absence of close boyhood pals has been noticed by many other researchers studying homosexuality.[4] Most homosexual men remember feeling "on the outs" with the other guys and unable to feel like an equal in their games and activities. This sets the stage for the self-concept of masculine inferiority, which leads to romantic longing and idealization.

In my own clinical experience, this absence of a really close boyhood buddy is very common. In fact, in the view of clinicians Gerard van den Aardweg and

Richard Fitzgibbons, this absence of boyhood buddies can be the deciding factor in forming a boy's sexual orientation. Indeed, they believe this problem may
be more influential than the boy's relationship with his parents.[5]

Richard Wyler describes how, instead of buddying with other guys and identifying with them, the men who tell their stories on his website remained developmentally stuck in their defensive detachment:

> Feeling deficient as males, we pined to be accepted and affirmed by others, espe-
> cially those whose masculinity we admired most. . . . At the same time we idol-
> ized certain male traits or maleness generally, many of us came to fear other boys
> and men.
>
> Born with unusually sensitive and gentle personalities, we found it was easy for
> many of us to feel different from and rejected by our more rough-and-tumble
> peers growing up. We came to fear their taunts and felt like we could never be-
> long. Many of us feared the sports field and felt like we could never compete.

Fear blocked them from trusting the men whom they so badly needed at that
time to be their mentors and role models:

> We were afraid to open our hearts to other men, to be truly "seen," to ask for
> help. We were afraid to trust men, afraid that they would dismiss or deride us,
> wouldn't keep confidences, wouldn't keep their word, or wouldn't really care.
> Some of us felt anxiety or even panic just being around men, getting near a ball
> field with them, or attempting to have a heart-to-heart with them.
>
> And fearing them, we ran from them. (<www.peoplecanchange.com>)

Almost without exception, my clients also recall a feeling of not measuring
up, which has imprinted the extremely destructive message "You aren't like
other boys." For example, Roger, a twenty-eight-year-old client, recalls an incident from the time he was twelve years old:

> I finally got picked for a baseball game. The ball came right to me, but I missed
> it and it landed a few feet away. I guess I was trying to look cool, but I walked to
> the ball instead of running. Everyone was yelling at me. The pitcher said I was
> walking like a girl. I felt humiliated. I didn't know if I should just stand there, run
> away, or punch the pitcher. It was the worst moment in my life.

Imagine how it would feel for a boy to have a distant father and also to be
teased by his same-sex peers. Imagine how it would feel to be called clumsy, a
sissy, a crybaby, or a mama's boy or to be labeled for any number of other fail-

ures. Often Mom, Grandma, or Sister is the only person in whom such a boy finds affection and sympathy. Because he tends to be emotionally sensitive, such a boy *believes* his classmates' teasing labels and gives up the struggle to prove they are not true. Their name-calling only confirms his hidden fear that he is not a "real boy."

Such are the childhood memories of the man whose story appears below—a client of mine now struggling with homosexuality in adulthood:

> My childhood and teen years were like so many others—an avoidance of and a dislike for football, baseball, and basketball, much to my father's silent disapproval; no rough-and-tumble play; no close buddies I could share with; asthmatic; aloof and emotionally guarded and isolated—even from my other siblings!
>
> What a devastating thing it is to believe at such a young age that you are utterly unworthy of your gender—the kind of son that no red-blooded father would want anything to do with. And when puberty arrived with its natural attendant urges, the male "eros" kicked in—and the rest you can probably guess.
>
> I sought comfort in TV, movies, books, and music, and although Bach and Mozart and Haydn have been great "friends" to me, music can never be a cure-all for loneliness. Like so many others, I have chosen to live in silence. A silence so painful and smothering that words are inadequate.

Rudy, a homosexual man, told me that when he was in grade school, his mother used to comb and part his hair and spray it until it was stiff with hair spray. The other boys always teased him about his hair because it felt so strange and bristly. Rudy would be sent off each morning in a clean white shirt, and carefully following his mother's daily admonitions, he would come home that night in that same, equally clean white shirt. As early as kindergarten, he became fascinated with another boy whose face he still vividly remembers today. This boy was exactly Rudy's opposite: dark-skinned, with long, curly, wild hair, disheveled clothing, and a loud voice; Rudy remembers him as looking like a "little savage." To this day, he still feels a romantic longing for the spontaneous, in-your-face type of male that his own lifelong role of "good little boy" prevented him from experiencing.

Fascination with such "outlaw" images appears, not surprisingly, as a common theme in gay life. Many homosexual men are drawn to leather bars, where men dress up in the roles of policemen, soldiers, and motorcycle gang members with leather chaps and chains. "By day," one of my clients told me, "a lot of these guys in these costumes are actually little accountants."

Acting, Fantasy, and Gay Icons

Fascination with image and role-playing is also seen in the gay world's adulation of female icons. Over and over among prehomosexual boys (as well as gay men), we see an absorption in fantasy and theater and acting. Many of my clients also played the piano as children. Some of this interest in music and theater can, of course, be attributed to the natural sensibilities of the boy born with the sensitive temperament. But fantasy, in particular, often becomes a form of escapism—a way of fleeing the painful challenge to participate in a gendered world.

Gay men are invariably captivated by larger-than-life feminine images, and they do not choose men as their icons. Instead, they become enthralled with Judy Garland, Barbra Streisand, Bette Davis, and Bette Midler (tough, assertive, "phallic" women) or Marilyn Monroe, Judy Garland, and Princess Di (tragic, misunderstood women). As children, they are captivated by images of Pocahontas, the Little Mermaid, and Cinderella. Adulation of female icons permits an escape into the secret feminine fantasy of childhood, providing an evasion to escape the challenge of developing their masculine potential.

"Why are gays drawn to Disney World each June?" asks Focus on the Family's Tom Hess. Anyone who doubts that gender conflict is at the root of homosexuality would likely lay that idea to rest after seeing Disney's annual Gay Day celebration. As Hess observes, "Infatuation with Disney icons like Alice is one of the top draws for homosexuals who flock to Gay Day each year."

"Snow White and the Seven Dwarfs have stepped down from their Enchanted Forest float and with wide smiles, they're inviting children, many of them under the age of 6, to join them in a dance," Hess notes. But this day, because it's Gay Day, there's a man dancing ecstatically with Snow White while wearing a little girl's diamond tiara. Watching him dance, Hess says, "are several thousand other homosexuals, all beaming like little boys . . . the sea of men erupts in adoring applause."[6] Another man jumps up and down with a polka-dot hair ribbon on his head as he leaps in delight while dancing with a costumed Alice.

One adult homosexual client of mine said that for a period of ten years, from the age of fifteen to twenty-five, every day he had to have some contact with Judy Garland. Either he had to hear her sing on one of his recordings (he owned them all) or he had to contemplate her photograph before he could leave his apartment for work. This female image was a symbol that soothed him.

One of the contributors to *Gay Soul,* a popular book in the gay community, discusses his own love of female icons, explaining why he himself sometimes wears a dress:

> Being involved in cross-dressing is a way of laying claim to all the possible arche-
> types of the universe. . . . In the divide between men and women, I like being
> right on the fence, to be able to sense the experience of both sides and to implic-
> itly point out that the divisions are artificial. . . . Who says gay men can't wear this
> particular item of clothing? . . . Or makeup? Why not?
>   The trouble is that people insist on an either/or, binary system of perception.
> . . . [But] we're not going to be just any old female. Aim high! This is part of turn-
> ing yourself into an archetype. . . . A lot of people . . . pick Bette Davis. . . . I
> pick Elizabeth I. They have similar characteristics; larger-than-life, imperious,
> and somewhat gender-ambiguous.[7]

Men who role-play as female characters say they do it because it offers relief from internal stress and conflict. Some keep an elaborate collection of women's underwear and nightgowns from the Victoria's Secret catalog that they wear in private as a relief from the pressure of having to present a masculine image to the world. And everyone has seen gay men in drag at a pride parade or in a gay bar wearing high heels and a wig. These men are reliving the fantasy option— the secret androgynous fantasy of childhood in which they decided they did not have to make a decision to be either male or female; they could be both. But because biology is (in the case of sexual identity) destiny, the consequence of taking the fantasy option does not result in *genuine* androgyny, but a pervasive and nagging sense of masculine *deficit.*

We are reminded of lesbian activist Camille Paglia's observation that "mas-culinity is risky and elusive—it is achieved by a revolt from a woman and con-firmed only by other men."[8] Gender-deficient men still secretly cling to the feminine identification that is proper to children in early infancy but that iso-lates them from the healthy challenge of a gender-polarized world.

An End to the Gender System?

Because gender is remembered as a source of pain in childhood, the annihila-tion of gender differences is, not surprisingly, a central demand of gay culture. Gay advocates often call for "an end to the gender system." Daryl Bem, who is an openly gay psychologist, describes his version of the ideal society—a "non-gender-polarizing culture" in which everyone (male and female) would potentially be everyone else's lover.[9]

By the time they are adults, many gay men feel a combination of self-hatred (which they label internalized homophobia), an intense desire to find masculinity in an erotic partner, and a defensive drive to celebrate their gender confusion as if it represented a superior condition. The anthology *Gay Soul* contains a series of chapters written by gay men who extol the superiority of the homosexual as "two-spirited." As one writer explains: "Gay men and women . . . [are] essential to the health of society, as people who are freed from the responsibilities of procreation . . . as people who point to an inner fusion of male and female, a holy androgyny, that all beings could aspire to."[10]

Says another: "Sex is an avenue to bliss in the soul, and that bliss I have followed all my life. . . . Bisexuality is natural; nature is pansexual. The soul is androgynous in everyone . . . gaiety makes us gods."[11]

And another writer agrees that homosexuality is a superior condition:

> I think the future of the world, the hope of the world, depends on us, that men who love men are the only people who can save this planet. That's our job, our purpose. We carry this other kind of energy that no one else carries. . . . The world is looking to us even though it doesn't know it.
>
> Because we live between genders, we also live between matter and spirit, between this world and the next. . . . Nothing has stopped us [from having sex with each other]. Not damnation, not imprisonment, not all kinds of psychological labels, because this energy in us is so strong. It allows us . . . to feed our souls and feed the culture.[12]

Changing attitudes about gender have begun to spread beyond gay literature into the courts. Some judges agree that the "gender system" is unfairly discriminatory. A court in Brockton, Massachusetts, recently ruled that a gender-disturbed junior high school boy must be permitted to attend classes while wearing girls' clothing. The boy had been suspended three times for using the girls' bathroom and wearing padded bras, wigs, tight skirts, and high-heeled shoes to school and for grabbing another boy's buttocks.

The boy's therapist had diagnosed him with gender-identity disorder. She said it was "medically and clinically necessary for [him] to wear clothing consistent with female gender." If he was not allowed to dress as a girl, the therapist told the court, he would be traumatized. The judge in the case—who is an open lesbian—agreed with the boy's therapist and obligingly referred to the disturbed boy as "she."[13]

Transgenderism is a theme the gay community has—for public relations reasons—long downplayed. Gay activists correctly suspect that the public senses something "not normal" about a boy thinking he is a girl. But with the recent political successes of the gay movement, the former effort to present homosexual men and women as "just as gender-typical as straights" is slowly giving way to a bolder approach. Activists have begun to lobby for new laws that assert the right of transgendered persons to dress and identify themselves in the workplace according to their preferred gender.

In contrast, Dale O'Leary, author of *The Gender Agenda,* observes that society must resist affirming a self-delusion:

> The boy in Brockton, Massachusetts is not a "she" no matter how many judges or therapists pretend he is. He is a boy with a severe gender identity disorder who needs real help. Unfortunately, many medical and mental health professionals— rather than working to find a cure for this type of psychological problem—have decided that *supporting the delusion* constitutes treatment. Or worse, they further the delusion through surgery aimed at "changing" a person's sex.
>
> Patients who suffer from the belief that they are men trapped in the bodies of women (or women trapped in the bodies of men) need real help. Cutting off a man's private parts, giving him breast implants, shooting him full of female hormones, and taking off his beard will not make him a woman—it will make him something less than a eunuch. Surgery will *not* change the fact that every cell of the man's body is clearly marked male (XY).[14]

All of these efforts, O'Leary accurately notes, are a part of a social movement aimed at the "destabilization of the categories of sex and gender."

But Is This Really an *Indifference* to Gender?

The gender-confused child does not truly feel an indifference to gender, says psychiatrist Richard Fitzgibbons. More accurately, he is explicitly *rejecting* the gender that should be his own.

> Children with gender identity problems don't inhabit a gender-neutral world where boys and girls play with the same toys. These troubled children reject certain types of play and clothing precisely because they ARE associated with their own gender, and they adopt activities because they are associated in their mind with the opposite sex. Boys with serious gender identity problems may use female

clothing to gain acceptance or soothe anxiety, and they become angry and upset when deprived of these objects.

Some parents may ask "What is wrong with a boy playing with dolls?" The answer is that the problem is as much what he is NOT doing—learning how to be a boy among boys—as it is what he IS doing—escaping into a female world.[15]

The feelings described by homosexual strugglers are not (as the gay movement often claims) a more highly evolved and superior attitude of androgyny. These are not healthy, positive, and expansive feelings, as psychologist Daryl Bem says—a mere "indifference to gender."[16] They are feelings of gender confusion and alienation.

Richard Wyler describes the origin of these feelings about males and masculinity: "Some of us began consciously or subconsciously to deride men as inferior . . . as 'Neanderthal' . . . less 'evolved.' Often, we succumbed to the common psychological phenomenon of being most critical of what we most envied. . . . Or most feared" (<www.peoplecanchange.com>).

Another powerful illustration of this experience of gender alienation comes from "Dan," a former client.

> We had an old farmhouse outside Sioux City, and you opened up this rickety trapdoor and went down these creaky steps into a dark and damp-smelling basement. My father would escape from the rest of us and spend hours there in his machine shop. But I was forbidden to go there—I might break his tools or get hurt, is what he told me. So I would lie on my belly up above, looking down and watching Dad work.
>
> What I'll never forget is that feeling of mystery about what was going on down below. Eventually my Dad let my two older brothers help him, and they'd be talking and working and laughing. It wasn't just the mystery of what was being done in the cellar . . . it was the whole mystery of who Dad was, because to this day, I really don't understand him.
>
> If I had to draw just one picture that would represent my entire childhood, it would be of me peering down into the darkness below at my father and my brothers.[17]

This hunger for male attention, affection, and approval—a yearning to share in the "masculine way of knowing"—is transformed in early adolescence into sexual strivings. When these needs begin to take on an intensely sexual nature, the boy may then identify his longings as his "being gay," particularly if this idea is supported by a gay counseling program at school or a chat room on the Internet. As Richard Wyler says:

> We saw ourselves as too fat or too skinny, too short or too awkward, not athletic enough or tough or strong or good-looking enough—or whatever other qualities we admired in other males but judged to be lacking in ourselves.
>
> It was more than low self-esteem, it was low gender esteem—a deficiency in our core sense of gender upon which our whole self image is guilt. Other males just seemed naturally masculine, but masculinity never came naturally to us. We aspired to it but were mystified by how to achieve it. Among other males, we felt different and lonely. (<www.peoplecanchange.com>)

Author William Aaron describes this same situation in his autobiography:

> Contributing to my retreat into homosexuality was that I was one of those sensitive, "artistic" children with neither the talent nor interest in any of the usual "masculine" pursuits. I hated physical activity—sports, and games most of all—and when I would make an effort to be part of the gang I would fail so miserably to perform well that for a long time afterward I would suffer from the shame of ineptitude . . . I was a classic case in that I (later) felt out of place in a man's world, and comfortable and capable in a more esoteric environment.[18]

The prehomosexual boy's longing may be with him for the rest of his life, along with the image of the window—the symbol of emotional detachment. Malcolm Boyd describes such a quality of detachment in his book *Take Off the Masks:*

> By the time I reached adolescence, I was a frail youngster who read a lot of books, was extraordinarily intense and solitary. My intermittent friendships with a few other boys usually ended abruptly and without explanation. I believed that the fault lay within me, a result of my personal ineptness in sustaining relationships. For the most part I looked at the outside world of boys my own age like a prisoner looking through a barred cell window. I felt locked in the cell of myself, and I ached to get out.[19]

Maximizing Masculine Potential

I believe these studies' implications for parents are clear. In order to grow up with a secure sense of themselves as males, boys must be encouraged to overcome their fears. There are many ways they can be helped to do so.

When boys relate well with their fathers, beginning to understand what is exciting, fun, and energizing about them, the relationship will evoke the boy's own masculine nature. Through his dad, the son finds a sense of freedom and power in being different from his mother, outgrowing her and moving on into a man's world, and finally maturing into heterosexual manhood.

Boys in groups have a unique power to actualize masculine potential in each other. Perhaps you, as a parent, have noticed how boys interact in a rough, mutually challenging way that toughens them up. Through a balance of challenge and support—teasing, ribbing, insulting, shoving, bolstering, and showing affection—we see a process of "iron sharpening iron." The good-natured putdowns and teasing that men engage in may well feel hurtful and confusing to the sensitive teenager. Boys will alternately put each other down and then lift each other up with the tough love that characterizes masculine affection and compassion. It is very different from the way girls get along together. That unique masculine way of relating is beautifully showcased in the movie *Stand by Me.* Males in groups teach each other an emotional resiliency and trust of other men that the prehomosexual boy misses.

Another way to help your son is to help him gain a basic proficiency in a sport he can enjoy—often an individual sport, such as swimming, running, or cycling—where he can learn to take the risks necessary to feel like one of the guys. A sensitive boy will probably never become a football player, but neither should he simply yield to his fears and retreat to girls' activities or solitary play and fantasy.

What's a Mother (or Father) to Do?

In her journal, Will's mother tells us more about how her son is getting along. Recently, the positive involvement of the boy's father has been dramatically affecting the way Will feels about himself:

> *May 21.* Will was sick last week, and with that, I saw a lot of regressive behavior. I don't know if it was my mothering attention to him, the TV being back on full time, or something else, or everything combined. He pretended to be Princess Toadstool. But he did wake up with a high fever and called for his Daddy rather than me—another definite first.

> *May 27.* At the Memorial Day picnic, he played baseball with a group of kids and he couldn't hit the ball at all. I know it was lack of confidence in front of the other boys, because when he plays with his father, he can hit the ball quite well. It was painful for me to watch.

June 17. Will went fishing with his father. Dr. Nicolosi had advised that my husband should give him something to look forward to, and this fishing trip was it.

June 23. He is still not very enthusiastic about playing sports, and he may never be, but he does play a little—baseball, basketball, catch, soccer, kickball. With his dad, he's really not bad when he plays, and he is becoming very aggressive with kicking and punching the heavy bag. My outlook is fairly positive at this point. Each night he plays rough with his father, even though it is not his favorite thing to do, and then they fall asleep watching a ball game.

July 2. Will started camp today. I was so afraid to send him—afraid that he was not ready to be out yet in the male world alone. I felt as though I was sending a lamb to the slaughter. I had until the end of the first week to get a refund for the camp tuition, and I held on to it for dear life, certain that I would have to cancel. Well, he loved it and is not afraid to go at all! They assigned him a buddy named Ivan. He was always playing with the boys (there are girls in his group also) when I saw him. However, he still lacks confidence and talks about magic and Disney.

July 20. Will was on a bike and said to a boy he was playing with, "Touch this leaf. It's magic. It will make you into a boy." Dr. N. interpreted this as meaning that he desires to be a boy, but for him it is still only achieved through fantasy.

September 1. Will was very popular with the boys at camp. He was the only boy from camp that his buddy Ivan invited to his birthday party, and David's mom says David talks all the time about the fun things he and Will did together. I got the same information from the parents of another boy, Brian. Meanwhile, I would say right now that Will's relationship with his father is awesome.

A big plus is that my husband gave him some shirts of his to wear today, and he put them on and was so proud to wear them. Before, he rejected wearing anything that even resembled his father's things. He would have agreed to wear something of mine before he'd wear anything of his father's. His dad also bought him a play toolbox, and Will looks forward to helping fix the truck. They continue to shower together whenever possible. Right now I am very pleased. Last night Will slept with his new basketball.

As you can see, Will began to make good progress when his parents did three specific things. As a parent, you will need to follow their example. Here are the three things parents need to do for their sons:

1. Dad: Get involved.
2. Mom: Back off.
3. Both parents: Bring other boys into the picture.

Parents have to make a point of bringing other boys around. As we have seen, prehomosexual boys typically do not have close male friends. They tend to be reserved, cautious, and emotionally distant from the friends they do have. There is an absence of the outgoing, aggressive camaraderie that characterizes most boy friendships. These sensitive boys don't know how to make male connections, so they have girl friends instead, because it is easier and it feels safer. You can help your son by indirectly discouraging female friends and actively soliciting and encouraging male friends.

Many parents complain to me that there simply are not many boys in their neighborhood. If that is the case, both parents will have to chauffeur boys back and forth so that their son will have boy friends. I encourage parents, whenever possible, to host some sleepovers in which one or two boys will spend the night.

But a word of advice: at the beginning of treatment, the gender-confused boy will feel uneasy when he is with two boys. He will easily feel left out. It is easier for him to have one boy to focus his attention on—or perhaps, more importantly, to have one boy focus attention on him.

It bears repeating again and again: friendship with boys is of inestimable importance. You will soon see how your son responds strongly to these male relationships. At first, he will be shy. But once his anxiety diminishes, you will observe the emotional connection—sometimes a deep emotional dependence, which can only be satisfied with a lot of continued friendship.

Caution: A Support Group to Avoid

One group you should be careful to avoid is P-FLAG (Parents and Friends of Lesbians and Gays). This is the gay-affirming support organization recommended by advice columnist Ann Landers and even by the U.S. Department of Education. Many schools and community agencies refer families to P-FLAG, which has affiliates in all fifty states and counts over seventy thousand families among its membership.

In 1998 we ordered P-FLAG's pamphlet "Be Yourself: Questions and An-

swers for Gay, Lesbian and Bisexual Youth," which included a list of books recommended for gay teenagers. A close look at those recommended books,
however, revealed an approach to child guidance that is consistently both sexually and socially radical. First-person stories aimed at teens described in pornographic detail the delight of a young girl's sexual seduction by her lesbian
teacher, of gay relationships between teenage boys and much older men, and of
the precise how-tos of masturbation. In these books teenagers are specifically
encouraged to use only their feelings as a guide to sexual behavior, to be their
own judge of what is right and wrong, and to "have fun" experimenting sexually. Furthermore, teenagers are encouraged to view religious traditionalists as
mean-spirited and hypocritical, while at the same time, to see gay consciousness as "sacred." Were similar books recommended by parenting groups for
straight teenagers, they would be considered violations of community standards
of decency.

Some of the recommended books are relatively tame on the surface, jus-
tifying teenage homosexual experimentation with the usual attitude of "This
is me. This is who I am." Others go much further, glorifying sex with animals, witchcraft, feminist goddess worship, worship of sexual pleasure as a
form of religion, promiscuity with hundreds of partners, bisexual orgies, and
voyeurism.

The P-FLAG pamphlet recommends that religious youth read *Gay Soul:
Finding the Heart of Gay Spirit and Nature,* a book that labels gay sex "sacred." In
it, first-person stories tell of gay men delightedly flouting their vow of celibacy
in seminaries, of a man reporting that he had a peak orgasmic experience during sex with God, and of sadomasochistic torture being enjoyed by a psychotherapist as a mystical experience. Another writer in the anthology labeled as
"sacred" the act of incest between brothers or fathers and sons.

After we made a complaint about P-FLAG's reading list to the U.S. Department of Education, P-FLAG was not, as one would expect, removed from the
government's list of recommended agencies. But the parenting group did remove their list of recommended reading for teenagers from the next printing
of their pamphlet.

At her local P-FLAG chapter meeting, one mother of a homosexual son told
us, there is a particular "attitude adjustment" that is expected of any parent who
participates. She wrote:

The group members were sharing positive feedback, and one single mother of a 29-year-old son, who had full-blown AIDS, shared with great pride that the next night her son would be performing "drag" for the first time at a gay bar near our city. She had obviously grown into this attitude of "pride" after months of being encouraged into this posture by fellow group members who had "worked" with her attitude of becoming totally accepting and encouraging of her son's drag behavior.[20]

Planned Parenthood Is No More Reliable

Neither can you, as a parent, look to the advice of Planned Parenthood or its website Teenwire <www.teenwire.org>. This group encourages teenagers to circumvent the authority of their mother and father in sexual matters. It bestows its enthusiastic approval on a homosexual orientation ("It's a fine thing") as well as sexual liberation in general. Teenwire tells your teenager:

> Frankly, a web page can't decide for you if you're ready [for sex] or not. Neither can your best friend, boyfriend, girlfriend, parent, brother, counselor, rabbi— well, you get the idea. The only person who can know when the time's right is *you*.
>
> The truth is this: if you're lesbian, gay, straight, or bisexual, that's what you are, and it's a fine thing. Don't sweat it, accept it, because no amount of denial is going to change what makes you hot.[21]

Three Categories of Sports

When parents are trying to find their way into new activities for their sons, I usually talk with them about the various kinds of sports that are available. Boys relate by "doing," and—like it or not—sports are the most popular and convenient form of "doing" for males in our culture. There are three categories of sports, which are presented in the order of benefit.

1. Solo sports, such as swimming, bicycling, running, skateboarding, skiing, and rollerblading. These sports give boys a sense of connectedness with their masculine bodies, and that is important. Part of the homosexual condition is the feeling of alienation from one's own male body. In solo sports, the boy has the opportunity to discover his physical competence by challenging himself.
2. Solo-competitive sports, such as tennis and racquetball. Beyond "me against me," solo competition challenges the boy to compete with a peer.

The prehomosexual boy is often afraid to compete directly against another male. Typically, he is fearful of matching himself against another boy's masculine strength. Solo competition offers the reparative opportunity of "me against him."

3. Group-competitive sports, such as baseball, football, basketball, soccer, and volleyball. These activities are the best of all for your son because they have the advantages of the previous categories plus the additional opportunity of group bonding. In competitive team sports, the boy is identified with a group of boys against another group. He must work as a team member, and his performance will affect the performance of the entire team. Now it is "us against them."

It is difficult, at times, for parents to know how far to push their son. How much should he be challenged? They struggle with the question, are we applying too much pressure or not enough? How to determine the proper balance is especially difficult, since these boys are often secretive and reluctant to express themselves. And they are not always truthful, because they deeply desire to please their parents, especially when their effeminacy has become an openly acknowledged problem.

As with every reparative activity, the boy must never be forced to do anything he strongly resists. Being forced to participate in an activity and failing (especially in front of other boys) will almost certainly result in an emotionally painful experience. Such experiences will only reinforce negative associations and deepen the sense of self as weak and inadequate. The boy should be actively encouraged, but if he strongly protests, then he is not ready for that activity. Instead, he might better be coaxed to try a less challenging sport.

Some Basic Guidelines

Here are four suggestions for dealing with the difficult situation of assessing the appropriateness of your interventions:

1. You should work with a counselor or therapist with whom you feel comfortable, who shares your goals for your son and can offer an objective evaluation.

2. When you are not certain whether you are placing too much pressure on the boy to develop his masculine self, give the boy the benefit of the doubt and back off. The need for affirmation and positive encouragement is as essential as participation in the desired activity.

3. In developing masculine behavior, positive reinforcement (praise, encouragement) is far more effective than negative reinforcement (coercion, intimidation). However, for extinguishing feminine behavior, gentle and consistent disapproval will sometimes be necessary. Still, a basic rule is that greater long-term results are gained by positive response on the part of the parent for masculine behavior than by negative response for feminine behavior.

4. We make a very important distinction between *shaming* and *correcting*. Shaming is about the person; correcting is about behavior. Correcting says that the behavior is bad; shaming says that the person is bad. The message to convey is "Mom and Dad want you to fix this or that *behavior*, but *you* are always okay with us."

One sentence, modified to a particular situation, can be a convenient tool for parents of gender-confused children: "(Boy's name), that's a girl's (behavior, activity, or gesture), but you're a boy!" The sentence has three benefits:

- It is short and straightforward (nonpreaching).
- It uses "boy-girl" language, which challenges the boy's androgynous fantasy "I'm special; I can be a boy, a girl, or both."
- It places the critical focus not on the *person* (which would communicate shame) but on his situational *behavior*.

The statement "but you're a boy!" should have an encouraging tone. The parental message is "We are reminding you who you are, and *who you are is good*."

When the Feminine Behavior Returns

Most parents and family members notice a connection between increased stress in the boy's life and the reappearance of effeminate behavior. A thirteen-year-old told me about Andy, his seven-year-old brother:

> I was watching my younger brother for a few hours, and some of my friends came over. And as soon as my friends walked in, Andy felt uncomfortable. He didn't know what to do, so he got into a kind of feminine behavior. My friends were sort of laughing at this, and I knew Andy was embarrassed about his own behavior, but it was as if he didn't know what else to do. It was like he didn't know how to just relax.

Andy did not know how to cope with the anxiety of being in the presence of older males. As a defense, he relapsed into the comforting defense of effeminate behavior. Another mother with a gender-disturbed son reported a similar observation: "I can tell what kind of day my son has had at the YMCA by his behavior. If he is acting effeminate, I know he's frustrated. On the other hand, if he is warm and verbal, I know that he was good at soccer."

This mother has made an important observation: she describes "acting effeminate" as the opposite of being warm and verbal. When her gender-disturbed son is not in his effeminate mode, there is more emotional contact; he is more connected and he is "real." There is something one-dimensional about boyhood effeminacy that tells us that, in large part, this effeminacy is more of a defense than who this particular boy really is. Many parents detect an unnatural quality of sham or caricature in the boy who is explicitly effeminate. In fact, one researcher reports that effeminate boys are actually more feminine-acting than girls.[22]

When a boy's behavior is not just gender-nonconforming but explicitly effeminate, it will inevitably lack the rich, expansive quality of a natural trait that emerges from the real self. Effeminate behavior represents a form of hiding from the challenge of masculine individuation. This is done by playing a role—much like the fantasy roles the boy imagines himself taking on when he becomes transfixed in front of the TV watching neutered or female Disney characters.

Will Your Efforts Succeed?

Wise parents will do their best to help a son or daughter feel comfortable as a male or female and to develop strong and intimate same-sex friendships. However, the struggle to help your child can be frustrating, and there are no guarantees about the outcome.

Possibly, your best efforts to help your child will not result in a heterosexual orientation. If that happens, even though you will likely disapprove of a gay lifestyle (and probably will make that very clear), we hope that you, as loving parents, will always cherish and keep a relationship with your child. Also, you should never give up hope for healing change at some time in the future.

As we see in the following journal entry, Will's mother has at last begun to enjoy some success in her own efforts. Her son's progress continues—intermittent at times, but moving forward. The effort to help her son feel better about himself with other boys, she now concludes, has been well worth the effort:

I do get frustrated and wonder if I should pack this in sometimes, but I know that I could never stop striving for this, because I think of how much progress he has made, how much more comfortable and confident he is about himself. I have been hugging him extra lately so he knows that I love him so very much.

Today at recess he played basketball with the boys. I might add that he invited two "real" (gender-confident) boys over to the house. Although he was still more reserved than they were, I think that it is part of his personality and intellect to be more serious. I was just so happy to see how he got along so well with them.

6

CONFRONTING ADOLESCENCE

The gay world is so wild and so much of a party scene.
If I could just keep the sex out and just have the
close buddies I've always been looking for. . . . Can it happen?

FIFTEEN-YEAR-OLD BOY

What parent, teacher, friend or minister would encourage
a child to engage in life-threatening behavior?

BOB DAVIES, EXODUS INTERNATIONAL

Keith's mother's voice sounded breathless on the phone. "I'm very concerned, Dr. Nicolosi. My son has been corresponding on the Internet with an older boy. Keith is just fifteen, and after reading some of the things he's been writing this young man, I'm afraid he's, well . . . maybe leading up to, umm, a homosexual-relationship-type thing. I don't know what to do. Can you help him?"

The boy with low gender esteem harbors secret, unrealistic expectations about male friendship. He looks for an intense emotional intimacy and deep, mutual dependency. His neediness either turns off the other guy or else goes the other way, crossing the line into mutual eroticism.

Keith did not want to come in to see me. He was very resistant to the idea of therapy. His mother, like many others, had done a great deal of research. It was after she found one of my books at the public library and realized that my office was located nearby that she decided to call me. And although she and Keith's father were anxious that he should receive help, both were doubtful that therapy could help him.

Eventually they brought Keith into therapy. He arrived at my office angry, defensive, and suspicious. He was incensed that his parents were "forcing" him to change. And he was deeply hurt that they did not respect his feelings, nor accept him for who he believed he really was.

Before we met for the first time, Keith e-mailed me the following letter. We hear his rage at control and manipulation by adults in power:

> I don't trust you, I don't respect you, and g— if I'm going to open any avenue to a relationship. You are the epitome of everything that I DO NOT need in my life right now. And the way I see you, good or bad, is crucial, and essential, to any client-counselor relationship. I'm sick and tired of my feelings, emotions, and thoughts not being respected because of my age, supposed maturity level, or my sexual orientation. If we were to work together, my feelings MUST be accepted as my reality.
>
> You sit there analyzing me and everyone else that comes into your office. WHO ARE YOU? What gives you the right? The license hanging on the wall? Your past "experience"? Those men that you've supposedly turned straight? None of that gives me the impression that I'm safe to give you any control of my life.

Despite his anger and suspicion, Keith decided to come in for just one session. I learned that Keith really admired Luke, the older guy (twenty-four) with whom he had been corresponding. Luke was lead singer in a local rock band, and Keith needed someone to hear and respect his deep feelings of attraction to this admired young man.

I spent our second session demonstrating to him that I could give him what his parents could not—I *could* understand and affirm the validity of his feelings for Luke. Clearly, this lack of validation of his feelings was the primary source of Keith's hurt and anger toward his parents. Indeed, I could honestly say that I did understand his deeply felt feelings of love and admiration and romantic attraction. Luke was the kind of guy Keith admired and wished he himself could be. My understanding of Keith's feelings for Luke would be the foundation on which we could build a trusting relationship.

In our second session, Keith expressed his anger that his parents were prohibiting him from seeing Luke. Attempting to separate emotional needs from sexual feelings, I asked, "So Keith, tell me, if you had complete freedom, what would you like to do with Luke?"

He thought for a moment with a wistful smile on his face. Finally he said, "All I would like to do is drive down Pacific Coast Highway with him. I'd have the windows down, and we'd be listening to the radio together real loud." Becoming more thoughtful, he added, "What I really want is for us to hang out together and for me to be Luke's best friend."

"Can you imagine," I continued, "if Luke said to you, 'Keith, I really like you as a friend—you're my best friend—but I really don't want to do anything sexual. That's just not what I'm interested in. Let's just be best friends; let's do fun things together'? Keith, if Luke were to propose that, would that be satisfying to you?"

He nodded emphatically. "Absolutely!"

For Keith, that realization was a turning point. After that, I was able to give him a picture of the kind of relationship that I believed he was really looking for, something he had been wrongly seeing as proof that he must have been "born gay." It turned out that his anger toward his parents emanated from the fact that they did not accept his *feelings*—his romantic, idealized, and even dependent feelings for Luke. While sex also sounded fun and exciting to him, it was those deeply compelling *attachment needs* that drove Keith to believe he was gay.

Later on, I asked Keith to draw a picture of himself. We can learn quite a lot from his self-portrait. Keith drew a picture of himself as an almost clownlike figure, reflecting his perception of himself as someone who could not be taken seriously—a soft, ineffectual male. We see a figure of an almost androgynous person—a one-dimensional character, which is a typical self-concept of most adolescents who are dealing with homosexuality. This reflects their idea of themselves as lacking in masculinity, individuality, and emotional maturity.

While Keith had no close male friends, he did have a few close girl friends, and his closest friend was Annette. "She's always there for me," he explained. I knew that Keith would need some close straight male friends, buddies rather than girl confidantes like Annette. Like many other boys in a similar situation, Keith was also poor in sports and had embarrassing memories of his earliest attempts to compete.

Many of his sexual-identity issues were confused with larger issues of personal identity and competence. "Who am I?" was the repeated theme in our early sessions. He had a preoccupation with appearance, and in the quest for self-image, Keith sought acceptance in groups of young people who shared his interest in heavy metal music. He soon realized that his preoccupation with a perfect exterior image was a defense against some hurtful experiences during early adolescence, beginning with his father and including other boys.

As the months went on, Keith began not only to understand but also to re-experience the deep pain of rejection from other males. He came to see how his emotional hurt was connected to his dependency on his friend. Luke, it now became obvious, was an idealized version of Keith. All that Luke was physically and in personality was what Keith wished he himself could be. Underneath Keith's feelings of admiration, however, envy would inevitably intrude on the relationship.

During those next months, after they had spent more time together, Keith ultimately became disappointed—literally "dis-illusioned"—with Luke. The young man, as Keith had by then discovered, "has his own insecurities."

Soon after he made this discovery, Keith developed a friendship with two straight male friends. He continued to grow in the ability to honestly assess his motivations, and it was clear that he was making significant progress. Then, a few months down the road, a brief sexual encounter with another boy showed Keith even more clearly that "what I really want isn't about sex." He had begun to see his remaining homosexual feelings as "a signal for other needs" and eventually terminated therapy with the self-understanding and tools to address those needs directly, which would help him to avoid eroticizing future male relationships.

The Long, Hard Road Through Adolescence

Adolescence is a time of dynamic emotional and physical growth and transformation of personal identity. It is a time of differentiating among conflicting values and of discarding some parental influences. It is a time of absorption and integration of peer, social, and pop-cultural values. Developing a sense of oneself as an adult in the world, as an autonomous person in society, is the primary challenge for the adolescent.

The teen who is conflicted about his sexual feelings must now confront his problem directly. By midadolescence, he can no longer avoid the erotic conflicts that he has suppressed or denied. He may begin experimentation with Internet gay chat rooms, online pornography, phone sex, and eventually, homosexual behavior in a search for masculine affirmation.

It is during this critical transitional stage that the young man can be most easily led astray. In today's culture, teens are sometimes actively encouraged to question and even test out their sexuality. A northern Virginia school psychologist recently told me that his caseload of teens reporting a sexual-identity crisis had doubled during one year.[1] Many other school counselors report seeing an increasing number of students who believe they are bisexual or homosexual.

A recent study in the *Journal of Sex Research* has revealed a surprising upsurge in homosexual experimentation and activity. According to that study, the percentage of U.S. women who say they had recently had sex with another woman increased fifteenfold during the ten-year period from 1988 to 1998. Rates among American men doubled over the same ten-year period. The number of men who said they had recently had gay sex climbed from 2 percent in 1988 to 4 percent in 1998, while rates among women skyrocketed from 0.2 percent in 1988 to nearly 3 percent ten years later.[2]

Television images of gay life are thought to have been influential in encouraging this homosexual experimentation. Positive images of gay people in the media, says the study's author, may have made it easier for people to recognize their same-gender sexual interest and to act on it. She noted that some of the increase is likely due to straight people involved in experimentation.

A Gay Identity Becomes Fashionable

My own clinical work also has reflected a growing proportion of younger teens questioning their sexual orientation. Thirteen-, fourteen-, and fifteen-year-olds are increasingly announcing to their parents that they are gay. A transition that used to occur in the mid to late twenties, or sometimes older, now takes place in the early and mid teens. More and more teens are coming out to their friends and parents. This is no doubt due to the increased presence of the gay identity as fashionable and in-your-face countercultural.

A provocative article appeared a few years ago in the *New York Times* that described a parent-faculty meeting at the Spence School, a private enclave overlooking Central Park, where a group of eighth-grade girls had declared themselves bisexual. The school hired a Harvard-educated psychiatrist, Dr. Justin Richardson (himself a gay man), to reassure the parents that lesbian experimentation is common in adolescence.[3]

A small but growing number of students have "come out" at these schools, or at least say that bisexuality is stylish. Dr. Richardson—who is described as "pedigreed, carefully-spoken, determinedly non-threatening"—was offered as the school's gay issues "consultant of choice" because he is "sane and clear," according to the school's headmaster.

Dr. Richardson told the parents to advise their daughters as young as *nine years old* that they, too, might have sex with other girls in the future. "It is a good idea," he said, "to mention that people have sex with members of the same sex sometimes, and that when they grow up they may have friends that do that— and that it may be something that they themselves do."

The mother of one seventh grader expressed some astute reservations after the meeting with Dr. Richardson. "It almost seems like they're presenting homosexuality to the kids as the cool thing to do. . . . Girls' schools . . . pride themselves on 'Girls can do anything,' so it almost gets to the point of, 'Who needs men?' "

Dr. Richardson agreed that students often tell him that "bisexuality is in vogue." Indeed, gay and bisexual issues provide students with an appealing countercultural focus for their adolescent rebellion.

Is Homosexuality a Normal Variant of Human Design?

But is homosexuality something you *are,* like being Asian or elderly or black, or is it something you *do,* like overeating or drinking alcohol?

Activists speak of the gay rights movement as a civil rights movement— which makes it extremely appealing to rebellious teenagers. Activists equate homosexuality, which is a psychological condition, with race and ethnicity, which are inborn qualities and morally neutral. But in reality, "homosexual" is no more "who a person *is*" than is any other behavioral propensity. Would it be meaningful to say, "Shy is who I am" or "Boisterous is who I am" or "Alcoholic is who I am"? We do not identify a "people" by their behavioral or psychological traits and then insist that no one criticize those traits or behaviors.

The gay movement has shifted the debate from *behavior* to *identity,* thus forcing opponents into the position of appearing to attack the civil rights of homosexuals. Activists succeed in making this equation through a careful choice of words, referring to homosexually attracted individuals as a "sexual minority," "a people," and "a community."

Many parents also become confused by the claims of gay activism. They are made to feel guilty and unenlightened for attempting to encourage their child's heterosexuality. A parent's efforts to promote heterosexuality in their child may seem, in some indirect way, to be opposing gay civil rights because homosexuality is said to define the person.

Gay Teens, Suicide, and Mental Health Problems

Teens always enjoy rattling the cages of the older generation, particularly when they can link their rebellion to a struggle for freedom, self-determination, and justice for a disadvantaged minority. But the real struggle that gay teens will face is much less glamorous.

A number of studies show that youth who are dealing with homosexuality suffer from a higher level of behavioral and psychiatric problems than do heterosexual youth. These problems include drug and alcohol abuse, suicide attempts, trouble with the law, and higher rates of running away from home.[4] One recent study found "compelling evidence" that gay and bisexual youth have higher rates of generalized anxiety disorder, major depression, suicidal thoughts, and even nicotine dependence.[5] Effeminate boys, in particular, suffer from a higher level of psychiatric problems, including a deep sense of inferiority.

When the studies are taken as a whole, it is clear that a teenager who self-identifies as gay is at high risk for infection with HIV or another sexually transmitted disease; for psychiatric problems, including suicidal ideation; and for self-destructive behaviors, such as drug and alcohol abuse and prostitution. Although social oppression must be considered as a contributing factor, no research has ever proved these alarming problems to be due solely to social oppression. The fact that these problems do not decrease in gay-friendly cities such as San Francisco and gay-tolerant countries such as the Netherlands supports the view that there must be factors at work that are intrinsic to the homosexual condition.

Activists bringing "safe schools programs" to the public schools often win support by using figures that show that one-third of all gay teens attempt to end their lives.[6] The problem of suicide attempts will only be remedied, these programs' proponents claim, when society puts its stamp of approval on homosexuality. Despite the inflated and inaccurate statistics used by these programs, it is indeed true, as we have said, that gay-identified teenagers are at greater risk for many psychiatric problems. Therefore, it is important to examine the possible contributing factors.

A research team led by Gary Remafedi compared gay and bisexual adolescents who had attempted suicide to a group of gay and bisexual teens who had not. In 44 percent of the cases, subjects attributed their suicide attempts to "'family problems,' including conflict with family members and parents' marital discord, divorce, or alcoholism."[7] Indeed, it has long been known that homosexuality is associated with dysfunctional structures in the family of origin.[8]

The claim that suicide attempts are due solely (or even primarily) to society's oppression seems to be a simplistic explanation for a much more complicated problem. The Remafedi study found that gay teenagers most likely to attempt suicide were those who also suffered from a host of other complicating problems, including the following:

- *Broken homes.* Only 27 percent of suicide attempters had married parents (versus 50 percent of nonattempters).
- *Sexual molestation.* Sixty-one percent of attempters had been sexually abused (versus 29 percent of nonattempters).
- *Early self-identification as gay.* Those who came out as homosexual or bisexual at an earlier age were at a higher risk for suicide.
- *Early sexual activity.* Teens who attempted suicide became sexually active when unusually young.
- *Illegal drug use.* Eighty-five percent of attempters had used illegal drugs (although 63 percent of nonattempters had also used those drugs).
- *Illegal activities.* Fifty-one percent of attempters had been arrested (versus only 28 percent of nonattempters).
- *Prostitution.* 29 percent of attempters had been involved in prostitution (versus 17 percent of nonattempters).
- *Gender conflicts.* More than a third (36.6 percent) of the male suicide attempters were classified as feminine, while only 17.7 percent of the nonattempters were classified that way.

The Feminine Boy Is Most at Risk

These statistics suggest that gay-identified teenagers in general are involved to an alarming degree with drug use and early sexual activity. Homosexually oriented adolescents classified as "feminine" are at the highest risk for suicide attempts, drug abuse, prostitution, arrest, and by implication, the deadly health problems associated with unprotected anal sex.

"The tragedy," the author of *The Gender Agenda* accurately explains, "is that boys who learn to be happy about being boys are far less likely to suffer the scapegoating and peer rejection that isolates them from contact with their own gender and thus prevents normal male bonding experiences." She says:

> Treatment is available for these children, but instead psychotherapists often use the politically correct approach to "accept oneself as gay" rather than addressing the root problem of gender alienation.

Parents concerned about prehomosexuality in their children are often told by their pediatricians not to worry, that no treatment is available, and that the child is genetically destined to be homosexual—even though research scientists know that homosexuality is likely due to a combination of temperamental characteristics such as sensitivity or risk avoidance, environmental influences, and learned behavior patterns, and is not simply "inborn" and predetermined like eye color. . . .

Statistics reveal that 61% of self-identified gay teens who had attempted suicide had a history of sexual abuse. Sometimes a boy may not recognize an early sexual experience as abuse, but instead sees it as confirmation that he is homosexual. Even adults may fail to see the incident as abuse when the abuser is another same-sexed child or adolescent. An experience of same-sex sex often establishes a life-long sexual habit pattern in a child who is starved for same-sex attention, affection and affirmation.

Today, schools issue dire warnings on the (comparatively minuscule) dangers of smoking, and tobacco companies have become liable in some cases for damages. Someday, perhaps, parents who have watched a son die of AIDS will decide to sue their pediatrician because when they brought the child for treatment for GID, they were told not to worry, or that nothing could be done. Perhaps the parents of another boy will bring suit against a school system which labeled the child as unchangeably homosexual and turned him over to a gay support group, where he contracted AIDS. In both cases, proper diagnosis and treatment might have prevented a negative outcome.[9]

"See if This Identity Fits"—Opening the Door for a Confused Teenager

Our children are being exposed to a value system that says homosexuality is perfectly okay—it is just a complement to heterosexuality. But as psychiatrist Jeffrey Satinover warns:

> The implication of such a set of values to an impressionable, possibly confused and certainly exploring youngster, is that there is no reason whatsoever not to go out and try it and see whether it fits. It's simply that a door has been opened, and a certain number of people will walk through that door and thereby expose themselves to terrible risks at an age where they are not really capable of making intelligent judgments about the risks. . . . A recent article in a psychiatric publication informed us that 30% of all 20-year-old homosexual men will be HIV-positive or dead by the age of thirty.[10]

Homosexual experimentation may result from feelings of normal peer infat-

uation, emotional dependency, need for belonging, search for pleasure, or sim-
ple curiosity. It may be an expression of anxiety about growing into adulthood
and a means of avoiding the challenges of heterosexual social relationships. A
youngster who feels socially inadequate, overwhelmed by the pressures of dating, or in conflict about his heterosexual impulses may also resort to engaging
in homosexual behavior by default.

A teenager's preoccupation with gay themes should cause parents serious
concern, and this requires appropriate professional intervention. Sometimes
these preoccupations are also accompanied by overwhelming guilt, self-con-
demnation, and even suicidal thoughts, particularly if you, as parents, are harshly critical of your teenager's identity struggles. You must take your son or
daughter's depression and suicidal thoughts with utter seriousness. But I believe
the appropriate response is to affirm your son or daughter as a person and to
recognize the child's deep need for same-sex emotional attachment, while re-
fraining from affirming his or her sexual attractions as normal and desirable.

When we consider how experimenting with homosexual behavior serves to
reinforce and deepen a gay identity, we see the absolute importance of early intervention. It is a highly favorable time to undertake treatment to address those
emotional needs that lie at the root of homosexual behavior. Untreated, adolescent sexual confusion becomes increasingly less receptive to treatment.

How the Adolescent's Sexual-Identity Process Unfolds

Unlike treatment of the younger child, which focuses on gender identity, treatment in the adolescent years encounters two additional problems. The first is
dealing with homosexual behavior, and the second is the issue of whether or
not the teen will choose to claim a gay identity.

Homosexual behavior. The critical developmental phase that lays the foundation for homosexual behavior is called the "Erotic Transitional Phase."[11] During
the early teen years, gender identification and same-sex emotional needs remain unmet in the prehomosexual child. With the onset of puberty, hormones
stimulate erotic interests, and sexual feelings are then directed toward satisfying
those unmet love needs.

It is precisely those emotional and identification needs that create the compelling quality that characterizes homosexual desire. While never satisfying
these childhood needs, homosexual behavior quickly develops into a compelling habit pattern. Gay pornography (now readily available on the Internet) and

access to partners (easily found by "cruising") reinforce this addictive dimension of homosexual behavior.

Gay identity. Popular culture portrays gay life favorably, even glamorously. Many schools have gay and lesbian clubs and organizations, and pro-gay counseling programs encourage all "sexually questioning" adolescents to try on a gay or bisexual identity.

The euphoric experience of "coming out"—of identifying oneself with an oppressed minority that is demanding social justice—appeals to the adolescent's romantic sensibility. Especially for youth, who typically feel misunderstood and unappreciated by parents and authority figures, the notion of a subculture with similarly oppressed youth, "where I can be accepted for who I really am," is indescribably appealing.

Further, because the gay subculture bestows great value on youthfulness, a young person who yearns to belong and who enters that world will quickly receive flattering attention, especially from older gay men.

Traditionally, mental health professionals understood much of adolescent homosexual behavior to be experimentation rather than a commitment to some permanent form of self-identity. They acknowledged that for the majority of adolescents, homosexual experiences represented nothing more than a period of developmental curiosity that would eventually be discarded as heterosexual interests came to predominate. And they recognized that, with proper guidance, the young person would sort out the real meaning of his sexualized longings.

But today, the teenager's natural desire to belong to an embracing community—along with the extraordinarily easy availability of gay sex—can quickly lead any confused young person into a deepening gay self-identity. In fact, quite a few of my adult homosexual clients have told me that they always assumed they were straight until their first homosexual experience; afterward, they believed that the pleasure felt in that experience must have proven them to be gay.

A national survey called *Sex in America* indicates that while only 2-3 percent of adult men are homosexual, 10-16 percent of all men go through a homosexual phase earlier in their lives.[12] What if these young men had been confirmed as "gay" by a school counselor or gay program during that transitional phase?

Another major study found that more than one-quarter of twelve-year-olds are unsure whether they are heterosexual or homosexual. This 1992 study polled 34,707 Minnesota teenagers and was published in the prestigious journal *Pediatrics.*[13]

This means that a school's gay counseling program, eager to identify and support every same-sex-attracted teen, will find that about one-quarter of all early teens *do* in fact suffer from sexual-identity confusion. But most alarming of all, such teens might erroneously be identified as homosexual if they are affirmed as gay by a counselor at age twelve.

One reason for this high incidence of gender confusion, mentioned earlier, is the media exposure of kids to glamorized gay images. Internet websites, television, films, rock music, teen magazines, and even public libraries offer appealing pro-gay messages. For some confused youngsters, these messages are quite seductive.

A teenage boy recently called in to a radio talk show's host, a psychologist, saying that he had attractions to men but that this created a conflict because he was a Southern Baptist. The psychologist advised him to accept himself as a "gay youth" and said that if he could not reconcile his "natural" gay identity with his religion, then he should think about jettisoning his religious beliefs and switching to the Metropolitan Church, a gay denomination. This sort of advice—the uncritical assumption that a young person's experience means that he is "naturally" homosexual (and that sexual feelings take precedence over deeply held religious beliefs)—represents the pervasive bias and misinformation that has permeated our culture.

Adolescent Boys and Risky Behavior

And there is further reason to be concerned.

Neuroscientists have recently gained a better understanding of the high-risk habits of teenagers.[14] The reckless experimentation characteristic of teenage boys, in particular, has traditionally been explained as a form of rebellion, but researchers have recently discovered that such risk-taking behavior is actually rooted in developmental changes that are occurring in the brain.

During adolescence, the brain undergoes a profound remodeling. The prefrontal neural cortex, which functions as the brain's command center, loses nearly half of its neural connections. Subsequently, decision making shifts toward brain regions that are governed by emotional reactivity.

These massive changes, a psychobiologist explains, predisposes adolescents to take more risks. Concurrently there is a drop in the brain's dopamine level during the adolescent years, which decreases the person's ability to experience pleasure. As a result, teens are drawn toward exciting and pleasurable but destructive behaviors, such as drinking, taking drugs, and experimenting with risky sex.

Beware: Gay Counseling Programs at School

So your teenage son's brain leads him to engage in foolhardy behavior. Is this the appropriate developmental period for a school counseling program to introduce him to the gay community, when his hormones are raging and his brain predisposes him to risk taking? One can hardly avoid noticing the irony: when a cigarette will be airbrushed out of a public figure's photo lest he model the bad behavior of smoking, our teenagers are being introduced *in their own schools* to a lifestyle that has been proven far more deadly than that of a smoker.

At the time of this writing, new HIV infections in San Francisco have more than doubled the rate of three years ago because safe-sex practices are being abandoned. "In Los Angeles and five other cities," reported the *Los Angeles Times,* "one in ten young gay or bisexual men is infected" with HIV.[15] Among young gay African Americans living in large cities, according to another report, the infection rate is even more alarming: one out of every three men is HIV-positive.[16]

The Los Angeles County Health Services Department interviewed fifty-three HIV-positive gay and bisexual men, according to the *Los Angeles Times,* and found that half of them, despite their HIV status, "had sex in public places such as bath houses or clubs with multiple partners without informing their partners of their status. Some did not use condoms." An AIDS Project Los Angeles survey similarly found that 31 percent of 113 bisexual men continued to engage in risky behavior, "even after being informed of their HIV-positive status."[17]

In another article, the *Los Angeles Times* reported that the rate of rectal gonorrhea among gay and bisexual men in San Francisco rose 44 percent during a recent three-year period, while in Los Angeles, new syphilis cases among gay and bisexual men rose more than 1,680 percent.[18] San Francisco is considered to be a "bellwether for sexual activity among gay men" around the nation, the *Times* noted.

Taken together, these news items have particular significance. We now have evidence that the adolescent brain leads teenagers into high-risk behavior, and we have evidence that young gays are increasingly engaging in unsafe sex. Also, wouldn't it seem that educators should reconsider the wisdom of introducing sexually questioning teenagers into the gay community through school-based programs?

Schools work hard to keep students from obtaining drugs and alcohol. They should also understand the wisdom of postponing the adolescent's exposure to a very, very high-risk lifestyle.

The Link Between Sexual Abuse and Sexual Identity

Early habituation into homosexuality can have lifelong consequences, as writers Bob Davies and Anita Worthen warn us. Both Davies and Worthen have held leadership positions within Exodus International, an ex-gay ministry. Anita Worthen says her own son, who is now living a gay lifestyle, was drawn into that lifestyle at age sixteen when he was molested by his school guidance counselor. Davies and Worthen explain:

> Sexual abuse is one of the foremost shaping factors that result in adult lesbianism. . . . It's also surprisingly common in gay men. One ministry leader said that half of the men coming for help were victims of past abuse, usually by another male.
>
> In a large majority of cases, the abuser is a male family member or trusted friend—not a stranger lurking on a dark street corner. In a few cases, the abuser is an older woman. Whatever the specifics, having one's trust violated at such a deep level causes widespread devastation that has lifelong effects. . . .
>
> In men, sexual abuse (from an older male) commonly brings great confusion about the boy's sexual identity. *Why did he find me attractive in that way?* the victim wonders. *Is there something wrong with me?* Typically, boys who are abused repeatedly experience some physical pleasure, and may seek to repeat the acts with other boys in order to duplicate the feelings of sexual pleasure and physical closeness.[19]

In fact, one major study found that childhood sexual molestation triples the likelihood of self-identifying as gay or lesbian.[20] Another study found that boys who identify as homosexual are much more likely than heterosexuals to engage in sex with other males before puberty.[21] And in a study reported in a recent issue of *Archives of Sexual Behavior*, investigating 942 adults who were not in psychotherapy, it was found that 46 percent of homosexual men and 22 percent of lesbian women reported homosexual molestation, compared to 7 percent of the heterosexual men and 1 percent of the heterosexual women.[22] Taken together, these studies tell us there is likely a link between early sexual trauma and later homosexual orientation.

Sexual abuse by an adult stimulates in the child the mixed emotions of fear, excitement, erotic pleasure, and anger. These feelings bond together and make the abused boy feel drawn, in a disproportionate number of cases, to reenact the sexual relationship later in his own adulthood with another child or young teenager. This cluster of mixed emotions, with sex tied to themes of control and domination, also stimulates an interest in the sadomasochism, domination, and "leather" themes that we see so commonly in gay culture.

Studies on Pedophilia: What They Are Overlooking

In the past few years, we have been seeing some scientific studies boldly making the case that boys who have sex with older men do not seem to be harmed by the experience. One recent study is by Bruce Rind, who was the lead author of an article published by the American Psychological Association (APA). That article created a public scandal as a result of its wide exposure by radio host Dr. Laura Schlessinger. Dr. Laura's outrage against the study actually led to a reprimand of the APA by Congress.

Then in a second Rind study, self-esteem and positive sexual identity were found to be the same in males ages twelve to seventeen who had engaged in sex with older men as among a control group. The youngest boys in the group, Rind says, "were just as willing and reacted at least as positively as older adolescents." Reactions of the boys (now college men) who had engaged in man-boy sexual relationships were "primarily positive."[23]

Rind does not use the terms "molestation" or "sexual abuse" because of their moral connotations, employing instead the values-neutral term "ADSR" (age-discrepant sexual relations). His second study added fuel to the contention among some psychologists that homosexual, "consensual" pedophilia may *not* in fact be psychologically harmful.

Aside from the fact that these studies may be unable to find "harm" because they were looking for the wrong indicators, they point to a more important issue: how will such research be used?

Obviously, such studies will be used to lower age-of-consent laws and to argue for reduced sentences for child molesters. After all, if there is no measurable psychological harm done by man-boy sex, at least if the act was "consensual," then why should pedophile acts be illegal? Research such as Rind's will, no doubt, be used as so-called "hard evidence" in the courts to promote the normalization of pedophilia.

In 1994 pedophilia was redefined by the APA's diagnostic manual *(DSM-IV)*; it was characterized as a mental disease only if the pedophile was distressed by his actions or negatively affected in his work or social relationships. By redefining the condition this way, the APA prepared the way, even if inadvertently, for the normalization of adult-child sex by making room within the diagnostic manual for the possibility of a psychologically normal pedophile. In the text revision of the *DSM-IV* the APA, possibly in response to embarrassing publicity, quietly restored pedophilia to its original definition, by which *any* person who acted on pedophilic desires would be diagnosed as having a mental illness.

Psychology, parents must remember, is inevitably a values-laden enterprise. How we interpret the data depends on our worldview and on what the researcher is expecting (or in fact hoping) to find from that data. But even more important, in any concept of what constitutes psychological health, we must not forget that psychological, characterological, and spiritual matters inevitably overlap—meaning psychology has no means of evaluating psychological health *without* making value judgments.

What if another researcher found that, even though the molested boys and teens had "just as high a self-esteem" as nonmolested boys, there remained other differences between the two groups that were characterological and spiritual? For example, we might wonder if the molested boys grew up with poorer moral judgment. Or we might wonder if they had left the religious faiths of their childhood and come to a dead end in their spiritual growth. Does that count as "harm"? Might they not also have more difficulty understanding and respecting gender and generational differences? Would they be living sexually focused lives, engaged in bizarre and unsafe sexual practices, and repeating their own sexual abuse on another younger boy? None of these factors were measured by studies that found "little or no harm" in pedophilia. But left to stand, such studies can easily convey the misimpression that there is *no difference between molested and nonmolested males*—and thus that pedophilia is harmless.

"Valuing" Versus "Tolerating" Sexual Diversity

The adolescent is often enthralled by the sociopolitical aspects of gay identity and the appealing thought of joining the fight against "the politics of oppression." Recognizing the role of adolescent sentimentality, pro-gay programs usually issue a "call to arms" for the student to take part in a broad political agenda alongside the personal issues with which the teenager is dealing. What should remain a focus on the youth's own personal experience instead becomes an expectation that the youth will join forces with the gay political movement. The teenager therefore comes to believe, *Society's oppression is the thing that is standing between me and the possibility of happiness.*

Many public school programs, such as California's Project 10, are designed to teach students to *value,* not just *tolerate,* sexual diversity. On the one hand, these programs address legitimate concerns (the needs of sexually confused students). But on the other hand, they move beyond emotional support and into active promotion of a gay lifestyle, thus validating homosexuality as a normal sexual variant and directly opposing the value systems of many families.

The referral networks used by Project 10 are organizations such as the Gay and Lesbian Community Services Center, Children of the Night, L.A. Sex Information Helpline—all gay-affirming social services. But how, we ask, can these organizations help the child who chooses to *resist* being homosexual? These groups will tell the teenager that gay is "who he is" and that his condition is unchangeable. Why doesn't Project 10's manual list any of the services of ex-gay support ministries and counseling centers?

The manual says its goal is to "provide education to help sensitize all students, faculty and school staff to the presence of, special needs of, and concerns of these minority youth."[24] But in reality, Project 10's goal is to *desensitize* students, faculty, school boards, and parents to traditional moral values by changing the way they think about homosexuality and by undermining parental and religious authority. One thing is clear: parents who do not share the gay-affirmative philosophy of Project 10 will face harsh discrimination and a tough uphill battle.

Ex-gay ministry leaders have spoken out against these programs. Leading a teenager into the gay world is sheer folly, says Exodus International's Bob Davies. "What parent, teacher, friend or minister," Davies asks, "would encourage a child to engage in life-threatening behavior?" Regeneration Ministries' Alan Medinger agrees: "It is absolutely criminal to take a confused kid and lead him into a life that could kill him."[25]

If you have concerns about your teen's sexual orientation, do not be afraid to discuss your concerns with him or her. You should try to bring up the subject. You very well may find that your teenager has been sending out a call for help.

One parent told me, "I found some gay pornographic magazines hidden under my son's bed—and he knows I vacuum under there." It was apparently the young man's indirect way of telling his parents something he could not bring himself to address openly. Almost without exception, adolescents admit that it was a relief for them when their parents finally learned of their struggle.

The Story of Dave

"Dave" is sixteen years old. His father is gay and lives in a gay neighborhood in New York City. Dave was sexually molested between the ages of eight and eleven by his uncle. The boy's parents divorced when he was twelve, and he went to live with his mother and new stepfather. While Dave's mother is very caring, she tends to be somewhat intrusive and overpowering, and her second husband is usually out of the house, involved in his hobbies of golf and bowling. A large part of the therapy with Dave has involved getting his mom to back off a bit so he can find his own identity.

At one point, Dave got so angry at his controlling mother and critical stepfather, and at the constant intimidation and abuse from his older brother, that he ran away from home. He went to New York City to live with his father and his father's friends for about two weeks. Fortunately, Dave got an up-close look at some of the common features of a life in an urban gay enclave. He was totally disgusted by what he saw. Bathhouses, pornography, and one-night stands repelled him. He came back convinced that even though he had thought he felt same-sex attractions, a gay lifestyle was not what he wanted after all. Instead, Dave became very clear that he wanted change.

He was a strong and dedicated Christian, and so we worked closely with the pastor of his church, who understood Dave's problem and his special need for male friendship. The pastor connected Dave with the church's youth pastor, made it possible for him to go to summer camp, found a way to involve him in a baseball team, and encouraged him to take part in group activities with other boys in the church.

David is not athletic, but he has been encouraged to push himself past his discouragement. His church has a recreational facility, and he has been able to spend time there, which keeps him away from the tensions at home. In counseling, he came to see that his stepfather is actually capable of giving him some of the male affirmation he craves.

David drew a portrait when I asked him to show me the type of man he is

attracted to. When we look at David's picture, we see a hypermasculine caricature of a super male. The figure is very physical and muscular. There is a virility
about the man's body. In describing the man in his picture, David wrote, "He
is in his twenties, he is muscular, handsome, athletic, spiritual, humorous, outgoing. He's flirtatious, fun to be around . . . kind-spirited, gentle, yet aggressive
if he needs to be. Flirts with the girls for fun, jock type, popular. His shirt is off
but I don't know if he's nude. He's straight, exclusively heterosexual."

David later abandoned his drawing. He explained to me that he did not
know what to do with the genital area, in which he had left an empty space; to
simply put shorts on the figure "would look ugly." This predicament, I thought,
was a good illustration of his conflicts about his own sexuality. He was intensely
ambivalent about male sexuality and did not yet know how to appropriately
represent it.

Poor Body Image and Homosexual Attraction

Another portrait of a young man was drawn by a frail fifteen-year-old whom
we'll call "Matthew." The picture depicts the type of guy he would most likely
fall in love with. The teenage artist described this excellent free-sketched figure
as that of a man between twenty and twenty-five years old and "buff." "He's
strong, really masculine; his looks are perfect. He's, like, really deep and insightful. If I saw him on the street, I would think, *He's perfect*. But I really don't know
him. He's mysterious; he's everything that I'm not; and he's what I look for in
a guy—what I look for in a role model." Indeed, the sketch was that of an idealized self.

Poor body image is very common among homosexuals. Drs. Richard Friedman and Lenore Stern studied seventeen homosexual men who were not in
psychotherapy, and of that total, thirteen as youngsters had suffered with markedly negative feelings about their bodies. Ten of the subjects described themselves as soft and flabby, and all identified their physiques as being "like a girl's."
In every case, they perceived their bodies as being easily damaged. All the subjects had a strong fear, should they engage in contact sports, of physical injury.[26]

In the same study, thirteen of the seventeen males reported chronic, persistent terror of fighting with other boys during the juvenile and early adolescence
periods, with the fear actually approximating a panic reaction. The researchers
theorized that "a certain amount of peer-to-peer aggression diminishes the
likelihood of exclusive, enduring homosexual outcome."[27] Indeed, the boy

who does not romanticize the strength of other males but endeavors to develop it in himself will be less likely to develop homosexually.

To Come Out or Seek Change?

For boys like Keith, David, and Matthew, "to come out or not to come out" is the most important question they must confront in their lives. Quite a few young men I counsel do, indeed, leave therapy and decide to embrace a gay identity. However, Keith, David, and Matthew all gained significant under-standing of the nature of their same-sex attractions during approximately one year of individual and group reparative therapy. As they deepened their own sense of masculinity and developed friendships with straight males, they experienced a significant diminishing of their homosexuality. As time went by, adopting a gay lifestyle seemed to be less and less of an option for them.

As Keith told me, "I used to envy those guys who are 'out.' I thought they were courageous, honest—they could be themselves. Now I'm not so sure that's what I want for myself."

Interventions for adolescent homosexuality must be broad-based and individualized, because the teenager's same-sex attractions likely stem from many different sources. He may have conflicted feelings about females, and he may feel fear and envy of male peers. Cruel teasing and peer labeling may have convinced the boy that "what they say about me must be true, so I might as well go ahead and call myself gay." All the while, the decision-making process is made more difficult by the easy availability of gay sex. In contrast, heterosexual longings (if the boy has any) would require a more complex social ritual of dating and the risk of rejection.

Since the popular "born that way" misconception has also influenced many psychotherapists, they may see it as their job to simply lead the client into accepting his "natural" homosexual or heterosexual orientation. In this simplistic scenario, the therapist supports the adolescent in his gradual "discovery of who he is" as the boy comes to know and accept his supposedly innate, predetermined sexual orientation. The assumption is that if sexual orientation is established at birth, then change is impossible. This popular myth, not grounded in scientific fact, has led many individuals into a gay lifestyle after they were told by their therapist that there was no hope of change.

In fact, change is entirely possible. A recent study in *Psychological Reports,* of which I am coauthor, describes 882 men and women who report achieving some degree of beneficial change in their homosexual orientation.[28] Further-more, another recent study (of which I am also coauthor), published in the same professional journal, shows that there are indeed mental health profession-als who believe that sexual reorientation is possible through therapy.[29]

Building Trust with Adolescents

Anger, rebellion, and hurt usually fester just under the surface as the teenager grapples with sexual identity. Although he may appear compliant, the homo-sexually troubled adolescent will be highly ambivalent about any adult who probes the deeper layers of his private life. Secrecy has always been his best de-fense against intrusion. Therefore, we can expect to encounter suspicion and hostility directed at both parents and therapists.

Fortunately, even deeper than the adolescent desire to hide is the healthy de-sire to be seen and understood by another male. This I have consistently found to be true: what the homosexually oriented man desires most is also what he fears most—to be truly "seen" by another man. Therefore, the first step in any kind of healing is to offer unconditional acceptance so that the teenager need not hide his sense of shame or his conflicted feelings and attractions.

The young man also needs to hear this message from his parents: "We love you, and nothing you do in your life will ever change that fact. We will do our best to respect your feelings and understand your perspective no matter what choices you make. But because we desire the best for you, we want you to se-riously consider the possibility of change. We do not think a gay lifestyle is a wise choice."

Separating Emotional Needs from Sexual Feelings

One sixteen-year-old boy was brought to me by his parents shortly after the boy had announced to them that he was gay. He came with them to the counseling session, but only very reluctantly. Yet even though the young man was resistant to being in therapy, a turning point in treatment occurred in our third session, when I asked him, "Tell me, when do you *not* feel homosexual attractions?

His answer was immediate: "When I'm playing soccer."

From that moment on, he was able to realize that when he was feeling ac-cepted and connected with other guys, especially on a physical level, his homo-sexual interests and preoccupations disappeared. It was during times of social isolation, loneliness, and rejection that his same-sex fantasies resurfaced to preoccupy him. By reflecting on this repeated pattern, the young man was able to realize that what he thought was an intrinsic, inborn part of "who he really was" was actually a situational reaction to feelings of gender inadequacy.

Surprisingly often the gender-confused adolescent has a physical handicap or limitation (such as asthma) that, in his mind, blocks him from gaining full acceptance from his peers. It is up to both the therapist and the parents to help the adolescent make a realistic assessment of that limitation and to show him that often this is an excuse to stay stuck in a posture of inferiority. His own obsessive focus on these limitations causes him to disqualify himself as equal with other boys.

As the healing process continues, the teen begins to understand that his same-sex attractions are all, in fact, attempts to repair an emotional deficit—his own perfectly normal and authentic (but unfulfilled) needs for male attention, affection, and approval. Homoerotic fantasies and romantic attachments come to be seen by many adolescents as a reparative drive (however misdirected when eroticized) toward gender wholeness.

Over the years, gay activists have been angered by the term *reparative therapy.* "You're trying to repair us," they tell me, "as you would fix a car or a transmission." In fact, "repair" does not apply to something being done to the client, but instead speaks of the nature of the same-sex erotic drive, which is itself a reparative attempt at health. Those authentic same-sex emotional needs are seeking fulfillment (and thus they are "reparative" in nature), but the person is approaching the task of reparation of the deficit in a self-defeating and ultimately unfulfilling way, namely through sex.

Most clients actually find the concept of homosexuality as a reparative drive to be comforting. They understand for the first time that they are not "strange," "weird," or "perverted," but rather they are simply seeking a completion in their natural identity—but in a misdirected way.

Parents and counselors alike must convey clearly to the adolescent that he is free to discuss his same-sex feelings. He has a normal, healthy yearning for deep friendship and closeness with other males. Conversations about such feelings are acceptable and important. They should not evoke shame. But we should talk more about what it means for those feelings to shift and become sexual. What, for your teenager, is the meaning or significance of such yearnings? What is it he is really looking for in other guys? How would sex derail that search for friendship and change his sense of who he is?

I often ask teens, "What does homosexuality mean for *you?*" or "What would you receive from such behavior?" Very often, what they say they are looking for has little to do with same-sex physical intimacy, but rather with a need to belong, to feel like an intimate part of one special male friend's life.

The therapist or parent should also evaluate the views of teachers, media stories, or websites that have introduced the child to homosexuality. Do these teachers and counselors dismiss principled dissent to homosexuality as nothing but "homophobia"? Do they represent homosexually oriented individuals as "a people," thus equating any criticism of a gay lifestyle with racial bigotry?

But don't our bodies say something profound about the design and purpose of human sexuality? Would it be normal if someone chose to drink, say, using a straw he put into his nose? Or is there some natural wisdom evident in our bodies' opposite-sex construction and the "perfect fit" nature provided for heterosexual coupling? All of these ideas make for helpful discussion.

Correcting Popular Misinformation

You can also help your teenager by debunking some gay mythology. Recently, a nineteen-year-old, gay-identified young man proudly informed me that Abraham Lincoln was gay. He had read this in a gay magazine. Fortunately, having heard the rumor myself, I was able to educate the boy on the historical reality. During Lincoln's times, travelers were often expected by an innkeeper to share beds, but the fact that Lincoln did this does not mean that he was homosexual. I was able to use this distortion about Lincoln to provide an object lesson in the politicization of history.[30]

The education of adolescents involves compassionately but clearly correcting popular misinformation, including these myths:

- "Sexual orientation is biologically determined—once gay, always gay." In fact, the lives of many ex-gays testify to the opposite conclusion.
- "Gay men can have long-term, monogamous relationships." In reality, the expectation of sexual faithfulness, gay researchers now admit, is more likely to destroy gay men's relationships than keep them together.[31]
- "Every other culture and society throughout history has accepted homosexuality. Ours is the only homophobic society." Actually, no culture has ever elevated homosexuality to the same status as heterosexuality.
- "Animals, too, are homosexual." Same-sex behaviors in animals are usually attributed by biologists to the stresses of captivity, biological pollut-

ants, domestication, nonavailability of the opposite sex, hormonal manipulation, misinterpretation of sex calls or odors, expressions of dominance, and immature sex play. But this does not mean the behavior should be considered normal.[32]

- "Attempts to change sexual orientation are dangerous; they only create greater unhappiness, depression and sometimes suicide." Serious depression due to failure to change is indeed a possibility, as it is whenever treatment fails for any other problem, such as obesity, anorexia, alcoholism, or drug abuse. But to put this risk in better context, remember that suicide attempts are also precipitated by being told one cannot change.[33]
- "Homosexually oriented people are identical to heterosexuals in every way psychologically and emotionally, except for the incidental detail of their sexual preference. As a group, they are as healthy as heterosexuals." In reality, homosexual men and women have been shown to suffer from a higher level of suicide attempts, substance abuse, and psychiatric disorders.[34]

These and many other myths call for education and correct information. Any youth confronted with a fundamental choice in lifestyle deserves accurate information in order to make an informed decision about his future.

The Difference Between *Gay* and *Homosexual*

Essential to the healing of homosexuality is clarifying distinctions about labels. Just because someone experiences homosexual feelings does not mean he is obliged to assume the label of *gay*. Unlike *homosexuality*, which describes a sexual orientation, *gay* is a social-political identity that says, in essence, "This is who I am; this is the 'real me'; and I can live out my same-sex attractions without any internal conflict."

Not all people who have same-sex feelings choose a gay identity. The confusion between *homosexual* and *gay* is the result of a popular ideology promoted within our culture and, increasingly, within our public schools. The sexually confused boy is encouraged to identify with his sense of masculine inferiority and gender confusion and to join forces with the other people who suffer from the same deficit. But in so doing, he separates himself from the majority of conventional society and identifies with approximately 2 to 4 percent of the population, while excluding himself from the remaining 96 to 98 percent.

For certain practical reasons, we object to the terms "gay child" and "gay youth." Children, adolescents, and teenagers are just too young to fully understand not only their personal identity, but particularly their *sexual* identity. And they certainly cannot yet comprehend the lifelong social and health implications of taking on a gay identity.

And there is another, philosophical matter: Is anyone "really" homosexual, or are we all designed to be heterosexual, with some people just suffering from a homosexual *problem?* Can a legitimate identity really be built around a psychological deficit? This is a philosophical issue more than a scientific issue.

It is an error to reinforce an adolescent in prematurely self-labeling himself or herself as gay or lesbian. Keeping this in mind, I hope you will remind your teenagers to fully understand the issues before they label themselves *gay* or *lesbian.* No matter what Dear Abby or Ann Landers say in their advice columns, teenagers should be encouraged to keep their options open.

A Look Inside an Adolescent's Heart

"Brian," who was fifteen years old when he began the following six-month diary, provides us with a close look at a young man who feels very much alone. He uses daydreams, fantasies, and escape from reality as a way of coping with his loneliness, his sadness, and his feeling of being unloved. His dream is always of "a bunch of friends" or one very special man to love him. The man he often dreams about is actually an idealized version of himself—in other words, a strong, salient man.

Depression is a continual problem for Brian, along with painful loneliness, low self-esteem, and feelings of being unwanted and uncared for. His willingness to share his diary with readers of this book speaks of his natural generosity. Its contents reveal his deep need to feel valued and loved by one special young man following years of isolation from his same-sex peers.

As Brian proceeds in individual and group therapy, he describes very well his intense struggle between the desire to reach out to others and his tendency to defensively detach.

April 6. I dreamed about having a bunch of friends again. If only I had someone to love and care about and who would feel the same way back. Someone taller than me and really built and gorgeous. Someone that would make me feel safe and loved and really wanted.

April 9. I wonder what it would feel like just to kiss another guy and to be cuddled and held by someone who really loved me. I love all kinds of guys, white, brown, and black. But I'm afraid I have no choice but to gaze upon male beauty from afar, full of desire and unfulfilled fantasies.

April 20. I don't know why, but lately I've been a little depressed. It seems like everyone in school is off doing their own things together, and I'm always the one left behind. I need someone, anyone. I want someone real to lift me up and take me in his arms and hold me, so I feel safe and secure and cared for and loved.

Each day I feel more and more alone. I wish all my dreams could really come true, that I would have all these friends, and that someone, when I say "I love you" to him, would say, "I love you, too" to me. If only, if only, if only . . .

May 19. I was so bored today. All I did was watch TV, and I couldn't think of anything to do. I kept dreaming about my new teacher, Mr. Jackson, and how gorgeous he is. Actually, I'm not even exactly sure what my attraction is toward him. I guess it's because he is exactly the kind of man I need. He's nice, sweet, and he made me feel like I existed. I haven't felt like anyone actually knew I existed in a long time.

July 5. I just had my first group therapy session. I was so nervous. But whenever any of them started talking, I felt so in tune with what they were saying. It felt good to be around people who knew what I was feeling and could understand completely.

One of the guys in the group—his name is Tom—said something that felt so true. He said a gay man has two options to fill himself up when he feels empty. On the one side, he could eat junk food, which represents sex, and on the other side, health food, which represents emotional intimacy. He could either have a quick fix and eat the junk food, but get sick later, or have the health food, which in the long run will be more satisfying and will really benefit him. I think Tom might be right.

July 21. Group therapy just ended. I talked a lot this session. I got a lot of issues out, and everyone's really helping me. I like it because everyone understands what you're saying and they try to help as much as they can.

I also really need some support from straight guys. But I'm afraid that they won't support me even if I tell them I'm in therapy trying to change.

July 25. Well, I've been fantasizing about a guy who doesn't even exist. His name is Adam. I don't know what he looks like except in my dreams, but thinking about him makes me feel happy. I guess there's no difference between this and my other dreams. I hate being alone and sitting in front of the TV by myself.

July 29. Now I don't know if I want to change or not. I'm wondering, *If I even wanted to change, could I?* I guess I just want to be in a relationship with a guy and see what it would be like. Maybe it would work?

I just feel so confused. On one hand, I think about the kind of life I was brought up to believe is right, with a wife and kids someday, and how much I would really like that. But then I think about how great it would be to be in love with a man. So I just don't know.

It was my mother who forced me to go to therapy. I kinda like therapy, but I'm so confused, I don't know what to do now.

August 2. Group therapy was really nice. Jack and Mark were there, and I was really impressed with Jack and the things he said.

Mark said we all do need intimacy with guys, and that's perfectly good, but the problem comes when I take it to a further step: sex. He said there's a fine line between love and sex, but a line no doubt. It would be wonderful if I could just get the emotional needs met and not go any further. It's true, deep down I really don't want sex. I want love and intimacy, holding and feeling safe and secure. That's what I need and what I want.

August 3. Dad is coming back from Europe tomorrow. I'm not exactly looking forward to it. It was nice with it just being Mom and my sister and me at home. Hardly any argument. It was so happy. I'm sorry, but that's the way I feel.

I've been lonely lately and fantasizing about Adam.

August 6. I've been thinking about that cool guy Jack and what he said at last week's group therapy session. Why do I kid myself like this? He's right. Like I'll ever meet the guys I dream about and just live happily ever after. The gay world is so wild and so much of a party scene. I know it's true. If I could keep the sex out and just have the close buddies I've always been looking for . . . Can it happen? Well, I'm only fifteen now, so who knows?

Clearly, Brian is at a crossroads in his life. His loneliness and detachment will lead him to accept an emotional connection wherever he can find it. After hearing another deeply depressed homosexually oriented young man express feelings of despair and self-hatred, psychiatrist Richard Fitzgibbons laments, "I don't know what is going to fill that void of peer acceptance, or of father love, or of mother love. What will fill it?"[35] The therapist alone cannot provide for those deep emotional needs; this is where church, family, and caring peers are needed so that the lonely and dispossessed young man won't by default have to look for the answers to his neediness within the gay community.

The Historic Spitzer Study: Change Is Possible

In May 2001, what the Associated Press's science writer called "an explosive new study" was announced in New Orleans at the American Psychiatric Association's annual conference. The study drew worldwide media attention. Dr. Robert Spitzer—the prominent psychiatrist who led the team that removed homosexuality from the psychiatric manual of disorders in 1973—concluded that a homosexual orientation (not just homosexual behavior) appears to be changeable for some people. "Like most psychiatrists," he said, "I thought that homosexual behavior could be resisted—but that no one could really change their sexual orientation. I now believe that's untrue—some people *can* and *do* change."

The change of viewpoint for Dr. Spitzer began on the opening day of the American Psychiatric Association's annual conference in 1999 when Spitzer was drawn to a group of ex-gays staging a demonstration at the entrance to the conference building. The picketers were objecting to the APA's recent resolution discouraging therapy to change homosexuality to heterosexuality. They carried placards saying, "Homosexuals Can Change—We Did—Ask Us!" Others said, "Don't Affirm Me into a Lifestyle that was Killing Me Physically and Spiritually" and "The APA Has Betrayed America with Politically Correct Science." Some of the psychiatrists tore up the literature handed out to them by the protesters, but others stopped to offer the protesters a few quiet words of encouragement.

Dr. Spitzer was skeptical, but he decided to find out for himself if sexual orientation was changeable. So he looked for subjects who claimed to have experienced a significant shift from homosexual to heterosexual attraction, and the shift had to have lasted for at least five years. He used subjects located by the National Association of Research and Therapy of Homosexuality, ex-gay ministries, and various clinicians working in private practice.

Spitzer interviewed 200 subjects (143 men and 57 women) who were willing to describe their sexual and emotional histories, including their self-reported shift from gay to straight. Most of the interview subjects said their religious faith was very important in their lives, and about three-quarters of the men and half of the women had become married by the time of the study. Most had sought change because a gay lifestyle had been emotionally unsatisfying. Many had been disturbed by promiscuous, stormy gay relationships, a conflict with their religious values, and the desire to be (or to stay) married.

Typically, the change effort had not produced significant results for the subjects during the first two years. They said they were helped by examining their family and childhood relationships and understanding how problems in those relationships had contributed to their gender-identity difficulties and their sexual orientation. Same-sex mentoring relationships, behavior-therapy techniques, and group therapy were also mentioned by them as particularly helpful.

To Spitzer's surprise, good heterosexual functioning was reportedly achieved by 67 percent of the men who had rarely or never felt any opposite-sex attraction before the change process. Nearly all the subjects said they now feel more masculine (in the case of men) or more feminine (women).

"Contrary to conventional wisdom," Spitzer concluded, "some highly motivated individuals, using a variety of change efforts, can make substantial change in multiple indicators of sexual orientation, and achieve good heterosexual functioning."

Orientation Change Is Gradual and Takes Place on a Continuum

Spitzer added an important qualifier: that change from homosexual to heterosexual is not usually a matter of "either/or" but exists on a continuum—that is, a slow, progressive diminishing of homosexuality and an expansion of heterosexual potential that is exhibited to widely varying degrees. Dr. Spitzer emphasized that complete sexual-orientation change—cessation of *all* homosexual fantasies and attractions (which is generally considered an unrealistic goal in most therapies) is probably quite uncommon. Still, when subjects did not actually change sexual orientation—for example, their change had been one of behavioral control and self-identity, but no significant shift in attractions—they nevertheless reported an improvement in overall emotional health and functioning.

The Spitzer study is believed to be the most detailed investigation of sexual orientation change to date. "Patients should have the right," he concluded, "to explore their heterosexual potential."

Significantly, if Spitzer's *own* son were gay and interested in changing, he said, he would support his son in seeking therapy and attempting to change his orientation from homosexuality to heterosexuality.[36]

But Will the Adolescent Stay in Therapy?

Young men who stay in reparative therapy, like Brian, the teenager who shared his diary, are those who agree that their homosexual desires in fact represent a far deeper need from males—they are in search of the three A's: attention, affirmation, and affection. With continuing counsel and inner work, many will take a path that leads beyond their same-sex attractions. But realistically, we must acknowledge that many other teenagers will drop out of therapy and make the decision to identify themselves as gay.

The road toward transformation is a long and winding one, and there will be continuing temptation to give up the effort to change when that "one special guy" seems to come across his path. Still, even if there is a setback—sometimes a setback that may last months or perhaps years—there is hope. All that parents or therapists can do is offer options to the adolescent; the final choice has to be up to him. Guilt, manipulation, force, or coercion will not free the client from his attractions but will only cause greater alienation.

It is important to remember that change is a matter of diminishing homosexual feelings and increasing heterosexual attractions. Change moves slowly, on a gradual continuum, and there will undoubtedly be regressions. It is not a matter of "once homosexual, now heterosexual." And like all psychological change, the transformation will probably never be total. Realistically, there will be some lingering attractions and temptations over the course of a lifetime.

Change gradually unfolds in three areas:

- Self-identity (the realization that "I am really a heterosexual man; I just have a homosexual problem")
- Sexual behavior ("I will not act on these temptations")

- Attractions (not even desiring another man)

The first two categories are the easier ones to change. Achieving change in all three areas is more difficult; the last category, in particular, will change to varying degrees and will progress very gradually over time.

As a parent, you will (I sincerely hope) always love and remain close to your child if he does not seek or achieve change. He will still be your son, or she will still be your daughter, no matter what. Recognizing that there are stubborn areas within your own life that are resistant to change (or that you have, in fact, chosen not to try to change) will make it easier for you to accept a deep disappointment in the life of your child. Still, you should never give up hope that your son or daughter may yet transition into heterosexuality.

In This Lifetime, We All Struggle

No one knows about the ups and downs of struggle better than John Paulk, author of the autobiography *Love Won Out*. John left his former life as a gay man, a drag queen, and a homosexual prostitute to marry an ex-lesbian and have a family. He believed that he had resolved all of his same-sex issues, but as a public spokesman for the Christian ex-gay movement, he experienced a setback when he found himself tempted to go back "just one more time" to visit a gay bar, where activists saw him and "outed" him to the media.

Viewing his life experiences in both psychological and religious contexts, John provides the background on his public "fall from grace." We make a mistake to consider any of our deep-seated struggles "finished" at a certain point in our lives; in truth, we remain human and vulnerable whether our struggle is with homosexuality, alcohol, food, drugs, or even pride. His account also reveals the insight he has found through his faith convictions:

> I began a process of coming out of homosexuality about more than 14 years ago, and for a variety of reasons became one of the more prominent individuals of this movement. I think that was due to the fact that my wife had been a lesbian. That was somewhat of an oddity. We both had very sensational stories. So for nine years we had been married and we had been in the public forefront and we are very vocal and thrilled that God has used us to spread this message.
>
> But that has a down side, because it feeds your ego and your flesh and your pride and all the things that are broken within you. When I came to work with [the ministry] Focus on the Family, three years ago, it increased the visibility even more. People wanted me to speak everywhere. I felt like a doll that someone

would wind up and say, come give your testimony, come speak here, come fly here, come fly there. In the mean time I was feeling great about my ministry. . . .

I started saying, "I am pretty wonderful. Everyone seems to think so." . . . So a year ago I wanted to escape. I wanted to escape my life. I wanted to escape everything. . . . My reputation. . . . I wanted off the treadmill and I thought I wanted to go back to a gay bar. Well, of course, because God loves me he is not going to let me go out on too long a leash, and I was discovered in there. . . .

I think that when you communicate in a media sound bite, and they ask you, "Have you changed and overcome homosexuality?" it's hard to answer that with a yes or no because sexuality is not a black or white issue. It runs on a continuum. I don't care who you are, there is a continuum to sexuality, sexual struggle, sexual temptation, behavior. . . .

I think homosexuality has components of idolatry. But I don't think it starts at that place; rather it ends up there. We know the real issues of homosexuality start way back in childhood for most people. The desires are the end results of a lot of dysfunctions—sometimes sexual violation, molestation, peer rejection, not bonding correctly with your own gender parental figure, abandonment. That is what is at its core. It begins with the individual feeling alienated, not feeling loved, and lonely. Where idolatry comes, is worshiping of other people in order to get those needs met.

I think what we have done in our movement is to respond the way the media wanted us to respond by saying, "Yes, I have changed. It's all washed up, and I am done with it, and now it's packaged and pretty. Here's my wife and two beautiful children."

I think we have realized the failure of this kind of answer. The leaders—myself included—need to say that in this life you may struggle, but God can give you victory over struggle. This is the paradox: that we can live a victorious life in the midst of struggle.

I have to say this past year has been the most difficult part of my life, but also the best year of my life—and I highly recommend it. [He laughs.] I mean, I highly recommend to people to allow the Lord to take you through brokenness.[37]

The Choice to Decline Therapy

Usually when adolescents come to me for treatment, it is because their parents have brought them in. Either the adolescent has "come out" as gay or the parents have discovered his homosexual behaviors or interests. The finding of gay pornography in the adolescent's room, or the discovery of letters or e-mail indicating a same-sex infatuation, have often alerted parents to the problem. For some time, mothers may have had the uneasy suspicion that there was another side to this obedient, compliant, lonely teenager.

Such detective work by suspicious parents presents them with a potential ethical conflict. They want to respect their child's privacy, yet they are afraid to neglect a serious problem. "I'm a sneak," confessed one mother, "and I admit it. But I'll do whatever it takes to save my kid." Most parents easily understand her sentiments. However, a commitment to doing "whatever it takes" may ultimately provoke angry rejection by the teenager.

When teens adopt a gay identity, some parents send the teenager to a therapist with the expectation that the therapist will "fix" him or "change" him. If the adolescent is resistant to participating in a reparative treatment program, and his cooperation is simply not forthcoming, then he should not be forced to participate. Richard Wyler explains this well:

> Some parents in particular are sorely tempted to try to take over their son's healing process for him. It won't work. He must decide he wants to change, and once he does, he must be at the controls. You may be along for the ride, offering support and encouragement, but not trying to run his life.
>
> Now, having said that you can't fix him doesn't mean you can't support him. You can be immensely supportive by creating a loving, nurturing environment that will be as conducive to healing as possible.... In some ways, many of us felt "loved out" of homosexuality either by God, by loving family and friends, or all of them. (<www.peoplecanchange.com>)

If the teenager does not want therapy, all that can be done is to provide information. We can only offer him the opportunity to make an educated choice—that is, to make a life decision based upon accurate information.

Even if your teenager decides to pursue therapy, there should be an open door policy, that is, he can leave at any time he chooses—and also return at any time in the future. A number of teenagers have come in to our clinic for counsel, have given themselves the opportunity to hear the option of reparative therapy, and have declined the invitation. The reasons for their refusal are varied.

One young man was deeply involved in a relationship with an older gay man and feared losing the security of that mentoring relationship. Others have become enchanted by the gay self-label or the gay subculture. Many young people have so deeply identified with their homosexual orientation that the possibility of giving up that identity is too frightening ("If I'm no longer gay, then who *am* I?"). In all these cases, if therapy continues at all, the therapeutic relationship must proceed very, very slowly, with much support and little direct confrontation.

Many parents, like you, refuse to simply abandon their son to a way of life that will involve painful adaptations, the likelihood of unfaithful long-term relationships, a high risk of serious or fatal disease, an extremely sex-focused gay culture, and significant social liability. It is in your child's best interests if you work toward maximizing the likelihood that he'll be heterosexual.

Alan Medinger, ex-gay ministry leader, talks about the change in his life that "set him free to love," desexualized his unmet emotional needs, broke the power of his addiction, and met the deep needs of his heart. Real and enduring change can happen, he affirms, "because I have seen it happen hundreds of times."[38]

And, as researcher Dr. Robert Spitzer said, if my *own* son were struggling with homosexuality, I would hope he would explore the possibility of change.

As another father told me emphatically, "Living life as a *heterosexual* man is hard enough!"

7

FROM TOMBOYS
TO LESBIANS

The feminine ideal—creative, expressive, intuitive,

receptive, empathic, connected to matter and spirit—has somehow been lost.

DIANE ELLER-BOYKO, COUNSELOR, EX-LESBIAN

For as long as she could remember, "Jessica" had hidden her intense crushes on female teachers behind a tough, sarcastic personality. Each day, after elementary school, when she was not playing sports with the boys, she retreated to her room to live in a fantasy world—an imaginary place in which she was a strong, heroic protector who "took care of" her favorite teacher or a little neighbor girl. Now and then she even wrote out her fantasies into dramatic stories, which she hid in a drawer in her bedroom.

By the time she reached junior high school, Jessica was using the name Jess and was wearing boys' jeans, flannel shirts, and cross-training shoes. She carefully hid her developing female body under thick layers of dark-colored fabric. Jessica was an excellent athlete, so her concentration on softball and lacrosse made sense to everyone. What did not make sense, however, was her angry repudiation of skirts and dresses, the way she refused to allow her hair to grow past her ears, and how she would not so much as listen to suggestions about wearing makeup or perfume or women's underwear. She identified herself with the labels of "lesbian" and "dyke" that she often heard used as slurs on the junior high school campus.

Jessica was contemptuous of her mother, whom she saw as weak, and their relationship was essentially nonexistent. The only thing the two shared, it seemed, was a mutual distrust. Her mother was so overwhelmed by the demands of keeping up the house (and often stayed in bed with bouts of depression) that she could give little time to her gender-confused daughter. She was a delicate, feminine woman, often sickly, who thought Jessica was just a "rebellious and incurable tomboy." On the other hand, the girl idolized her often-absent father.

Jessica began therapy, and I found her to be a sincere young woman with a genuine desire, just beneath her defensive exterior, to understand her conflicting feelings about accepting her gender. After a period of time, she told me that for many years she had been sexually molested by her uncle. The mother adamantly denied the repeated sexual abuse, which the woman's own brother had apparently committed since before the girl's fifth year. "He'd never do such a thing!" she insisted. "Jessica is just making up stories to get attention. You can never trust the stories she tells you."

The major conflict at the root of lesbianism, I believe, is the girl's unconscious rejection of her feminine identity. Women who become lesbians have usually decided, on an unconscious level, that being female is either undesirable or unsafe. Sometimes this is because the girl experienced early sexual molestation by a male. Other times (the more common scenario) it is because her mother appeared to the girl as either a negative or a weak identification object. The narcissistic and controlling mother who forces the girl into rigid, stereotyped behavior (providing her daughter with a negative object of identification) and the depressed, abused, or inadequate mother who provides a weak object of feminine identification are the two most common scenarios observed among mothers of lesbians. For some lesbians, probably a small minority, biological factors have set the stage for a gender-conflicted identity.

One former lesbian client, now married with children, describes the unequal distribution of power that was a defining issue within her family and a factor in her unconscious refusal to identify with femininity:

> I always thought of my mother as weak, while my dad was strong and had a charismatic personality. I still remember thinking, when I was very young, "I am not going to grow up to be like Mom." I also remember deciding that I was going to behave and even look like my brothers and my dad. My brothers had lots of friends and played sports, and my Dad was the guy in charge, the one who had a job, the one who had a life. He was smart and kind of sarcastic and always seemed

to have all the answers. My Mom stayed home, and she just idolized him.

My mother and I never seemed to have much to say to each other. She never really understood me, and looking back, I guess I never tried to understand her, either.

Jane Boyer, an ex-lesbian, also tells us about her own early family life, which she says was dominated by an abusive father. As the oldest of four children, Jane fell into the role of taking care of her siblings, including her depressed and withdrawn mother. She developed a strong aversion for her mother's role as the passive victim:

> We saw my mother get beat up quite a bit from my dad. There was a lot of domestic violence. Because I was the oldest of four, I basically took on the role of taking care of my mother because she not only was alcoholic, but she felt very helpless.
>
> My mother took a very passive role, and there were times that she would be drunk and crying with an icebag over her face. Her face would be all bloody with black eyes, and she'd be saying, "I don't know if I should leave him," and on and on.

Then, as early as the age of five, Jane found herself admiring the strong, masculine women she met—the exact opposite of the abused women in her family whom she had resolved she would never emulate. In later life, she came to understand that her mother had probably done the best she could with the overwhelming problems she faced. But just the same, Jane said, "I know that there were many, many times that I just hated what I saw in her. Even her sisters were a lot like that. They were kind of passive and weak, and didn't have a whole lot of backbone."

So what Jane (unconsciously) decided as a child was *If this is what it means to be a woman, I don't want to be one.* As she explained, "Women, to me, symbolized weakness . . . as I got older, when I did get involved with other women, these women were very butch, very dyke and very tough."

Whenever her parents argued, she sided with her dad—a phenomenon that Freud called "identification with the aggressor." This is a primitive psychological survival mechanism that is the equivalent of saying, "If someone hurts me, I'll be like he is so I won't get hurt. I'll be the one in charge." As she explains: "My father used to say degrading things about women all the time. My father truly hated women. They were sex objects. He used to call women the 'c' word and the 'b' word." As Jane explains, "He [Dad] was powerful, he was in control. She was weak, she was powerless. I didn't want to have anything to do with that."

Jane later married and adopted a child, but she continued to find herself romantically attracted to "butch" women, with whom she was vulnerable to developing a strong emotional dependency. One night, just for a lark, a friend encouraged her to go along with her to a lesbian bar, and Jane soon found herself caught up in a lifestyle that would nearly break up her marriage. She found herself continually drawn to the "very strong, very tough" woman of the type that were everything her mother had not been. "When we were together," she said of herself and her lovers, "[people] would always look at us as a man and woman."

At one point, driven by alcoholism and severe depression, Jane consulted a psychotherapist to see if there was a way she could reconcile her family life, her strong religious faith, her marriage, and her same-sex attractions. "I had been told that I was [born this way], so I thought gosh, if I was born this way, then I have to leave my husband, and I have to hurt my kids. . . . Because people were telling me that if I went back to my husband, I would never find peace."

The therapist—herself a lesbian—told Jane that to be true to herself, she should live out her lesbianism. Jane said,

> But when I finally left there, I was convinced that she was not at peace. She was talking about men, saying things like, And just because they have a penis . . .! She went on and on—just a lot of unresolved issues with men . . . a lot of anger towards men and a lot of unresolved issues with her mom, too. A lot of hurt . . .
>
> So I walked out of that appointment thinking, She's not at peace. *She's living her brokenness, that's what she's doing.* She has not recognized anything.

It was through her religious faith that Jane ultimately came to the life-changing conviction that "lesbian love is a counterfeit, and we are far too easily pleased with the counterfeit."[1] Jane decided that rather than "living out her brokenness," she would leave her lesbian lover and work toward change, rededicating herself to her marriage.

The Wounded Female Psyche

Male homosexuality tends to follow a relatively predictable developmental pattern, as we have explained in the previous chapters. But lesbianism is less predictable and more likely to alternate, during the woman's lifetime, with periods of heterosexuality. Many lesbians believe their sexuality is a choice they made as an outgrowth of their feminist political interests. Still, I believe the most common pathway to lesbianism is a life situation that creates a deeply ambivalent attitude toward femininity, conveying the internal message "It's not safe or desirable to be a woman."

This wounded female psyche may be why so many lesbians are champions of feminist political causes. Psychotherapist Diane Eller-Boyko, a married ex-lesbian, observes:

> Our culture especially honors the masculine—strength, dominance, achievement, striving. That creates in many women a neurotic split from their authentic natures. The woman represses the inner hurt and pain, and starts to identify with the masculine. It is out of the unhealed places of the wounded feminine psyche that she becomes aggressive and loud. Many women today are depressed, shut down, and overfunctioning.
>
> Lesbianism quite naturally allies itself with feminism. In the lesbian community you hear, "You don't need a man, you can do it on your own." Or, "What good are men? They only want one thing. Who needs them?" This, combined with a rebellious attitude toward the idea of receptivity, is part of lesbianism.
>
> Yet receptivity is the very core of the feminine. Rather than championing a war against men, we must bring back the life-giving spirit of the feminine.

Unknowingly, many mothers convey an unattractive image of femininity to their daughters. As Eller-Boyko explains:

> Mothers who cannot honor the feminine in their own natures become unavailable, dull, depressed, angry, compulsive—living by neurotic rituals which they use in order to fill the empty core of their being. Their daughters are wounded by this. And so the daughters carry on this wound to the feminine spirit for yet another generation.

Such a young woman may seek a deeper connection with the feminine through an intense same-sex relationship. Women naturally seek creativity, tranquillity, a feeling of centeredness. But, Eller-Boyko says, when a gender-deprived woman gets close to another woman, "Lesbian feelings may surface because she thought it felt kind of sexual. That emotional, rich experience becomes sexualized. But it's not so much about sexuality."

What feels so good about a lesbian relationship is that a woman gets "filled up" and connected with what she has lost touch with—her own femininity:

> The connection with another woman takes her into her own inner life, into that part of herself where she starts to experience her own feminine nature. . . .
> But when a woman has rejected her own femininity, she pays a price. Because

in seeking to unite with other women, she is trying to unite with herself—and this type of union will not, ultimately, heal the psyche. With another woman, she will have only the illusion of wholeness. The "Shadow"—representing those real developmental needs that were never met—will continue to haunt her.[2]

One Family Dynamic in Lesbianism: The Narcissistic Family System

Psychoanalyst Elaine Siegel, Ph.D., is a former supervising analyst at the New York Center for Psychoanalytic Training and the author of *Female Homosexuality: Choice Without Volition*.[3] Siegel says her lesbian patients fit a surprisingly predictable pattern: they grew up in narcissistic family systems that "tried to force their emerging identities into rigid, idealized forms of behavior alien to them."

Having been molded and manipulated by their parents' expectations, she says, these women experienced a "severe arrest in ego development." In rejecting their mothers as identification objects, these women also rejected the femininity their mothers represented. Siegel said her lesbian patients had been unable to successfully complete the separation and individuation phase during which the child establishes a separate, secure, and individual sense of self.

Despite having sometimes outwardly well-adjusted personalities, they were "unable to identify with either parent," and in a psychodynamic sense, they never "owned" their own female anatomies. Not all her patients had been blatantly tomboyish, but all showed some signs of gender conflict. Within the tensions of a narcissistic family system, in which the child is expected to meet the parents' expectations and never learns who she is as a separate individual, many of these women had long struggled with uncertainty and confusion in carving out their own personal identities.[4]

While Siegel is aware that this family model does not explain all forms of lesbianism, she is nevertheless struck by the commonality she found among the patients in her own practice. She has blunt words to describe the mothers of the lesbian women she saw in her practice:

> The little girl who turns to homosexuality never has a chance to create herself. She is a creation of her mother, whose self-love she was meant to enhance. . . .
>
> Mothers seemed to use their children as sometimes desperately needed, sometimes desperately repudiated extensions of themselves. . . .
>
> When these little girls tried to turn to their fathers, they did not fare much better. Preoccupied with their business deals, the men sporadically paid attention to their daughters, overstimulated them, and then appeared to forget that they were around.

. . . These fathers, when they took the time to react at all, responded to their daughters as persons who had to be made over in their own, masculine image.

Siegel describes the mothers of her lesbian clients as generally immature, emotionally fragile, and aloof from the needs of their daughters. They did not treat their daughters as whole and separate persons but rather as narcissistic extensions of themselves, and as such, their daughters were expected to fulfill the mothers' own needs. As a result, these girls never developed a stable sense of either self or gender.

In childhood, Siegel's lesbian clients provided the following indicators of gender conflict:

> None of them as little girls, were interested in playing with their dolls or in the usual games of family, and they had a marked aversion toward normative feminine clothing.
>
> A very strong indication for concern is a girl's rejection of urinating while sitting, or insisting upon standing while urinating. Other causes of serious concern is her assertion that she has or will grow a penis, or, in older girls, that she does not want to grow breasts or menstruate.[5]

In adulthood Siegel's lesbian clients, who had been unable to identify with their mothers, sought to repair their defective body images by seeking an intimate partner who was similar to themselves. Because they were unable to integrate their sexual organs into their body image, these women also developed a profound denial of gender differences ("Women can do everything that men can do." "Who needs a man?"). This attitude often carried over into a political position of radical feminism and of resentment toward men in power.

In my own practice with men, I have found this same sort of phenomenon—a denial of the male body in my male homosexual clients. Indeed, Siegel and I are in agreement that a primary therapeutic task is the need for both lesbians and homosexual men to "claim" their female or male bodies, from which they have become emotionally detached, as part of their fundamental sense of self.

The Aftermath: Gender Narcissism

"Gender narcissism," says psychoanalyst Gerald Schoenewolf, is a condition in which a person "takes one's own body as an object of desire." Schoenewolf sees this as the fundamental syndrome characterizing the homosexual condition: "Gender narcissism develops in reaction to feelings of inferiority about one's gender, and might be defined as excessive love or concern for one's gender, one's genitals, or one's gender identity, and an aversion to the opposite sex."[6]

We often see gay men and lesbians joining forces on the political front to protest against patriarchy. The lesbian who feels wounded in her feminine spirit—unsafe in claiming her feminine nature—will be powerfully drawn to a political movement that buttresses "woman power" and condemns patriarchy. She joins forces with the gay man, who shares her anger because he has been wounded by his male peers and has long felt on the outs in masculine company, particularly in relation to straight males in power. So the gay-lesbian political alliance in support of feminist goals is not surprising:

> A number of both female and male homosexual [patients] had politicized their feelings about homosexuality. Not only their gender was idealized, but also homosexuality as well. Homosexuals, they held, were more sensitive, more humane, more refined, and more moral than heterosexuals. "If straights were as peace-loving as gays, the world would be a better place," was an often expressed sentiment.[7]

More on Family Dynamics

As Siegel has pointed out, a narcissistic mother who interferes with her daughter's separation and individuation can propel the girl in the direction of lesbianism. But still another pathway to lesbianism is the experience of severe hurt by a male, which communicates the same internal message: "It is unsafe to be a female." As psychiatrist Richard Fitzgibbons explains:

> A number of women who become involved in same-sex relationships had fathers who were emotionally insensitive, alcoholic, or abusive. Such women, as a result of painful childhood and teenage experiences, have good reason to fear being vulnerable to men. . . .
>
> Women who have been sexually abused or raped as children or adolescents may find it difficult or almost impossible to trust men. They may, therefore, turn to a woman for affection and to fulfill their sexual desires.[8]

Dr. Charles Socarides agrees that the girl who feels lesbian attractions harbors a sense of gender inadequacy: "In my practice, I have found that lesbians had deep feelings of inferiority as little girls. Anything that parents can do to make their kids feel proud of their identity—as young men, as young women— will help the [treatment] process."[9]

Rejection of One's Own Gender

Little clinical attention has been paid to the tomboy phenomenon in girls because there are far fewer gender-disturbed girls than boys. And boyish girls do not attract the same degree of concern as "sissy boys." Girls are allowed much more latitude in contemporary culture for a wide range of gender nonconformity, while effeminate boys have been (and continue to be) rejected or marginalized. Therefore, the girl must display more extreme cross-gender behavior than the boy before parents seek out professional help for her.

Another issue is that tomboyish behavior in girls is, in reality, often a passing phase, while sissyish or effeminate behavior in boys usually is not.[10] Many girls will normally engage in, or even prefer, masculine activities during their childhood years, while still maintaining a basic feminine identity. Later, these girls will increasingly expand their feminine interests as they approach the adolescent years.[11] So, as Dr. Selma Fraiberg says in her classic book on children, "It is only when the personality of a girl is dominated by masculine tendencies, and femininity is repudiated, that we need to feel some concern for the future development" of the child.[12]

For a small percentage of girls, tomboyish behavior and rejection of their femininity continues through adolescence. Such girls are more likely to become transsexual or lesbian.[13] Strong rivalry with brothers and other boys, especially in the physical-athletic sphere, is another indication that there may be lasting gender adjustment difficulties.

Dr. George Rekers describes a case of a tomboyish girl referred to treatment:

Becky was referred for psychological treatment at the age of seven years, 11 months, by a psychiatric nurse specialist who had assessed her at the request of the girl's mother. Becky had two younger sisters, age 2 and 6 years old. The girl's father was absent from the home due to divorce.

For as long as the mother could remember, Becky had been dressing exclusively in boys' pants, and she often wore cowboy boots. At the same time, she consistently rejected any feminine clothing such as dresses and she had no interest in female jewelry.

Becky's only use of female cosmetic articles that her mother could recall involved drawing a mustache and/or a beard on her face several times. Becky appeared "masculine" in her gestures, mannerisms, and gait. It was reported that she would occasionally masturbate in public and rub her body up against other girls in her peer group. She frequently projected her voice very low so she would sound like a "man."

She repeatedly expressed her desire to be a boy, and she adopted male roles in her play. She definitely preferred the company of boy playmates and did not interact very well with other girls. Her behavior was described as excessively aggressive. She had a very poor relationship with her 6-year-old sister who displayed a typical preference for feminine play activities.[14]

Dr. Elaine Siegel reported that her lesbian patients never played the usual girlhood games, such as dressing up dolls and playing house, but rather substituted active games and sports more typical of boyhood. She describes the treatment of three of her clients who were experiencing gender confusion. While these children knew their biological sex—that is, they understood intellectually that they were male or female—they had no understanding about what being a boy or girl would mean within the context of their own lives. In fact, she says, many of her female clients emphatically turned away from their feminine natures with an attitude of what Siegel calls "omnipotent triumph"—an in-your-face rejection of their femininity.

The Roles of Mothers and Fathers

Dr. Robert Stoller, a pioneer researcher in gender-identity problems in children of both sexes, says that if one wishes to promote the gender identity of a girl, there should be a warm mother-daughter intimacy, along with a father who does not promote identification of the daughter with himself. Indeed, a healthy relationship with Mom provides the most important foundation for the incorporation of femininity and heterosexuality.

In Stoller's study of a group of very masculine females, he generally found too little emotional closeness with the mother and too much relationship with the father.[15] In some cases, the father was disappointed at having a daughter and treated her as if she were a son, resulting in the "forced choice" to abandon her feminine aspirations to gain her father's love.

Severe Depression in the Mother

Studies of severely gender-disturbed girls often uncover a traumatic interruption in the early mother-daughter bond. This appears to be due, in most cases, to a severe depression in the mother. The father—taking over in the child rearing where the mother has withdrawn—sees his daughter as a "buddy," encouraging her to behave like he does and to share in his masculine interests. With little influence by the mother, such girls often become masculinized by the age of three or four.

A history of severe maternal depression was prominent in the histories of twenty-six GID girls whose histories were reported by Zucker and Bradley. Nearly 77 percent of the mothers had histories of depression, and all had been depressed during their daughters' infant or toddler years, during the sensitive gender-identity developmental period. Here we see the phenomenon of the mother as a weak or negative identification object. These researchers offer a detailed picture:

> The girls had difficulty in forming an emotional connection to their mothers. In some instances, it seemed to us that a girl either failed to identify with her mother, or disidentified from her mother because she perceived her mother as weak, incompetent, or helpless. In fact, many of the mothers devalued their own efficacy and regarded the female gender role with disdain. . . .
>
> In a smaller number of cases, it seemed that the daughter's "significant medical illness" or difficult temperament during infancy had impaired her relationship with her mother.[16]

The mother who has been abused by men will likely convey the message that it is risky to be a woman:

> Six of the mothers had a history of severe and chronic sexual abuse of an incestuous nature. The femininity of these mothers had always been clouded by this experience, which rendered them quite wary about men and masculinity, and created substantial dysfunction in their sexual lives.
>
> In terms of psychosocial transmission, the message to the daughters seemed to be that being female was unsafe. The mothers had a great deal of difficulty in instilling in their daughters a sense of pride and confidence about being female.[17]

The Father's Role

The proper role of the father in developing his daughter's feminine identity is to reflect his daughter's gender-differentness from himself with respect and appreciation. At the same time, he provides love and positive regard so that the girl will feel worthy of another man's love. In contrast, the father who is absent or aloof will hinder the girl's ability to accurately perceive men and will distort her idea of what she rightly deserves and should expect from a relationship with a man.

We also sometimes see the well-known psychological phenomenon, mentioned earlier, of "identification with the aggressor." When the father or older brothers victimize the family, and when the mother feels acutely put down by her husband and cannot stand up for herself, the daughter may make the unconscious decision that it is unsafe to claim her feminine identity and thus place herself in a similar position of vulnerability. Instead, to avoid overwhelming anxiety, the girl refuses to identify with the helplessness of her mother and defensively identifies with the same masculinity she fears.

Not surprisingly, many explicitly gender-disturbed girls are, as Zucker and Bradley note, "preoccupied with power, aggression and protection fantasies."[18] As adults, such women may become involved in sadomasochistic and "domination" or "leather" sexual activities. These activities act out an unconscious approach-avoidance conflict regarding issues of gender. The girl who has been unable to make a satisfactory identification with a same-sex love object (the mother) will harbor repressed rage against the very thing she loves because, on the one hand, she desires it but, on the other, she has been hurt by it.

Sadomasochism is, in fact, somewhat common within the lesbian community. As one lesbian-activist psychotherapist has observed:

> I can't remember the exact moment when I started to notice that many of our lesbian publications, erotica anthologies, conferences and books were referring to sado-masochism in an approving or erotically positive way.
>
> Suddenly, it seemed, s/m has become mainstreamed, even celebrated, particularly among younger lesbians. The whips, chains and master-slave role-plays don't seem to shock us as they once did. . . .
>
> Instead of challenging s/m, so many lesbians are now embracing it as glamorous and hip, a way to be "sex positive" and "in-your-face queer."[19]

The author of the above observations, it should be noted, is disturbed by the growing popularity of S&M within the lesbian community—*not* because it violates any moral norm of decency, she makes a point to assure the reader, but because S&M threatens the lesbian community's *political* objectives. She is concerned that the practice "reflects and perpetuates oppressive attitudes toward women, minorities and economically disadvantaged people in our society."[20]

The Specter of Sexual Abuse

A girl's poor relationship with her mother and unhealthy interaction with her father are certainly key issues in her gender confusion. But reports of experienced ex-gay counselors and ministry leaders also consistently support the observation of a higher than average frequency of childhood sexual abuse by a male. Ex-gay ministry leaders Anita Worthen and Bob Davies have found that in the histories of lesbians they have known or counseled, sexual abuse is one of the striking common denominators:

> In women, abuse can lead to a deep fear and even hatred of men if the perpetrator is a male. Men are no longer "safe." The woman's deep need to connect with another individual leads her right into close relationships with other women, often women who have been wounded in similar ways. This sets the stage for lesbian bonding to occur.[21]

The trauma of sexual violation can have enormous repercussions in a young woman's life. From the girl's perspective, her femininity somehow provokes sexual abuse; consequently, in self-defense, the girl must relinquish the vulnerable, feminine part of herself. Typically, this rejection of her feminine identity is an unconscious choice.

Lesbian Relationships and Emotional Dependency

Lesbian partnerships can, some ex-gay ministries observe, take on a quality of "relational idolatry." Unlike the characteristically open relationships of gay men, the bond of two women tends to involve an intense enmeshment. Psychotherapist Andria Sigler-Smalz, a former lesbian who is now married, describes the nature of such relationships:

> Female relationships lean toward social exclusivity rather than inclusivity, and it is not unusual for a lesbian couple to increasingly reduce contact with family members and previous friends. This gradual withdrawal serves to insure control, and protects against separateness and perceived threats to their fragile bond. . . .
>
> The propelling drive in the lesbian relationship is the woman's same-sex emotional and nurturing deficits, and these deficits are generally not sexualized to the same degree as seen in male homosexuality. For the female homosexual, "emotional attraction" plays a more critical role than does sexual attraction. . . .
>
> Within these relationships there appears to be a capacity for particularly strong attachment. However, a closer look reveals behaviors that indicate a fragile relational bond ridden with fear and anxiety. . . . For example, we see fears of abandonment and/or engulfment, struggles involving power (or powerlessness) and control, and desires to merge with another person to obtain a sense of security and significance.
>
> While lesbian partnerships generally are of longer duration then male relation-

ships, they tend to be fraught with emotional intensity and held together by the "glue" of jealousy, over-possessiveness and various manipulative behaviors.

During the course of the relationship, the "highs" are very high, and the times of conflict, extreme. Excessive time together, frequent telephoning, disproportionate card or gift-giving, hastily moving in together or merging finances, are some of the ways separateness is defended against. In such relationships, we see the counterfeit of healthy attachment—that is, emotional dependency and over-enmeshment. . . . There is often a desperate quality to the emotional attraction in women that struggle with lesbianism.[22]

Generally speaking, females discover their sexual orientation later in life than do males. This may be due to several factors—particularly, because girls tend to be less sexually active than boys, and because a lesbian identity usually emerges gradually and from within the context of deep emotional attachments, rather than as a result of sexual experimentation. Boys, on the other hand, are more likely to become aware of their homosexuality through brief, experimental sexual encounters.[23]

Transsexualism

Gender conflict in girls is not always outwardly observable in the form of "butch" behavior and masculinity. Some lesbians, in fact, are quite feminine. Yet masculinization in some girls can be extreme.

An example of an adolescent girl with extreme gender confusion is "Cindy." Her rejection of gender identity led not only to lesbianism but also to an even more dramatic rejection—that of her own body.

Cindy was fourteen years old and lived with her mother in a rural community. Her mother had never been married but lived with a few boyfriends on and off over the years. Cindy had no memory of her father and had experienced little affection from any adult male figure.

When Cindy first appeared at my office, she was wearing a distinctly masculine and oversized shirt, faded blue jeans, and boots. She sat with legs apart and elbows on her knees. Her voice inflection and way of communicating were quite manly, as were her gestures and mannerisms. At times I had to remind myself that she really was a girl.

Cindy told me with pride that no one had ever been able get her to wear a dress. She said that she had felt like—and wanted to be—a boy all of her life. A recent TV program about female-to-male sex-change surgery had fascinated her, and now she was just "waiting it out at home" until she could move out and have the same surgery done.

Cindy stated that she had a deep emotional attachment to another girl and that it was sexual. She was not gay—she was just a guy who, like any other guy, wants his girlfriend. This did not sound so much like rebellion or desire to shock as an emphatic and uncompromising statement of personal conviction.

While Cindy seemed intelligent, her grades were poor. One particular problem at school was that she insisted on using the boy's bathroom. Her social interactions were largely limited to other boys at school. At every opportunity she reminded people her name was not Cindy but Rick, a name she had taken in honor of a male rock star she admired. She was disgusted by anything feminine, including her own physical maturation as a woman, and she would wear a lumberjacket to hide her breasts, which she said she hated.

The vast majority of her peers at school rejected Cindy. Her few male friends were the rebels, the radical fringe, the dropouts and dopers. Not surprisingly, she suffered frequent depressive episodes accompanied by suicidal thoughts. She repeatedly stated that she must live as a male, or else she would kill herself.

This is a remarkable and instructive case, but Cindy's story is very extreme. In such a case the therapist's task is to sort out the mix of biological and psychological factors that cause the client's difficulty and to determine whether the client is willing to work toward claiming her feminine nature, in which case reorientation therapy can proceed. Many such severely conflicted clients seek out a therapist who will support them through sex-change surgery, which we do not support. Mutilation of the body, we believe, provides no long-term answers.

Unfulfilled Nurturance Needs

Some lesbians do not suffer so much from unfulfilled basic identification needs as from unfulfilled longings for nurturance. These women retain an unconscious need to repair a fragile mother-daughter bond. For them, the issue is a deficit of same-sex nurturance. Therapist (and ex-lesbian) Diane Eller-Boyko explains this unfulfilled longing, which she calls her "own personal story":

> A client will . . . tell me—in words more or less like this—"Connecting with another woman felt like an ancient longing fulfilled. A homecoming." When I hear

this, I know that something of the feminine is missing within her. The feminine ideal—creative, expressive, intuitive, receptive, empathic, connected to matter and spirit—has somehow been lost.

In falling in love with another woman, she is really seeking to connect with herself.

Looking at lesbianism developmentally, I would suggest that she is seeking to unite with the archetypal "good mother."[24]

As Eller-Boyko explains, many lesbian women who seek change do not persist in therapy. For them, giving up the emotional connection of a lesbian relationship seems too threatening—much like a death. She notes:

> We can say to a teenage boy, "OK, you can get your emotional needs met but it doesn't have to become sexual." A girl, on the other hand, may perceive that the therapist is asking her to give up a relationship upon which she feels deeply dependent and needy. She very likely feels as if she can't live without her love interest or "significant other."
>
> A lesbian may say, "When I'm involved sexually, it's the only time I feel I'm loved and cared for." Particularly for the girl who has been sexually molested, same-sex behavior offers a sense of control in the relationship with the other person. Such girls view their lesbian sexuality as a way to gain mastery of a threatening situation. It is the only time they feel "safe" with their sexuality.

Checklist of Questions About Daughters

The following is a list of questions for parents who suspect that their daughter may be gender-confused. Reflect on the following questions, then discuss them with your spouse and, if possible, with a qualified therapist. This list will not fit all prelesbian girls, since the roots of lesbianism are more complex than those for male homosexuality, but they do provide an important starting point:

1. Is your daughter markedly gender-atypical?
2. Does she reject her sexual anatomy?
3. Does she go to her mother with questions? Does she ask her mother to do things with her? Does she show Mom her toys, games, and activities, or does she prefer to go to Dad? Does she have a warm, comfortable relationship with Mom? Does she enjoy doing "girl things" with her mother?
4. To what extent does your daughter interact and relate comfortably with other girls?
5. Does your daughter adamantly reject the possibility that she will grow up

to be married and have children someday?

6. How early and how often have you observed any of the following behaviors?

- Dressing like a boy and refusing any girls' clothes
- Opposite-sex gestures and mannerisms, including voice inflection
- Preferring opposite-sex toys and activities
- Rejecting or having no interest in girls and their games
- Insistence on using a boy's name

7. Does her father encourage the girl in developing her femininity?

Autobiography of Chastity Bono

Entertainers Sonny and Cher divorced when their daughter Chastity was four years old. As Chastity tells us in her autobiography, *Family Outing,* she found herself emotionally stuck between a distant, disapproving mother who was prone to unpredictable angry outbursts, and a generally unavailable father. At the same time, she was estranged from her female peers. Chastity, who today self-identifies as a lesbian, explains how her parents enmeshed her in their marital disputes as a way of getting back at each other:

> In a way, I think I was the son my father never had. . . . When my father encouraged my tomboyishness, my mother would get annoyed. I think in some ways they acted out their frustration with each other through me: my father would aggravate my mother by encouraging my boyish behavior, and my mother became more uncomfortable with me because she saw me mimicking my father.[25]

Cher was upset by her daughter's masculine clothing and lack of female friends and tried, without success, to persuade Chastity to wear a skirt to school. In fact, at one point Chastity "vowed never to wear anything girlie again." Clearly, the markers for future lesbianism were in place at this time.

When the Girl Is Brought to Therapy

When a girl has been found to be involved in a lesbian relationship, the parents will probably be focused on stopping their daughter's sexual behavior. But the girl herself is primarily concerned about her own feelings of loneliness, alienation, rejection, and poor self-esteem. A skillful therapist can offer concern for the girl's feelings.

Feeling misunderstood at home is often a major source of unhappiness. The father will need to assess his involvement in his daughter's life. This will probably require a more supportive, less intrusive role for him. The mother, at the same time, will need to share her emotional self and her vulnerabilities with her daughter, and build a relationship of greater mutuality.

Lesbianism, as we have said, follows developmental patterns that are not always identifiable in childhood. But we can begin by asking the mother to reflect along the following lines:

- What is my relationship with my husband like?
- How do I feel about my daughter's femininity?
- How do I encourage, support, and reflect the expression of my daughter's developing womanhood?
- What is my attitude toward my daughter's relationship with her father?
- Do I feel threatened by my husband's attention to my daughter?
- Do my husband and daughter seem to have a special relationship that stirs negative or uneasy feelings in me?
- Do I feel envious or competitive regarding my daughter's relationship with her dad?
- Do my husband and daughter make me feel left out?
- Would it be helpful for me to talk to a qualified professional psychotherapist about these issues specifically and about our family relationships in general?

Concerned parents should give immediate and serious evaluation to a gender-confused girl's relationship with her mother. This, of course, is true if the girl displays outright symptoms of gender disturbance, but it is also true if her gender nonconformity is less explicit and is accompanied by a hostile or conflicted relationship with the mother.

Lesbianism "by Default"

Some women seem to develop normally as girls, and in fact function well heterosexually and marry, but then, to the complete surprise of their entire family, fall into a lesbian relationship in adulthood. Dr. Richard Fitzgibbons explains that the emotionally fragile woman with unfulfilled nurturance needs may turn to a lesbian relationship out of disappointment and loneliness or after she has become disillusioned by a bad marriage or a divorce.[26] Such women may vacillate between lesbian and heterosexual relationships several times throughout their lives.

The public romances of lesbian entertainer Ellen DeGeneres and her partner, and of singer Melissa Etheridge and her partner, both illustrate the fluidity of sexual attraction in some women. Each of these women had a partner who was once heterosexual, who then identified herself as lesbian for several years, and who later went back to living a heterosexual lifestyle. Such fluidity is more common among women than men.

Tasks in the Healing Process

Psychotherapist Diane Eller-Boyko explains the process of therapy for an adult client. Describing her own healing pathway out of lesbianism as well, Eller-Boyko says she works toward building a gradual reconnection with the client's own feminine nature. Client and therapist will be looking at the blocks in the client's psychological development that started an "erosion and devaluation of the feminine spirit." Eller-Boyko further explains, "Instead of looking for another woman, I'm trying to connect her with that reservoir within herself. . . . Only when she has been nourished by that deep connection, can a woman move on to connect with the masculine."[26]

As we have said, many factors lead to a lesbian or homosexual outcome, so parents should not take the attitude that all the responsibility for their daughter's lesbianism falls on their shoulders. Your daughter's sexual identity was also shaped by peer influences, her own temperament, the choices she herself made, perhaps an experience of sexual abuse, and sometimes biological factors that have influenced her gender nonconformity.

Cultural influences, as well, reinforce your daughter's developing attitudes. The culture we now live in does not reinforce a healthy appreciation for growing more deeply into one's gender. In the next chapter, we'll take a closer look at the cultural politics of homosexuality and how this may have magnified your child's gender conflict.

8

THE POLITICS OF TREATMENT

There is no doubt that ultimately, an enlightened and civilized society

must rid itself of its homophobic fears and prejudices. . . .

This is a mental-health issue of the first magnitude.

JUDD MARMOR, M.D., PAST PRESIDENT
OF THE AMERICAN PSYCHIATRIC ASSOCIATION

One of the greatest challenges faced by parents is the political war that rages around homosexuality.

As cheerleaders for the gay-activist cause, the mental health associations hold to a one-sided worldview that tolerates no dissent. The American Psychological Association, for example, admits that homosexuals are not "born that way," but then its leaders refuse to investigate the family and social factors that shape sexual identity. "Why ask why?" they say. "It doesn't matter."

Complicating the issue of treatment is the perfectly understandable sympathy that both parents and therapists feel for the pain experienced by the gender-confused child. This sympathy, I believe, often leads to a denial of reality wherein adults are tempted to label that troubled child "perfectly normal."

And no matter how often evidence is offered to the contrary, many people still continue to reason that same-sex attractions must be normal because homosexuals are simply "born that way."

As we have noted, scientists know the "born that way" argument is not true. They recognize that a homosexual orientation results from a combination of biological, social, and family influences, reinforced by lifestyle choices along the way. Yet the gay-rights movement has convinced many psychotherapists that homosexuality is intrinsic to a person's deepest identity, so it would be a violation of a child's rights to influence him or her toward heterosexuality.[1]

What Does Psychology Know About Human Design and Purpose?

In the vast majority of graduate programs in clinical psychology, students are taught that homosexuality is part of a person's core nature. Does this mean, then, that psychologists know something about human nature of which the rest of us remain ignorant? In fact, psychology knows nothing about human design and purpose that you and I aren't aware of.

No matter what the profession claims or implies, most people still have the instinctive awareness that something "just isn't right" about homosexuality. And they know that something is very odd and sad indeed about a fellow who prefers to dress in a wig and high heels, or a man who expects to give motherly love and nurturance to a baby, or a father who wants to "nurse" an infant using a mechanical device attached to his own nipple.[2]

Most people intuitively sense that what is "normal" must be—as one psychologist said more than fifty years ago—"that which functions in accordance with its design."[3] Our visceral reaction—shock and disgust—to the image of a man trying to nurse a baby using his own nipple is very likely part of an instinctive, nearly universal "gut sense" given to humankind to warn us that there are gender boundaries that cannot be crossed without violating our natures. Religious traditionalists, of course, see that same "gut intuition" confirmed and enlarged upon through biblical revelation.

For many years, our culture thrived under the influence of the shared worldview that we were designed creatures. People tend to understand the design argument intuitively. So when a boy is born with something like, say, attention-deficit disorder, psychologists do not say, "You were born like this, so attention deficit must be a normal and healthy way for you to experience the world." Instead, they help the boy learn focusing techniques so he can concentrate better on his schoolwork.

Of course, being *designed creatures* does not mean we are limited to a narrow way of functioning. We can still sacrifice normal function for a higher purpose; a priest can choose to be chaste for the sake of his vocation, for example. Or we can expand on a normal function—such as making use of a calculator to improve on arithmetic we do in our heads—as long as that expanded function does not subvert the original created purpose. But homosexuality violates our human design by subverting it to an unnatural purpose. Instead of seeking out the "other" who is designed to be complementary to him, both psychologically and anatomically, the homosexually oriented person falls in love with a mirror image of himself.

Traditionalists who believe there is a moral order grounded in nature's design find supportive evidence in social science research because studies show that gay male relationships are likely to be unstable, nonmonogamous, and destructive to the body. Surely this should be a warning that humankind does not have un-limited freedom.

The Limits of Science

Misunderstanding of the scientific evidence by educated people never ceases to amaze us. "If science is in any way a part of your life, then you just can't agree with them," said a Republican political strategist, referring to members of her political party who oppose gay activism. This woman, an outspoken supporter of the normalization of homosexuality, has evidently formulated her entire view on the fallacy that "science has proved homosexuality to be normal."

Contrary to what this politician believes, science has proved nothing of the sort, nor can it. This is because the concept of "who we are"—what is normal, healthy, adaptive, self-actualizing, or high-functioning in a fully human sense—is not ultimately a scientific concept but a philosophical concept. Science is an invaluable tool, but it is of limited value in answering the ultimate questions in life: "Where did we come from?" "What is our purpose in life?" "What is wrong with the world?" "How should we live?" Science is blind to the human spirit. It cannot tell us about our core identity—who we are.

Gay activists gained much public support by promoting the concept that "science reexamined homosexuality and has found the condition to be normal and healthy."[4] It was this illusion of psychiatry as *hard science* that allowed gay activists to radically overturn public opinion, religious theology, and legal pre-cedent on homosexuality.

Scientific data describes the world and provides the facts we need to guide us toward an understanding. But "who we are," in the fullest sense—that is, our core identity or human essence—is a matter that must be resolved by philoso-phy and religion. Science functions only on a descriptive level as what we call a "servant discipline." It is the disciplines of philosophy and theology, however, that give us a larger perspective that reaches beyond the material world to provide us with an image of what it means to be fully human.

Clinicians Who Devalue Religious Motivations

When homosexuality was removed from the psychiatric manual in 1973, many observers have noted, nothing new had been discovered about human sexuality. What actually happened is that gay advocates had gained the sympathy of psychiatrists for their social activism. As psychiatrist Jeffrey Satinover explains: "The normalization of homosexuality was a classic example where the American Psychiatric Association knuckled under to a victim group's pressure tactics. In that instance, no substantive data was presented either to 'prove' that homosexuality is an illness, or to 'prove' that it is not."[5]

Most parents, not surprisingly, do express alarm about the possibility that their child may grow up to be homosexual, transvestite, transsexual, or bisexual. In support of these parents, a small number of clinicians have openly defended the right of parents to influence their child's gender identity—and subsequent sexual orientation.[6]

One such advocate, and a very unlikely one, is Dr. Judd Marmor. As a popular former president of the American Psychiatric Association, he was a leader among those psychiatrists who supported the normalizing of homosexuality in 1973, and is the author of several highly respected texts on homosexuality. Yet in spite of his belief that homosexuality should be considered normal, Marmor states that "the issue of preventing [homosexual] development where possible, is a legitimate one."[7]

In what seems a puzzlingly frank admission, Marmor acknowledges that homosexuality often develops through a "poor relationship with a father figure which results in a failure to form a satisfactory masculine identification, and a close but ambivalent relationship with a mother figure." But after acknowledging that pathological *foundation* for much of homosexuality, Marmor then rejects labeling the *outcome* of this development as a developmental disorder! Why? All he says is that the psychotherapist has a duty to "remove stigma" from people "whose early life experiences, through no fault of their own, have rendered them erotically responsive to members of their own sex."[8] This is an odd statement indeed. Why should it be psychiatry's role to compromise clinical understanding in order to serve as agents of social activism?

Marmor then contemptuously dismisses people who believe that God created men and women heterosexual. He speaks of "pious religionists" who consider biblical condemnations of homosexual acts to "represent 'the word of God.' "[9] Although he has scathing words for a biblical worldview, he nevertheless does sympathize with a parent who desires to avoid homosexual development in his or her children because of the *social* disadvantages of homosexuality.[10] In other words, utilitarian values (happiness, social adjustment) are acceptable, but biblical views (human beings are created heterosexual by design and have a responsibility to live in a way that is satisfying to their Creator) should be summarily rejected.

Dr. Kenneth Zucker, a prominent clinician in the treatment of childhood gender-identity disorder, holds a similar attitude to Marmor's. Zucker recognizes gender-identity disorder of childhood as a developmental disturbance, and he understands and supports a parent's desire to maximize the likelihood of his or her child growing up heterosexual due to the social disadvantages to a gay lifestyle. But he, like Marmor, is disparaging of a family's religiously based disapproval of homosexuality.[11] In effect, he treats as suspect parents' religious convictions about sexuality—typically, a belief system that envisions human wholeness and fulfillment in terms of gender complementarity and heterosexuality.

When clinicians like Marmor and Zucker marginalize and disrespect the religious values of their clients, they overstep their bounds. They incorrectly imply that science knows something definitive about the purpose of human sexuality of which a religious belief system is ignorant.

When the Data Is Interpreted to Suit Ideological Purposes

Because they are usually caring individuals who are motivated to help, most psychotherapists do not want to theorize about the meaning of research findings that might be offensive to a group of people. For example, while recent evidence shows a higher level of psychiatric illness among homosexual individuals, most psychologists remain silent about the obvious possibility: that this dysfunction could be due to the homosexual condition itself.[12] Instead, psychology routinely blames the problems of gay life on society's oppression.

One major recent study has broken this ideological resistance. The study, which showed a higher level of psychiatric problems among gay men and lesbians, opened the door to speculation among researchers that the higher level of psychiatric problems among homosexuals could also be due to loneliness, promiscuity, and the difficulty in finding and keeping long-term partners due to the instability of gay relationships.[13] Another researcher suggested in the same prestigious journal that homosexuality—to the extent that it is biologically based—may be a "biological error."[14] This was a particularly bold statement, given that when television talk show host Dr. Laura Schlessinger offered the same idea, she was hounded off the air by gay activists, who used that comment out of context ("Dr. Laura says *we* are biological errors").[15]

But such frankness, as we have said, is unusual. The politically correct explanation (and the safest explanation, in terms of a psychologist's career advancement) is that, among gays, social oppression can be the *only* source for the higher rate of psychiatric disorders and substance abuse problems.

Sexual-Liberationist Philosophy Dominates the Professional Associations

Political correctness continues to plague all of our mental health associations. A 1999 American Psychiatric Association annual convention was scheduled to include a debate on whether sexual orientation could be changed through therapy. But that debate was canceled when two of the scheduled speakers withdrew, saying that the subject of homosexuality-as-changeable was too politically charged for a scientific meeting. Psychiatrist Jeffrey Satinover and I were originally proposed as members of that panel, but the gay-activist psychiatrists refused to participate if either Satinover or I took part in such a discussion.[16]

So you are in graduate school and you think heterosexuality is normative? Good luck expressing your viewpoint, publishing your thesis, and getting along with your colleagues. You had better keep that view to yourself, or you may find yourself squeezed out of the social club from which you are trying so hard to gain approval. Psychology is made up of a "herd of independent minds," as the saying goes, all loudly trumpeting their love of diversity while insisting that you think exactly like they do.

Is the profession aware that there is any irony there? As president of NARTH, I took heart recently when the president of the American Psychological Association, Norine Johnson, published a prominent editorial that made a passionate plea for intellectual freedom. She said: "I am strongly supportive of open debate in the APA, regardless of the volume or intensity of the debate. Debate is healthy. Disagreement is healthy. . . . A productive and healthy science requires freedom of inquiry and freedom of expression."[17]

What motivated Johnson's impassioned statement? Not, unfortunately, concern for people seeking a change of sexual orientation. Dr. Johnson had actually been concerned about a public uproar that had embarrassed the association: APA had published an article that found that pedophile relationships are, surprisingly often, remembered by the molested boy as positive. In response to a wave of public criticism, the association had expressed regrets about that article. Dr. Johnson's passionate plea for scientific freedom was, instead, in defense of the authors' right to discuss a *pedophile-friendly viewpoint!*

Nevertheless, encouraged by Johnson's willingness to deal with controversy, NARTH wrote asking for permission to announce our scientific meetings in APA publications, just as gay organizations do. (NARTH's requests have been denied in the past.) The result? We received a response, not from the APA president, but from Clinton Anderson, head of the Office of Gay, Lesbian, and Bisexual Concerns. Unfortunately, Anderson represents a politically different group of people—gay advocates. He is adamantly opposed to NARTH's perspective on homosexuality, and he strongly rejects the treatment of prehomosexual children. Sending NARTH's letter to the desk of Anderson was like sending a complaint about law-enforcement abuse to City Hall, only to have it routed back to the police commissioner. Of course, our request was denied.

If the APA truly wants scientific openness, then organizations like NARTH must be invited to participate. Scientific freedom requires the inclusion of those with different understandings of the meaning and significance of human sexuality. Yet parents struggling to find a like-minded therapist may be interested to know that, as of this writing, the door at the APA remains essentially closed to alternative viewpoints.

Nature Itself Is "Heterosexist"

A number of writers—mostly gay activists—condemn therapy for gender-identity disorder, and of these, many attack the treatment as being "heterosexist."[18] In a sense, of course, they are right, because nature itself is inherently "heterosexist"—that is, biased toward heterosexuality, which is essential for our survival. Gender complementarity and heterosexuality are the norm in animal and human biology.

But not everyone seems to understand this. I recently received a call from a producer of the *Oprah* show, requesting that I participate in a show on gay teens. "I don't believe there is such a thing as a 'gay teen,' " I told the producer, "although there are heterosexual teenagers who have homosexual feelings."

Dead silence on the other end. Then: "Well, if you think there's no such thing as a gay teen, do you know of any other psychologist who would do our show?"

Apparently the show's producer had no curiosity as to why I did not believe that "gay teens" exist as a separate category of people. My premise is that all people are, by their nature, heterosexual; some people, however, have a homosexual *problem*. More accurately, I consider the word *homosexual* to be shorthand for "a heterosexual person with a homosexual problem."

A further source of confusion is the use of the term *gay*. Whenever I give a speech, I remind the audience of the distinction between *gay* and *homosexual*. *Gay* is a sociopolitical term, and it communicates a positive identification with one's same-sex attractions. Someone who calls himself "gay" believes homosexual attractions represent "who a person is" in that person's core nature. But to call oneself "gay" is only one of many possible responses to same-sex attractions. My adult clients may indeed be homosexual, but they are not gay. They are working toward developing their natural heterosexual potential.

What *Is* a Psychiatric Disorder, Anyway?

Psychiatry has long struggled to define the term "mental disorder." To this day, it has found no comprehensive definition.[19]

In recent years, the list of psychiatric disorders has grown into an ever larger and more incoherent jumble. Not surprisingly, various advocacy groups have come forward to demand that psychiatrists label yet more conditions as disorders.[20] Radical feminists insist that male chauvinism is a mental disease; some black psychiatrists say that racism is a disorder; and some gay psychiatrists say "homophobia" should be labeled a disorder![21]

Science can offer much useful empirical data to help people resolve their problems in living. Ultimately, however, it cannot offer purely scientific answers to such essential issues as "What is the purpose of our sexuality?" and "Can homosexuality really be part of a person's core identity?" Social scientists Stuart Kirk and Herb Kutchins, for example, frankly admit that their own views on such matters are, like the American Psychiatric Association's, not purely scientific but actually value-laden opinions. Yet the average person, Kirk and Kutchins point out, misunderstands psychiatry as representing some sort of neutral "wisdom of the rational."[22]

The knowledge of "what is" can never tell us "what ought to be." This is the fundamental flaw of psychology, Dr. Jeffrey Satinover reminds us; it is meaningless without the backdrop of a framework of values.[23]

Should Homosexuality Be Considered a Developmental Disorder?

The APA's own categories for defining a mental disorder are "distress" and "disability." Among gays, we see widespread drug abuse; higher rates of depression, suicide attempts, and sexual addiction; and ravaging sexually transmitted diseases. By what logic can these negative factors—which are multiplied, not reduced, in gay-friendly cities such as San Francisco—be redefined as healthy?

It has often been said that the higher level of psychiatric problems within the gay and lesbian community should be blamed on society's oppression. Logically, there must be some truth to this assertion. However, is society's oppression the entire story? One research study was designed to measure whether distress would decrease in societies where homosexuals enjoyed a high level of tolerance.[24] The researchers compared gay-friendly societies, such as Holland and Denmark, with societies more hostile to homosexuality. The study found a higher level of distress among homosexuals in *every* culture, not just those that disapprove of homosexuality.

The Problem of Defining the Term *Disability*

Let us further consider the homosexual condition in light of the APA's yardsticks for defining a disorder. Without a foundational philosophy to guide us, however, we shall see that we uncover more questions than we do answers. In fact, the meaning of "disability" is itself endlessly negotiable.

Reparative therapists point out the widespread promiscuity characteristic of the gay world, saying this is evidence that homosexuality is inherently unhealthy. Gay theorists reply by *redefining promiscuity as normal and healthy for gay men.* Says activist Gabriel Rotello (who is considered a conservative by the gay community), "I believe that for many people, promiscuity can be meaningful, liberating and fun."[25]

Next, reparative therapists point to the characteristic unfaithfulness of "committed" gay relationships and say this is evidence of emotional disability.

In response, gay theorists *redefine the meaning of "committed."* Two gay clinicians, for example, studied 156 long-term gay relationships and found that *not one couple* was able to maintain sexual fidelity for more than five years. So the researchers *redefined monogamy itself as negative,* saying it denotes sexual "ownership" of one's partner.[26]

A Related Problem: Should GID Remain a Disorder?

We believe treatment of the gender-disturbed child is justified for several reasons. The following useful list is a paraphrase of the views expressed by clinicians Zucker and Bradley in *Gender Identity Disorder and Psychosexual Problems in Adolescents and Children:*

1. GID causes distress in the child. It is a maladaptation to a gendered world. The child typically experiences peer ostracism, unhappiness and a high level of interpersonal anxiety from the experience of interacting within a world that expects gender-appropriate behavior.

2. GID is indicative of a deeper maladaptation. Rather than something natural and intrinsic, it is likely to be symptomatic of an intrapsychic problem.

3. GID is a strong predictor of future homosexuality, transvestitism or transsexualism—conditions which many parents desire their children to avoid.

Although Zucker later modified his views to acknowledge the likelihood of an underlying neurodevelopmental problem in *some* children, he remains convinced that treatment of GID can be effective.

As we mentioned earlier, the psychiatric profession has created an internal inconsistency when it categorizes gender-identity disorder as a psychiatric illness while labeling the adult outcome (homosexuality) as normal. Not surprisingly, gay activists say, "Why should the *pre*homosexual child receive a psychiatric diagnosis and treatment when the adult homosexual is considered normal?" Another way of putting the question is this: "How can the outcome of a diagnosable *disorder* of childhood be considered a *normal* condition in adulthood?"

Clearly, the contradictory thinking here reminds us that the psychiatric profession remains unable to formulate a consistent definition of the concept of disorder. Taking advantage of that confusion, gay activists have been steadily working behind the scenes for the removal of the GID diagnosis. It would not surprise us if they eventually succeed.

Gender Confusion Is at the Heart of the Homosexual Issue

It is through our maleness or our femaleness that we grow to maturity. This is one reason, in our opinion, why we see so much immature behavior in the gay community. In gay men, we see sexual impulsivity, narcissistic self-absorption, fascination with image, and a high rate of indulgence in drugs and alcohol. In women, we see emotionally dependent, can't-live-without-you relationships and a similar high rate of difficulty with depression and substance abuse. Without a secure sense of gender, it is much more difficult to get past the roadblocks of adolescence and settle into maturity.

If anyone doubts that a distortion of gender is at the heart of the homosexual issue, a good look at the writing of gay theorists will quickly set them straight. "Put an end to the gender system!" is one of the principal rallying cries of gay activism. Psychologist Daryl Bem, as one example, defines his idea of a utopian society as one where everyone would potentially be everyone else's lover and gender would be insignificant. He envisions a "non-gender-polarizing culture that [does] not systematically estrange its children from either opposite sex, or same sex peers. Such children would not grow up to be asexual; rather, their erotic and romantic preferences would simply crystallize around a more diverse and idiosyncratic variety of attributes. Gentlemen might still prefer blondes, but some of those gentlemen (and some ladies) would prefer blondes of any sex."[27]

But rather than entering a so-called "ideal" world where gender does not matter, the gender-confused child must in fact enter the *real* world, where gender differences are a biological fact of life. If he does not understand gender, he will feel misunderstood, and he, in turn, will not understand the world. In fact, there is evidence that GID children have difficulty accurately perceiving basic male/female categories.[28]

The Effeminate Boy Suffers, Even Within the Gay World

It is impossible to overemphasize the negative social effect of effeminacy on a boy. The condition causes stress, unhappiness, isolation, and relentless peer rejection. Feminine or gender-atypical homosexual teens are also more likely than other homosexual teenagers to attempt suicide (see chapter six).

Many mental health experts think our society is supporting a system of arbitrary and meaningless sex-role stereotypes. They believe it is their job as psychotherapists to change society so it will approve of cross-gender behavior and homosexuality. But does the gay world itself believe gender to be an irrelevant construct?

Gay men typically chuckle at the straight man's "narrow" idea of masculinity. Yet despite all the rhetoric about throwing off traditional sex stereotypes, masculinity still remains the gay ideal. Many researchers, some of whom are gay men, have observed this phenomenon. One such observer notes that masculinity is "the single most desirable feature" among gay men. Effeminate men, this researcher says, "are held in much lower esteem than are masculine-looking homosexuals."[29]

The following was observed by a social scientist who studied the gay male community:

> In the gay world, masculinity is a valued commodity, an asset in the sexual marketplace.... If there is a consensus on any subject in the gay world, it is that masculinity is better than femininity. The norm in the gay world is that one should be masculine. One should "be a man" and not "a sissy." Statements such as, "Those nellie queens make me sick" are typical.
>
> This preference for the masculine involves not only the area of sexual attraction ... in the friendship groupings and homophile organizations I have studied ... status differentiation ... is highly related to masculinity-femininity, with the most masculine being nearest the top of the status hierarchy.[30]

In a major study on homosexuality that is cited approvingly as a landmark work by gay activists, researchers Bell and Weinberg said of gay men: "A chief interest which many of our respondents had in a prospective sexual partner was the degree to which he conformed to a stereotypically 'masculine' image."[31]

The Politics of Gay Counseling Programs at School

The most popular pro-gay school counseling programs—such as Project 10 or the Rainbow Project—assume that if a child has homosexual feelings, then he or she is inevitably gay.

Suppose your son discovers that he feels some same-sex attractions. In his confusion, he goes to consult with the Rainbow counselor at school. The counselor, according to the guidelines of the Rainbow program, will himself be gay. The Rainbow counselor says to your son, "I certainly understand what you're going through. I had those same feelings too, when I was your age. Those feelings mean you're gay, like I am. By the way, you don't have to tell your parents. They're straight, so they wouldn't understand. And there's a generation gap, too, so your parents probably have old-fashioned values."

Most parents do not know that, according to most state laws, this divisive gay-affirming counseling can be provided without parental consent. Because of his feelings and attractions, this young teen is now "one of them." The immediate result is that a huge family division is created—"us against them." That is, the confused child and the gay Rainbow counselor are "on this side"; the child's mother, father, society, religion, and traditional family values are "on that side."

The National Education Association has instituted a Gay and Lesbian History Month as another means of promoting homosexuality to your children as normal and healthy. Some great and honorable individuals in history no doubt have struggled with homosexuality, but they would not necessarily have identified themselves as "gay and proud" (even if the term *gay* had existed during their time). Many, no doubt, would have seen their desires as an affliction to be overcome. Yet the NEA is determined to promote these individuals as sources of inspiration for sexually confused children.

Textbooks on adolescent development confirm that a certain amount of homosexual experimentation is not uncommon and that most teens who experiment will eventually move on to heterosexuality. But the real damage takes place when young people are encouraged to put the "gay" label on that adolescent experimentation. They find out that there is a whole support network that will quickly plug them in to a whole new sociopolitical identity. A few years ago, the label "gay" did not come with a ready-made member ID card.

Joe Dallas is a therapist who has spoken out strongly against these sex-education programs. Dallas lived for several years as a gay man himself, and he saw firsthand the destructiveness of affirming a confused teenager into a lifestyle whose implications a boy cannot yet fully understand. "Confusion about sexual identity during adolescence is common under the best of circumstances," he says, "and teenagers shouldn't be exploited with premature suggestions about what their sexual identity is or isn't."[32]

Dallas cites the Minnesota Adolescent Health Survey of 1992, which studied 34,706 students and found that fully 25.9 percent of twelve-year-olds were unsure whether they were heterosexual or homosexual. This underscores the vulnerability and confusion common in the early adolescent years. Therefore, he says, "If they're encouraged during those same confusing years to experiment sexually, and if they're taught that virtually all forms of sexual expression are legitimate, then when parents are told, 'Don't worry, we don't recruit; if your kid is not gay, these programs can't make him gay,' can they really be expected to buy it?"[33]

Teens' sexual feelings are, paradoxically, the most intense when their personal identity is the most uncertain and most fragile. Premature self-labeling as "gay" can be especially damaging at this age, because adolescents are not adequately equipped to make decisions that carry profound—and potentially life-threatening—lifestyle consequences.

The Truth About Kinsey

The school program Project 10 takes its name from the claim that 10 percent of the population is gay. This figure, promoted since the early 1950s, has since been proved inaccurate. Several large recent studies place the percentage of homosexuals in the population at about 2 percent. (However, given the enthusiastic support for a homosexual lifestyle among school counselors who work with sexually confused teenagers, that 2 percent figure is almost sure to increase in the future.) Still, the old 10 percent figure has had tactical value in the defense of the normality of homosexuality. "We used that figure when most gays were entirely hidden," Tom Stoddard, onetime head of the Lambda Legal Defense Fund, candidly admits, "to try to create an impression of our numerousness."[34]

Reevaluations of Kinsey's work (most notably, by Dr. Judith Reisman in her book *Kinsey, Sex, and Fraud*) suggest that Alfred Kinsey, who is the originator of the 10 percent figure, had an investment in inflating that figure in order to promote a sexually permissive society. Since Kinsey's time, other studies on the actual percentage of homosexuals reveal a far lower number.

Evaluating eleven of the most comprehensive research studies on prevalence available through the year 2000, psychologists Stanton Jones and Mark Yarhouse conclude, "The rate of men who manifest a sustained and exclusive commitment to homosexual practice is certainly less than 3%."[35]

Are Homosexually Oriented Individuals "a People"?

The main factor driving the normalization of homosexuality has been the political theme that "gay" denotes a class of people in the same way one would describe a racial or ethnic group. Homosexuality was formerly understood as a psychological condition, period. But since gays have been established as "a people," then one can speak of "exclusion," "discrimination," and the need for employment and housing quotas.

By this same logic, should we also call feminists and ACLU members a people? What about Roman Catholics and Southern Baptists? Should mere identification with a group be grounds for official status as "a people" with special legal rights, quotas, and privileges?

When radio psychologist Dr. Laura Schlessinger said that a gene for homosexuality—if one exists—should be considered a "biological error," her detractors grabbed hold of that phrase immediately, saying, "Dr. Laura called *us* biological errors!" These activists implied that because they were in fact *a people,* Dr. Laura was actually saying they had a questionable right to exist.

Meanwhile, Back at Your Local School, Notice the Changes in Terminology

While television shows like *Oprah* have picked up the activist banner of "gay is good" politics, let's consider the political activism going on in the schools. Currently, gay activists are promoting Rainbow and Safe Schools curriculums in the name of tolerance and diversity, while health classes present homosexuality in value-neutral terms and students are taught about all forms of sexual expression as if they were normal and healthy variants. Much of this instruction is presented as necessary to stave off hatred and violence.

The blurring of *is* and *ought* is facilitated by psychology's gradual replacement of the old, morally laden terminology. Words like "perversion," "child molestation," "promiscuity," and "adultery" are either gone or are rapidly on their way out of today's social science textbooks. In their place, students hear new, sanitized terms like the following for pedophile relationships: "adult-child sex," "age-discrepant sexual relationships," and "intergenerational sex." Instead of the term "promiscuity," we hear the terms "extradyadic sex," "frequent sexual exposure," and "open relationships." As if a term like "sexual exposure" could in any way capture the meaning of an intimate relationship!

Wherever we see a shift to value-neutral terms, we know that the philosophy of " 'is' equals 'ought' " is being conveyed right along with these words. And when this idea that "is" equals "ought" filters down into the general culture, we can call that the "philosophy of Oprah." Here is a group of people who are telling their stories, and Oprah's spin is simply "Well, *here they are.*" This philosophy of "whatever is, ought to be" worked when gay activists appealed to the American

Psychiatric Association in 1973, and it still works today on daytime television.

Here is a textbook example of the "philosophy of Oprah." The National Gay and Lesbian Task Force (NGLTF) sponsored a conference for college students called "Creating Change," and it is described in their brochure as follows: "Public sex is a reality of campus life. . . . We will present a sex-positive approach to facilitate practical, non-judgmental solutions."[36] The NGLTF's reasoning says in effect, "This particular phenomenon *exists* . . . and that is all we need to know. There is no requirement to evaluate and understand it." Instead, the NGLTF simply searches for ways to "nonjudgmentally" (meaning, permissively) respond to the existence of public sex in the college community. They call this a "sex-positive" approach.

This same "sex-positive" philosophy guides many licensed counselors in their psychotherapy practices. In the clinical literature, some gay clinicians actually advocate public sex, open relationships, and group sex as good strategies to resolve sexual boredom. An advocacy piece of this sort appeared in a mainstream psychotherapy journal called the *Family Therapy Networker*. The author clarified that he makes no "pious judgments" about sexuality, instead searching for whatever "works" to keep gay men together in their relationships.[37]

And what else are our young people dealing with? The Gay Men's Health Crisis is a safe-sex foundation that publishes a pamphlet written for the benefit of gays, particularly teens and young people. When we requested permission to reprint drawings from their graphic sex-education publication in this book, not surprisingly, we were turned down. In fact, the pamphlet's drawings were so perverse that they would not actually have been suitable for reprinting. The pamphlet describes "safe" ways of dealing with grotesque, unnatural, and unhygienic sexual practices.

Because Your Values Are Different

So, as a parent who is taking steps that may succeed in establishing a normal heterosexual orientation in your child, you need to realize that a noisy, vocal minority is going to insist that your child's sexual orientation just should not matter to you. But that minority does not speak for you.

In the next chapter of this book, we'll take a look at some transcripts taken from sessions with the parents of gender-confused children, as well as a teenage boy who is troubled by emerging homosexual attractions. And we'll offer encouragement to you—a parent who has refused to give in to the idea that any choice of gender or sexual orientation is as good as another.

9

THE HEALING PROCESS

Dads, hug your sons. If you don't, someday another man will.

A. DEAN BYRD, PH.D., PSYCHOLOGIST

If there's one thing I've learned from being a father," said a client I'll call Gordon, "it's that each child is different." He settled down into the chair in my office with a look of sad resignation.

A successful financial analyst, Gordon was the father of four sons. "When Gloria and I were married, we couldn't wait to have a family," he said. "I didn't have a great relationship with my own dad, so I really wanted to have that closeness."

The couple had three boys in rapid succession, all of whom idolized their dad. Then came Jimmy.

Gloria, seated in the easy chair next to her husband, looked at me with sad, worried eyes. "By the time I was pregnant with Jimmy," she said quietly, "I wanted a girl *so badly*. Jimmy was to be our last child. When he was born, I was disappointed to tears."

Perhaps Jimmy and his mother had unconsciously worked together to remedy that disappointment, because at the age of eight, Jimmy was now his mom's closest friend. A caring and gentle boy who showed a gift for playing the piano, Jimmy was the kind of child who is naturally attuned to what other people are thinking and feeling. By this age, he could read his mother's moods like a book, but he did not have a single male friend his age. In fact, he was already showing many signs of prehomosexual behavior. Gloria had recently become concerned about the boy's increasing social isolation and depression. In contrast, their older boys were happy and well adjusted.

Jimmy's gender confusion had first become noticeable years before, when he started putting on his grandmother's earrings and trying on her makeup. Gloria's gold and silver hair barrettes had been especially captivating for the little boy, and he soon developed quite an astute sense of what he liked and did not like about women's clothing—all this before he ever started school. He was just four years old at that time.

"I treated Jimmy just like I treated all my other sons," said Gordon. "And I guess that didn't work, because he always seemed to take my criticism the wrong way. He'd go off to his room and refuse to speak to me for a couple of days."

Now, having grown older, Jimmy was presenting many other troublesome signs—immaturity, an overactive imagination that he used as a substitute for human relationships, and a contemptuous rejection of his athletic older brothers and the friends they brought home. Gordon recalled that their other sons had always rushed out to meet him when he arrived home from work, but not Jimmy, who had always acted as though his dad was unimportant.

Right now, it was Jimmy's fantasy world that caused everyone the most concern. He had a make-believe life in which he spent hours alone in his room drawing cartoon characters. And Gloria had observed another disturbing pattern—whenever Jimmy became frustrated as a result of a painful event in his life, he retreated into the world of feminine make-believe. When one of his brothers' friends was visiting the house and teased or slighted him, he would revert into an exaggerated version of feminine conduct.

Finally, Gloria and Gordon agreed to do something to help their son. And they followed through on their decision as well—so much so that after the first month of family intervention, one of the other boys, Tony, began to complain that he was feeling left out. To me, that meant the parents were working overtime to follow my directions. So at this point, I suggested that Gloria and Gordon explain to Tony that "the whole family needs to work together to help Jimmy with his problem of 'forgetting to be a boy.'" Then, despite that rough start, Tony began to cooperate in helping his brother.

Gordon could see that his youngest son had, for a long time, retreated from him. "When Jimmy was little, I went through a tough time. Our marriage was stretched to the max, and I was having a lot of trouble at work. I guess I just didn't want to be bothered reaching out to a temperamental little kid who pouted and stomped off to his room whenever I said something he took as criticism."

The other boys, in contrast, had always been eager to play with their dad and to seek out his attention. "So I just let Jimmy choose *not* to be with me," Gordon admitted. "I have to admit, my way of thinking was, *Well, if Jimmy doesn't want to be around me, then that's his problem.*"

"Our strategy, then," I explained, "is to do just the opposite of what you've been doing. That means, Gordon, that you need to actively engage Jimmy. Gloria, you'll need to learn to back off from him. And the whole family has to keep working together to remind Jimmy that being a boy is a good thing."

My strategy for Jimmy included encouraging Gordon to give his son special attention, take the boy out with him on errands, and engage him in contact-type physical play. I try to sensitize fathers to the many mundane opportunities, such as going out to gas up the car and allowing the son to hold the gas pump. All of these small efforts are part of building the male-male bonding that lays the foundation for a strong father-son relationship.

Sometimes Gordon invited Jimmy to go with him into the backyard to help him work in the garden or start the barbecue. Gordon made it his business to be home when Jimmy had his weekly piano lessons and to go to all the boy's recitals. At other times he included the boy in sports outings with his older brothers, hoping to draw Jimmy out from his habit of isolation and his resentment of his brothers.

At first, Jimmy responded with explicit rejection of his father's invitations. When invited to go along with him to the office, for example, Jimmy turned the invitation down in no uncertain terms. But as he developed a more comfortable relationship with his father, Jimmy began to act more like a boy, and at school he was beginning to find himself teased and scapegoated less often.

With my encouragement, Jimmy's parents decided to send him to a day camp that encouraged sports participation (without being competitive) and that had more boys than girls enrolled. Jimmy's mother, Gloria, made the special effort of soliciting the help of the camp supervisor, a college-age man who was willing to give Jimmy the special male attention he needed.

Boys like Jimmy must understand that their parents are supporting, encouraging, and uplifting them, not being judgmental and critical. For example, when Jimmy was eight, one day he took a stuffed panda along to school. Gloria visited the playground around lunchtime and saw her son playing all by himself with the panda, pretending to talk to it. The next day, with Gloria's prompting, Gordon spoke to his son and said, "Jimmy, boys your age don't take their stuffed animals to school. But I brought you something else you can take instead." He gave Jimmy a new hand-held computer Game Boy, which the boy took along with him the next day. To his surprise, his classmates surrounded him, begging for the chance to play with it, and of course Jimmy was included in their play because the toy was his.

As a result of his parents' consistent intervention, Jimmy displayed a gradual diminishment of gender-inappropriate behavior. This included not only his effeminacy but also his peer isolation, general immaturity, and fear and dislike of more masculine boys.

Gordon told me, "When Jimmy dismisses me and acts like I'm not important, I've got to admit it's kind of a slap at my ego, and I'm tempted to walk away. It's so much easier just to coast along and accept the status quo. But then I remember that Jimmy's attitude toward me is a defense. Underneath all that rejection and contempt, he really does want to connect with me. So I put aside my feelings and just keep pursuing him. I dropped the ball with him when Jimmy was younger, but now I'm not going to let my son just turn me away."

The Challenge to Affirm Masculinity

As we have seen, boyhood gender confusion is really a retreat from the challenges of masculinity. And many studies indicate that gender confusion is also associated with other problems, which—as in Jimmy's case—usually include a boy's rejection of his father, social isolation, and compensation in a fantasy world. Successful treatment helps the boy find his way in a world that is naturally divided into males and females. With the dedicated help of the two most important adults in his life, his mother and father, the gender-confused boy can begin to abandon his secret androgynous fantasy and discover the greater satisfaction of joining the gendered world.

As a parent, you will need to be sure that you carry out your interventions—with or without a therapist—gently and affirmatively but clearly. While discouraging unwanted cross-gender behavior, parents must be sure that the child

feels affirmed as a unique individual. This means your child need not be expected to become a stylized boy or girl, with nothing but gender-stereotypical interests. There can be a fair amount of gender role crossover. But at the same
time, healthy androgyny must first be built upon a solid foundation of security
in one's original gender.

It is essential that you always respectfully listen to your child. Do not force
him into activities he hates. Do not make him conform to a role that frightens
him. Do not shame him into covering up effeminate mannerisms. The process
of change must proceed gradually, through a series of steps that are accompanied by loving encouragement.

Shaming can, in fact, have a negative effect. "Alex," a homosexual man in
treatment with me, recalls:

> One time, when I was around five years old, I had been given a box of perfumes.
> I remember a lot of little bottles of different perfumes in some kind of box with
> different compartments to hold them. I thought they were really something, and
> I carried them around with me wherever I went.
>
> I remember taking them with me when my dad and I went to visit some rel-
> atives. I guess I was excited about them, because I remember showing them off
> to my Aunt Margaret. When I did, she looked down at me and said something
> like "What are you doing with perfumes? Are you a little sissy?" Well, I started to
> cry. She must have felt bad, because she immediately tried to comfort me.
>
> I don't know too much about this incident, but I still remember it. This per-
> fume thing didn't last long, but it was something that made me feel both good
> and bad at the same time.

It may be helpful to emphasize to your son, if he is still very young, the re-
alities of his own biological makeup—particularly, that he possesses a penis and
that it is a healthy and normal aspect of who he is. His father should be actively
involved in this educational process. Many fathers find that showering with
their sons opens the door for these conversations. Dads should stress that this
anatomical reality makes the youngster "a boy just like all other boys." More important, impressing on him that he has *male* genitals (which the very young prehomosexual boy likely will have a subconscious wish to deny) will powerfully
dispel any fantasies regarding his feminine or androgynous imaginings. The
boy's male body is the one reality, the one undisputed part of himself that proves
his masculinity and inevitably distinguishes him from Mom. It is a symbol that
he is indeed like Dad.

Showering with Dad

The experience of taking showers together has the potential to strengthen a boy's identification with his father and his father's masculinity, as well as with his own male anatomy.

Dr. George Rekers, a prominent expert on gender-disturbed children, provides detailed guidelines for father-son showering so that the experience will be positive. Dr. Rekers says, "Fathers should not react harshly or negatively if their son raises questions about sex or sexual anatomy while they are in the shower together. Any such questions should be answered positively, with natural interest, with information suitable to the son's developmental level, and with positive encouragement and affirmation to keep communication open on such important issues."[1]

The father should also be told that it is normal if his son stares at the father's sexual anatomy or if the boy spontaneously reaches up to touch him. If that happens, the father should be careful not to react as startled or upset, and not to react negatively, harshly, or in any punishing way toward his son. Instead, the father should make some reassuring statement to tell the boy that he will have a similar genital anatomy when he is a teenager.

If the son happens to touch the father's privates, typically the boy's curiosity will be satisfied, and he will probably stop touching the father's privates after a moment. The son is not likely to touch him there again very often, if at all. But in the unlikely event that the son persists in touching the father's penis, Dr. Rekers advises the father to be prepared to give his son a competing instruction, such as "Here, take this washcloth now and wash behind your ears, making sure you get real clean," without directly telling the son not to stay focused on his dad's sexual anatomy.

If the son repeatedly touches his father's privates every time they take a shower together, Dr. Rekers advises the father to say, "I don't mind if you look at my penis, because I'm your dad and seeing what my grown-up penis looks like helps you learn how your body will grow up to be like mine. But now that you've already touched it to see what its like, I need to teach you that we guys don't touch each other's penises—unless we're a doctor examining a patient or a parent giving a little boy his bath or checking if a boy needs medicine if he complains his privates hurt or itch." Furthermore, the father should explain that when any boy touches his own penis, he should do so in private.

Dr. Rekers describes one tragic event that traumatized a little boy and induced cross-gender behavior. The father stepped out of the shower, and his little boy reached up out of curiosity and fascination and touched his father's penis. The father immediately slapped the boy, shouted at him harshly, and called him a "pervert." From that time on, the little boy began exhibiting cross-gender behavior. When the boy took a bath himself, he tucked his penis between his legs to look like a girl, and he told his mother that he wished he did not have a penis. Nevertheless, if the father-son experience is handled tactfully, Dr. Rekers says, "the boy is better prepared for taking public showers together with other males in the future in the men's locker room at school or away at a college dorm."

Besides suggesting that fathers shower with their small sons, I also ask fathers to have regular, aggressive physical contact with the boys. Fathers can also help by encouraging assertive behavior and physical expressions of aggression. This helps counter the timid, "good little boy" role that the gender-disturbed boy often exhibits. Wrestling, roughhousing, "beating up Dad" are ways a boy can discover his physical power, feel his bodily strength, and make contact with this frightening and mysterious male figure.

The Importance of Touch

Without exception, my adult homosexual clients describe a painful absence— typically an aching void—of physical contact with their fathers. Richard Wyler tells us how this isolation from touch can lead to a lasting sense of deprivation:

> The cultural message is clear: Real men don't touch. Unfortunately, this taboo often carries over to fathers and sons, even when boys are still very young, and to brothers and close friends. Men in our culture seem afraid of being perceived as homosexual, or even of "making" themselves or someone else homosexual by hugging, holding or touching them.
>
> But the very thing they fear is the thing they are creating: a society of touch-deprived boys who grow up longing to be held by a man. If the need to be touched and held isn't met in childhood, it doesn't just go away because a boy grows into a man. For us, the desire was so primal, and so long denied, that some of us sought sex with a man at times when all we really wanted was to be held. We just didn't know how else to receive the non-sexual touch we craved.

Without this normal touch, a young man is much more vulnerable to settling for relationships that prove to be inappropriate or even abusive. Wyler, again, says:

It is not surprising that many of us were drawn into dysfunctional or unhealthy relationships, even from early childhood. If we found something that felt like love and affirmation, we often clung to it, no matter the consequences.

This sometimes even included other males who used us for sexual pleasure, or whom we used sexually to feel close to and loved by. (<www.peoplecanchange.com>)

Remember the story of Olympic diver Greg Louganis, whom we described in chapter three? He was a lonely boy who was misunderstood and teased by his schoolmates and alienated from his father. Not surprisingly, Louganis was emotionally vulnerable to the attentions of the older man he met on a beach. He "kept going back for the affection, the holding, the cuddling—more than the sex. I was starved for affection."

One important task of parents is to encourage the boy's expression of what he is really thinking and feeling. Since we know that he is probably fearful of growing up and of meeting the challenge of a male role, the boy should be encouraged to verbalize these anxieties and to communicate his ideas about gender, which will inevitably be distorted. "Sean," for example, was an effeminate seven-year-old, and his father made a decision that "we won't talk about Sean's problem; we will just affirm and love him." That approach is a start, but it is not good enough. Parents need to find opportunities to clarify male/female distinctions. Asking questions like "What do you want to be when you grow up?" and "Who do you want to grow up to be like?" will open up a window of opportunity to correct fantasy distortions as well as to offer encouragement.

It will also be necessary for you, as parents, to gradually replace toys, games, and articles of clothing that support your son's cross-gender fantasy. Some mothers tell me they have secretly dumped certain objects. While understanding their frustration and need to act in a hurry, I suggest a more open approach. You can encourage the boy to participate in the transfer of these items by having him decide which ones to give to which little girls he knows. Some parents have even made a ritual out of disposing of the feminine toys in a ceremonious packing and removing of girl's stuff to be given away to a needy neighborhood girl or a female cousin.

A "bye-bye ceremony" might be helpful in the case of a toddler. Get a box, put the dolls inside, seal it up, and say "Bye-bye," all the while acknowledging how hard it must be for the boy to give these toys away. Explain, "Now Daddy is going to take them to a little girl in the neighborhood who doesn't have any Barbies to play with."

It is important for your child to feel and express his sadness and loss. More difficult, perhaps, is your sympathetic "hearing" of his pain while going through with the disposing of the items. The "bye-bye ceremony" can be difficult, but it should not be traumatic. And your decision to do this should not be impulsive but rather well thought out. Is the boy ready to let them go? Perhaps all he needs is a nudge? Or will the ceremony leave him feeling betrayed and angry? If it will, then it is too soon for such dramatic action.

How aggressive these corrective interventions should be depends on your child's response. If he becomes withdrawn, depressed, angry, frustrated, or nervous, then you will know that you are moving too quickly. One enthusiastic couple hoped to "fix" their boy all in one week. The result was an anxious, alarmed child. The dramatic, negative change in the boy's mood indicated that he was not given time to adjust to his parents' changed expectations.

Some parents take the opposite approach: they are hesitant to make the most obvious, commonsense changes. Much of this hesitancy is due to the mixed message from our culture and, as we discussed, the conflicting advice given by child development professionals. These parents look for explicit permission from a professional to say to the boy gently but clearly, "Bobby, no more sissy stuff. You're too old now for this girlish behavior." They say they fear discussing the problem with their son lest they hurt his feelings.

Nevertheless, the most effective intervention is for the parental team to convey together, through a gentle but unified and consistent message, "This is not who you are—you're a boy." This style of treatment is gentle, caring, loving, and should not happen all at once, yet it is explicit and unambiguous. Most important, it should involve parental unity and consistency, because that is the type of approach that is most effective in the long term.

One mother summed it up well: "Helping my son overcome effeminate behavior is like growing roses. It doesn't require a lot of work, but it takes a lot of consistent mindfulness."

The first step in healing begins when parents acknowledge that there is a problem and then decide to work together to correct their child's difficulty. The second step is conveying to the child that they, as parents, are committed to helping him, and that change is necessary. Once the child realizes that both parents, as a team, will no longer ignore his inappropriate cross-gender behavior, he will begin to adjust. This clear (and often unexpected) message will, however, predictably create some discomfort.

Stages in the Growth Process

Based on my clinical work with gender-disturbed boys and their parents, I believe there are four stages in the growth process: (1) resistance, (2) apparent conformity, (3) secretive resistance, and (4) the parent-child working alliance. If your son is engaged in obvious cross-gender behavior, these stages should serve as a general framework for you to construct a pathway for your child's progress. Of course, as with all constructs used to explain a complex phenomenon, these stages bleed into each other somewhat; a child may slip back one stage before he moves forward to the next. These steps can, however, serve as general guidelines.

Stage 1: Resistance. Confronted with the new limitations that have been placed upon him, your child may express anger, hurt, and rebellion. He is coming to realize that Mom and Dad will no longer allow him to engage in the feminine fantasy behaviors that once gave him pleasure and comfort. Once he gets the idea that he will not be able to gratify his make-believe self-image, he may withhold his affection and emotionally pull back from you. Gender-nonconforming boys are especially sensitive to criticism and being challenged. Be careful not to be overly critical or to impose severe corrections.

You can show your son special appreciation, saying things like "You know, you're really lucky to be a boy." Highlight—even exaggerate—boy-girl differences. Reinforce the boy's emerging masculine identity by asking such questions as "What kind of a girl are you going to marry when you grow up?" "What kind of a daddy are you going to be when you grow up?" As parents, you will need to be creative in finding and using opportunities to emphasize gender differences.

Stage 2: Apparent conformity. With enough gentle consistency, most parents soon notice—at least on the surface—their son's cooperation with their new expectations. Often the change is so dramatic that the parents may wonder, "Is he really changing, or is he just trying to please us?" Because he is motivated to make you happy, your child may simply act out the transformation in compliance with your wishes. In fact, these earliest changes often represent mere behavioral conformity without authentic internal transformation.

But over time, if he has sufficient emotional attachment to you, your son will incorporate these behaviors into his sense of self. Because you, as his parents, are the most important people in his world, he should reluctantly but steadily shed his cross-gender fantasy.

Stage 3: Secretive resistance. You may be delighted by your son's quick response to your newly applied interventions. However, there will probably be a regression of some secret effeminate behavior, which will quickly disillusion you and make you think your efforts will be futile. To help avoid frustration and discouragement, I advise parents to expect setbacks. In other words, do not be surprised at them.

This is the pattern of ambivalence: Your five-year-old son seems to be cooperating. Then, one day, he is carrying that doll around again and perhaps has even gone back to sucking his thumb. You say, "Honey, didn't we talk about that?"

He says, "Huh?"

"Son," you reply gently but firmly, "you know what we talked about—about you being a boy and about big boys not playing with dolls. Now, go put the doll away, and then let's find another toy of yours."

You should expect the boy to go two steps forward, one step backward. At such times, parents need to be reassured that nothing in the universe moves in a straight line, including their son's progress.

You will probably notice that your son is most likely to revert to girlish behavior during times of pressure upon his self-esteem. As one father observed, "When my son feels bad, he goes into his effeminate behavior." When he is feeling happy and buoyant and affirmed by others, he is likely to avoid the feminine regression. Realistically, we can anticipate some regressive behavior when the boy is fatigued, sick, stressed, or has experienced a particular discouragement or rejection. The effeminacy is a self-soothing response to stress.

After such a regression, parents express concern that their son may be "just pleasing us" or "making us happy because he knows it is important to us." They want to know if their son is really changing on the inside. Indeed, growth into one's gender involves much more than *acting* differently—it requires an internal shift of perception.

The family should take a hard look at the boy's male role models. If the father remains a negative model—particularly, if he is involved in an ongoing neglectful or abusive relationship with the boy's mother—the child may harbor the unconscious perception that it is unsafe to identify with maleness. In such a case, the boy needs his feminine armor as a defense, and any behavioral changes made will likely not be internalized.

Indeed, we should empathically appreciate the difficulty of the little boy's struggle. There is an internal conflict going on. As one boy explained, "There are two parts of me inside that are fighting each other."

Stage 4: A working alliance. Nothing is more gratifying for parents than to begin to see their son's willing cooperation with the growth process. While her son was watching a television program featuring an alluring female cartoon character, one mother of a very young gender-disturbed boy—"Aaron"—had a rare opportunity to observe his internal conflict:

> I could see that Aaron really wanted to get lost in the female character. Before, he would have danced around the room like a ballerina, as he watched.
>
> Next to him were some boy figures from a toy farm set, along with a couple of cars. I could also see that he was trying to move his eyes away from the TV and pick up one of the boy figures. He was trying to avoid the temptation of fantasizing about being this female character. My heart broke for him because I knew exactly what he was feeling.

In the working alliance phase, not only will you observe your son's newly cooperative attitude, but also he will begin to verbalize his inner struggle. One couple reported that their little boy confided to them, "It's hard growing up." Remember that for these children, growing up creates conflict because it means meeting the challenge of being a boy. And *not* growing up remains attractive because it provides the comfort of staying in a feminine or androgynous role, and often staying in an overintimate mother-son relationship because it provides a place of hiding from the challenges of the male world.

Another boy said, with apparent frustration, "I'm trying to forget about them," referring to the collection of Barbie dolls that he had given away. His mother told me, "He seems willing to change now, even though I can see that it stresses him."

The Role of the Psychotherapist

Since parents naturally become emotionally enmeshed with their child, often they find it difficult to stay with a program of effective change on their own. Whenever possible, I strongly encourage them to find the right psychotherapist to help them.

A professional psychotherapist who shares your values and objectives will assist you, first of all, by providing further education, and second, by correcting blind spots you may have as individuals and as a parental team. The psychotherapist may observe, for example, that you are not communicating effectively with the child. He may see that your son never verbalizes his stresses and conflicts and only *seems* to be complying with what you ask him to do. He may point out how mother and father convey different (perhaps even contradicting and confusing) messages about gender.

To correct childhood gender confusion, a strong parental team is highly important. Your best assurance of change comes when there is commitment by both parents. The fact is, with the commitment of only one parent, a positive outcome is much less likely. Remember, there is no such thing as a neutral member of the parental team. The uninvolved parent is perceived by the child as implicitly giving permission to remain effeminate and as negating the message of the committed parent.

Traditional psychoanalytic treatment for prehomosexuality focused on the child being seen alone by the psychotherapist. The parents were excluded from the sessions, with the child being seen from two to five times a week for many years. This treatment was very expensive and its success rate was disappointing. Instead, what appears to be most effective is for the therapist to work on a regular basis with the parents and not the child. After a few weekly sessions, the therapist should usually see the parents only on an as-needed (perhaps monthly) basis to coach them and monitor the boy's progress. Usually it is necessary for the psychotherapist to see the child only for an initial assessment and then from time to time afterward.

I have often found that my professional support and advice only confirm what parents already intuitively knew. In their hearts, they feel strongly that something is not right with the child, but they need permission to intervene. Most mothers are well aware that the boy's father should have been more involved and that his distance increases their son's difficulties.

But—as we discussed in the last chapter—parents often become confused by contradictory messages from the media and many child development professionals. These parents need an informed therapist who will support *their* goals, not the therapist's idea that gender is irrelevant. The therapist should prepare the child for life in a gendered world, while helping to reduce the possibility of his later homosexuality.

Unconditional Love

One of the most important responsibilities of the therapist is to help parents express disapproval of the effeminate *behavior* without conveying disapproval of the *child*. The therapist helps the parents learn to convey explicit expectations to the boy that his effeminate behavior is unacceptable and to gently but firmly discourage such behaviors. But at the same time, the boy must not experience his parents' expectations as a deeply personal criticism or a rejection.

As you work through these issues with your son (or daughter), someone is bound to tell you that a healthy person is not limited to a narrow version of gender identity. This person will say that our personalities should include aspects that are both masculine and feminine.

This popular view derives, to some extent, from the work of psychoanalyst Carl Jung, who lived during Freud's time. Jung believed that mature adult development requires the integration of opposite-sex characteristics. There is, of course, some truth to the notion that we grow by integrating opposite-sex emotional characteristics, but this can be achieved only *after* the individual has securely identified with his biological sex. Such integration should never compromise the fulfillment of one's appropriate gender identity.

A popular misinterpretation of this principle is seen when parents promote gender bending in their children. Some "liberated" mothers say they are perfectly delighted to see their boys wear dresses or nurse baby dolls, and they have no problem with their daughters adamantly refusing ever to wear a dress. But this is a serious mistake. It is foolish to encourage your son to integrate feminine qualities before he has assumed his masculine identity. And it is certainly not wise to support your daughter's rejection of all things feminine.

Measuring Success

Successful treatment of gender confusion should diminish cross-gender behavior and identity, improve peer relationships, and ultimately lower the level of stress in the child's life. The goal of treatment is to diminish the boy's sense that he is different from, and somehow inferior to, other boys. This will maximize the possibility that your child will develop a normal heterosexual orientation.

To check your progress, take note of the following markers of success in the treatment of gender-disturbed boys:

1. *Decreased effeminacy.* Parents observe a diminishing of the behaviors that first caused concern. We should see less indulgence in girlish activities and mannerisms.

2. *Increased self-esteem.* Parents begin to see their son conveying an overall

positive feeling about himself. They find that their son seems proud of having accomplished a difficult personal challenge. Parents notice that their child has a more secure sense of who he is.

3. *Increased maturity.* Parents describe a happier, more self-assured child who has a naturalness about him. One mother, as if searching for a word, explained, "He seems more . . . real." The boy has become less shy, self-conscious, and self-preoccupied. He will evidence more emotional connectedness and appropriate responsiveness toward others.

4. *Diminished anxiety or depression.* Researchers have found a connection between boyhood effeminacy and a higher than normal level of anxiety or depression.[2] As their son resolves his gender-identity conflict, parents remark that he seems less nervous and uneasy and generally seems to worry less about little things. The experience of fitting in with other boys decreases the associated symptoms of anxiety and depression.

5. *Popularity with other boys.* It has been generally observed that boys who displayed characteristic "real boy" behaviors are more popular, and those who show less masculine behaviors are less popular. (This scenario is not as true for girls.) Masculine boys are more likely to have good male friendships than are feminine boys. Boys who suffer with gender-identity issues are often the victims of extreme cruelty by their same-sex peers. Feminine boys, my clinical experience suggests, are also more likely to be molested by sexual predators, who seem to be aware that the peer-rejected boy is attention-deprived and will therefore make an easy target.

6. *Diminished behavioral problems.* While most prehomosexual boys are compliant "good little boys," a smaller percentage are openly disruptive. Either way, when appropriate gender behavior is incorporated, the child's parents, teachers, and other supervising adults observe more socially cooperative behavior. They notice fewer temper tantrums and emotional outbursts and less withdrawn behavior.

7. *Better relationship with Dad.* Parents report that the son spontaneously seeks out his father, wants to be with him, and enjoys his company.

8. *"Happy to be a boy."* Parents perceive that their son seems proud to be a boy, to be doing things that other boys do and doing them well. This will ultimately give him a sense of satisfaction in being one of the guys.

Dr. George Rekers, prominent researcher on childhood gender-identity disorders, describes the results of treatment of over fifty GID children suggesting that permanent changes in gender identity were achieved. Rekers is convinced that a preventive treatment for "transvestism, transsexualism, and some forms of homosexuality has indeed been isolated."[3]

Drs. Zucker and Bradley also believe that treatment for gender-identity conflict can be successful:

> It has been our experience that a sizable number of children and their families achieve a great deal of change. In these cases, the gender identity disorder resolves fully, and nothing in the children's behavior or fantasy suggest that gender-identity issues remain problematic. . . .
>
> All things considered, we take the position that in such cases a clinician should be optimistic, not nihilistic, about the possibility of helping the children to become more secure in their gender identity.[4]

Other researchers who report success working with effeminate boys say effective treatment helps these boys understand the motives for their cross-gender behavior and reinforces signs of their developing masculinity. Their approach, like ours, calls for a therapist who is of the same sex as the child and who will solicit the help of the child's father. They also bring the child's family into the therapy and draw upon peer-group reinforcement.

Coming Along in the Change Process

We want to share the results of treating gender-confused children by revealing the transcripts of several real-life case studies. These cases were not picked out as success stories—actually, they are rather typical examples of families that have experienced some tangible success, along with some disappointments. All case examples here are of boys, whose gender confusion is much more likely to draw the attention of parents.

Our hope is that as you read, you will have a point of comparison by which to track your own son's condition and progress. All these boys were originally brought to my office because of gender confusion. Their parents returned for follow-up assessments several years after completion of their sons' treatment.

Remember that the goal of treatment is to diminish the boy's sense that he is different from, and somehow inferior to, other boys. This will maximize the possibility that the child will develop a normal heterosexual orientation, although it will likely be one or two decades after treatment before a child's sexual orientation can be known.

The Continuing Need for Self-Assertion: "Tommy"

Here is a transcript of an interview with a mother of a gender-confused son several years after the end of treatment. This boy had improved markedly in regard to effeminacy, and he is doing much better. Some relational and self-esteem difficulties continue to interfere with his progress, though, because Tommy still allows himself to fall into a passive role in both male and female relationships.

Dr. N.: It's been four years since you last came to my office. How is your son doing now?

Mother: Overall, Tommy is doing much better. He's less moody and you wouldn't call him effeminate.

Dr. N.: Now, what about your son's popularity with other boys?

Mother: Unfortunately, that hasn't really changed.

Dr. N.: That hasn't increased?

Mother: No. The problem is that he has given up on some children that he has tried to make friends with when they haven't responded back to him. He has just stopped calling them and talking to them at school. He tends to do that—just give up whenever things discourage him.

Dr. N.: Does he have any close friends?

Mother: Well, there's Marianne, the girl down the street. They're still good friends. Thank goodness, they are not that attached like they were before, where they had to be seeing each other all the time.

Dr. N.: Right. I remember that when he was acting very girlish, Tommy used to spend a lot of time with her.

Mother: Yes. He used to let Marianne just "mother" him and also kind of boss him around. And he used to take that behavior from her and, despite the way she treated him, kind of "be there" for her whenever she wanted him. Back then I didn't realize that a relationship like that was not good for him.

Dr. N.: What about his male relationships?

Mother: He has a best friend, but I really don't see the closeness that I'd like to see, although this boy also considers my son to be *his* best friend. But when they're together, Tommy doesn't really talk that much. I can see that he's very quiet. The other boy is kind of the leader and is always saying, "I'm the greatest, I'm the best."

Clearly, although the effeminacy is now gone, Tommy still needs help with his tendency to fall into relationships where he is disempowered. I suggested his mother get him into a club or volunteer work where he could be in a leadership position helping younger boys, in order for him to grow in confidence and self-assertion. He could also benefit from therapy with a male counselor.

Dad Is Accepted as a Loving Adviser: "Tim"

Tim's father has learned that his gender-fragile son requires special attention, and since Dad has provided that attention, the boy has made steady progress.

Father: For the past year now, I've become an observer; I try to pay real close attention to how Tim acts with his peers, both male and female, and in all social aspects. His school just had a fifth-grade play, and I helped build the set. I made sure that I brought Tim in beside me, doing a lot of the construction work and getting him involved with some of the other guys as well as some of their sons. It was a treat for us both. I've tried to do this in the past, but Tim wasn't interested; I think it was a confidence thing with him—confidence that he couldn't hold up his end.

Mother: I just want to say something, Jack. I think it was more than that for our son. I think Tim was actively rejecting you and what you were all about.

Dr. N.: But that's a defense against his feeling inferior. His attitude of superiority, basically, was a cover for his sense of inferiority.

Father: I think you're actually right. He was thinking, *If I accept my dad for what he is, then I have to accept the fact that I might not be able to live up to what he is. But now I can strive to be more like him; I really can accomplish this.* I see this now more and more in every aspect in dealing with our son. Now I talk to him about things that, if I had talked to him about them a year ago, he would have been very defensive and would have literally just shut right down.

Dr. N.: This is an attitude that holds over into adult life. Many gay men—as we see when reading gay literature—say that homosexuality places them above the average guy. They are the artists; they are the sensitive people; and the average guy is just a worker. But paradoxically, at the same time, they're sexually attracted to the same type of guy they have contempt for. It's a defensive attitude that goes back to just these types of painful childhood experiences that your son has been struggling with among his peers. So you've tried to make it clear that he *is* one of the guys, he *does* measure up.

Father: Right. It's that sense of inferiority, of not measuring up in the male world, that we want to protect him from. But before, Tim didn't want to open up to me. I think he felt that if he opened up and spilled the beans to me from his perspective, either he would get this feeling we were rejecting him—like *Here they go again; they're not really interested in me* or else he'd think, *They aren't really comprehending what I'm trying to tell them.*

And I have learned that when Tim does open up and he wants to talk, I had darned better pay attention to what he's saying. That's no time to read a magazine, and if there's some special thing on TV I want to watch, too bad. Better detach from what you're doing and listen, I've learned. Because, if you don't, he picks up on it immediately, and once he shuts down, he shuts down.

Now he'll actually come to me and he says, "Is it okay if I do this?" In other words, he is actually asking me how to act like one of the guys. I take the time to explain to him why, if he's doing that with his buddies, he probably shouldn't go down that path if he wants to be more accepted by his peers in school. Stay away from that kind of girl stuff altogether. And when I talk to him in that way, I can feel the connection. I can feel him looking me in the eye and going, "Okay, Dad. This is good; I'll try it."

Before, I never really point-blank sat down with him and told him why he had so many problems with the guys at school. Now I approach him in a loving way as an instructor and a father and say, "If you want to go through life without all the bumps and the pain, there are certain things that are appropriate and certain things that are not appropriate. Certain behavior is going to cause you nothing but heartache."

I don't see the flippant hand motions anymore or the giddiness. I see more and more of a mature young man than I ever expected in this time frame. It's like taking a book and turning each page and just going, "Wow!" It keeps getting better for him.

Of course, real change for Tim is not just a matter of changing effeminate mannerisms, but when he projects a different image to the world, his male peers act differently toward him, and gradually Tim actually begins to feel different about himself as well.

A Father's Effort to Heal the Relationship: "Evan"

This father has a son (Evan) who was involved in a sexual encounter with a camp counselor three years ago, when the boy was thirteen.

Dr. N.: When Evan was a child, did he seem different from your other sons?

Father: Oh, sure. Early on, I saw the kinds of toys Evan chose. And he was a very expressive child, very social and emotional. We saw him as our creative and sensitive son. Then as he got a little older, we began to notice the gravitation toward things that our culture doesn't consider to be masculine.

Dr. N.: Did that concern you?

Father: Not really, because we have many creative people in our family and we just figured that would be who he was. I never had it in my head that my son had to be macho or even especially athletic. Much later, though, when we saw the interest in gay things he was developing as he approached puberty, I found out that you have to deal with this kind of son differently.

Dr. N.: What would you have done differently?

Father: I would have been less critical and picky about the little things. Trying to force him into doing things a certain way—it didn't work with my son, even as far back as when he was still in preschool. Evan got really stressed out from criticism. My other sons didn't, but he did deal with mental stress in that way. And it caused a rift between us that stood in the way of our relationship for many years.

The shame of it is that it took me so many years to realize that my son did not do well with this "Just get hold of yourself, kid, and tough it up" kind of attitude from me. Evan, probably more than most boys, needed to see that his dad was a man with a heart who had the ability to cry, was willing to listen, and would say, "Let's talk about how you feel about this," instead of, "Son, you'd better get talking—now!"

Dr. N.: What do you hope for in your son's life?

Father: Most of all, I hope that my son finds peace, and I hope he learns to be happy about who he is. Whatever turmoil and discomfort he's feeling today, I hope that he can be healthy in a way that he himself sees as healthy. And because our family is Christian, I also hope that he can find God's will in his life.

Dr. N.: But what if he comes to you someday and says, "Mom and Dad, I've tried. I can't change; I'm gay." What would you do?

Father: Oh . . . Well, that would be very painful for me to hear, but of course, without any question, I would still love him.

Dr. N.: Would you still keep up the relationship?

Father: Absolutely. How could I ever stop? He's our son.

Dr. N.: Exactly. They are always our children . . .

Father: There have been many times recently that we've cried together and Evan's poured his heart out to me about what's going on in his life. Listening to him, I found out that there were many things I had been doing that I meant in a loving way, but back then, he didn't see that. Evan was interpreting them critically.

Dr. N.: What convinced you that something was wrong?

Father: When he came into his teenage years, I could see that Evan was in pain. He saw himself as flawed, not lovable. He was not comfortable with who he was. Then there was the sexual incident with the camp counselor that was the real wake-up call. Getting closer to my son, I could see that it was very hard to convince him that I really loved him and was interested in his life. He just didn't seem to be able to believe it.

Dr. N.: So he couldn't accept what you were saying?

Father: No, and we've cried together over this quite a few times.

Dr. N.: That must have been very hard.

Father: It's so painful to hear what your son has struggled with. You just wish you could take away all the pain, the bad memories, the mistakes being revealed to you now—just erase them.

Dr. N.: There are so many things that *all* of us parents wish we could just undo, aren't there?

Father: But now, Evan and I can talk through all these things together, especially when he's down and he's feeling pain. Now, most of the time, I don't give advice anymore or try to fix the problem. I just listen, and I try to let him hit me with all his feelings, his anger, and just receive that anger but not defend against it.

Dr. N.: What advice would you give to other fathers of teenagers?

Father: Well, we were fortunate enough to have a son who didn't want to be gay. That made a very big difference. But it's been a few years now since that sexual incident, and we realize there's no quick fix.

Dr. N.: Nothing changes overnight.

Father: Right, and you're going to have days when you say, "Nothing is working;

he's not changing," and other days when you're sure the problem is completely gone. On those days, you say to yourself, *This is going to work, thank God! I'm going to have a heterosexual kid.* So I'd say to parents, "Know that this is going to be a long haul, and it may possibly get more painful before it gets better."

But looking back, I can see that this is not just about fixing mannerisms. It's not just about, "I wish Evan wouldn't walk this way," or "I wish he wouldn't wave his hand that way."

Dr. N.: Of course. It's about much more than just the way your child presents himself to the world.

Father: At its heart, it's about helping Evan to be happy and, ultimately, to feel comfortable and at peace with himself. He recognizes the choices that have been set before him, and he doesn't want to be gay. My relationship with him is far better now. I believe we can now be very confident that we've done all we can to lay the right foundation.

An Uninvolved Dad: "Simon"

Simon, five years after his parents started intervention, had also given up his effeminacy. His mother reports that he's doing well in school and has matured. He is no longer as moody, and his gender problems appear to be resolved. However, Simon's dad has dropped the ball, and—like Tommy—this boy has a remaining struggle with self-confidence.

Dr. N.: Mrs. Martin, how old is your son now?

Mother: Simon's now twelve.

Dr. N.: Do you think there is a decrease in his effeminacy?

Mother: Absolutely. I don't see femininity. I don't see that at all. When he was younger, I saw the dressing and attempts at femininity, the dancing. I'm trying to remember back, it's been so long.

Dr. N.: Right. What about his self-assertion?

Mother: He's not exactly aggressive, because that's not his nature, but he's had coaches that are very positive, and they build him up, make him more confident. I've tried to pick the coaches for him, and I've requested their particular teams.

Dr. N.: Do you think there is a decrease in Simon's anxiety and depression?

Mother: Absolutely. I don't see that anymore.

Dr. N.: What did you see before?

Mother: I remember I definitely saw anxiety years ago. I especially saw it when he would go to a class with both boys and girls. That's when I first noticed that he had a problem, when he had to go face other children. He would cry. He was not confident. He wanted to stay home with me.

Dr. N.: Does he feel better about himself than he used to?

Mother: I do know that my son has confidence in certain areas. For example, when it comes to schoolwork, he is certainly far and above the other kids. He just got his report card and he has an A average. School is easy for him. And I don't see real babyishness anymore, although once in a while I still hear a bit of that babyish voice and I have to remind him. And as far as maturity level, I see him as very responsible and considerate of me, and he's always on time whenever we go somewhere.

Dr. N.: I don't recall any behavioral problems with Simon in the past. Anything come up since then?

Mother: No, he's always been good. I consider him to be highly intelligent, because he has always had that calm way about him, and the intelligence is there too. Where other kids might get into a little mischief, Simon's thing is to absorb knowledge.

Dr. N.: What about those male friends?

Mother: He has a lot of boys now calling up and asking his opinion on homework, so I know that he is mingling and I know he is liked. But I personally think that, because his posture is not good, I would see that as an indication that he doesn't have a high self-esteem. But even though he's liked, I still consider him to be a loner, even though he has lunch with the boys and he plays all the sports. He's not a super athlete, but he's doing okay. His coach says he has it mentally together, so everything will fall into place for him.

Dr. N.: How is Simon's relationship with his father?

Mother: Not so good. My husband hasn't learned anything. He'll yell at Simon, and I can see that Simon's feelings get hurt. Afterward, my son retreats to his room and doesn't see his father for days. Now, my husband should pick up on that and see it as a problem, but he doesn't. He doesn't have the smarts or the compassion or whatever it is.

Dr. N.: Does he observe? Does he know there's a problem?

Mother: No, I don't think he does.

Dr. N.: So he doesn't even notice. So let me get this straight: sometimes his father will scold him, and Simon's reaction is to withdraw and sometimes he'll avoid his father for days. And his father will either not notice or, for whatever reason, he doesn't want to reach out and connect with the boy?

Mother: Yes. And I see that as a lack of compassion. As a mother, my first instinct would be to protect my children. And that's why we've had trouble in the marriage. And now it has gotten to a point where I just don't bother reminding my husband anymore. It hurts me to see my son that way, and I just don't want to deal with him about Simon anymore. We've fought about this, and it's hurt our marriage.

Dr. N.: So, if you didn't prompt him—

Mother: We would all stay home for the rest of our lives and do nothing. The only thing my husband would do with them is watch TV—and watch what *he* wants. My husband is really very childish.

Simon's mother has worked hard with her son, but the boy still needs an encouraging role model, hopefully a male relative, to take the place of the boy's abdicating father.

Dad's Loving Attention Gets Results: "Brian"

Brian's parents notice that he blossoms when his dad remembers to seek him out. The key is consistency.

Dr. N.: Mrs. Jones, how old is Brian now? It's been four years since you were in here.

Mother: He's now ten.

Dr. N.: How would you evaluate his decrease in effeminacy? Has that changed at all?

Mother: Yes, a lot. He still has some feminine gestures. Of my four sons, he is the most feminine; however, he is not making what we call "girl choices" anymore. We call it "being healthy" or "acting like a boy." I think he still struggles with that a little bit, sometimes his gestures, his body language. We still have to occasionally remind him. But I notice that his choices are much more appropriate, and this has been true for a couple of years.

Dr. N.: Do you think he is changing because he knows he'll get disapproval if he doesn't or because he's truly losing interest in acting this way?

Mother: I haven't seen anything inappropriate. The choices he makes now even when we're not around are the right ones, the appropriate ones. I do check, and have for a couple of years.

Dr. N.: So you think there is a significant diminishing of his girlish choices.

Mother: Yes, a lot.

Dr. N.: How would you rate his self-esteem? I remember that he had an issue with low self-esteem.

Mother: I think that is going to be a battle that will last his whole life. I do see it gradually getting a little better, but it's a real hard battle for him. Sometimes he'll come to me and say, "I think I'm getting popular" or "I think I may be making more friends." I hear this a lot. He's kind of giving himself positive affirmation, whereas my other three boys have never questioned their popularity.

Dr. N.: What about his anxiety and depression? That used to be a big problem for Brian, especially his depression.

Mother: That has almost gone.

Dr. N.: Really?

Mother: Actually, I would say that during the last year I've hardly noticed that at all. He still is moody. But I've recognized that he is just my moody child. He's introspective and looks inside of himself and likes to discuss his feelings with me, not his dad. But no, he's not depressed. I don't see that. I would say he's a happy boy.

Dr. N.: That's great. Let's talk about Brian's male friendships. How is that going?

Mother: He still worries about friends and relationships. Since we've seen you, to help Brian, I started to be a Cub Scout leader so I could at least have a group of ten boys at my house once a week.

Dr. N.: Did you really?

Mother: Yes, and I'm still doing it, so we have boys in our house all the time.

Dr. N.: Does he connect with them?

Mother: He didn't connect with them when I started Cub Scouts, but now he does. I started the group when he turned eight, and I could tell he was a little awkward—not comfortable. Now he's actually out of my Cub Scout group, but he's my helper with the ten other boys that come here, and he is very comfortable.

But I still see him as having a bit of a negative self-image regarding being popular. He's really been trying hard, I would say, in the last couple of years, to make friends in school that he can keep. And he'll come home so thrilled and he'll say, "I have a new best friend." The other boys always seem to be calling him, and the teacher says he's quite popular in school. But that doesn't yet seem to have quite sunk in.

Last school year, we put him in soccer and he hated it. So we let him stop that. But he did just recently ask us if he could play tennis and join the tennis team. We told him, "Sure." That's the first time he's asked to play a sport. But it's not that he's unathletic. He's not sissyish in the way he handles his body.

Dr. N.: Well, then, I'd say he's making some progress. What about those terrible temper tantrums and dramatic outbursts Brian used to have?

Mother: Those hysterics? All gone.

Dr. N.: All gone . . .

Mother: That was an awful, awful stage of my life for about four years. I look back on my notes written during that time and I can't believe how far we've come. Our house was in turmoil. And now that's all gone.

Dr. N.: I think it's a very good thing for parents to keep a journal, so they can have a perspective on the change. Because we live so much in the day to day, we lose sight of the big picture. Keeping a journal gives parents a sense of progress for their efforts.

Mother: That's true. Honestly, when I think of my life with Brian from the time he was two to at least six, it was a real nightmare. I never dreamed that he would be as normal as he is. Never. I honestly didn't think he'd be ever be able to cope with society or anything.

Dr. N.: Has his father continued his involvement?

Mother: He has, as long as I keep poking him when he forgets. Bill forgets that he should stay involved, but when I remind him, he doesn't get angry, because he knows it's important.

Dr. N.: Does he make gentle corrections with Brian?

Mother: Not as often as I think he should, and Bill and I have had battles about this.

Dr. N.: Does Bill not notice the same effeminacies that you do? Or does he notice but just doesn't make the connection between the amount of his involvement with Brian and Brian's effeminacy?

Mother: It has to be right in front of Bill's face and pretty obvious before he'll notice.

Dr. N.: Does Brian reach out to his father?

Mother: Yes. But I notice that he's much more friendly to his dad after they have spent time together. In other words, if Bill and Brian spend time together, then Brian will reach out to his dad more spontaneously. Both of us see it.

Dr. N.: That's typical. Brian has lingering negative impressions of Dad, and of the masculinity Dad represents, remaining in his unconscious mind. But when he spends enjoyable time with his father, his inner image of "bad Dad" or "just plain unimportant Dad" is replaced with "good Dad." His immediate experience of his father is in conflict with that lingering, unconscious image.

Mother: I used to tell Bill it's like he's an "injection" to Brian. That's the best way I can describe it. Bill gives Brian a "shot" of attention, and immediately, for the next two or three days, Brian's all over Dad. But then the injection wears off if Bill doesn't keep up the attention. However, I see that Brian doesn't need as big of an injection now. He just needs a consistent, everyday pat on his shoulder or an arm around his neck. That type of thing.

Dr. N.: Exactly. That's right. That's how it works. And do you see a connection between his diminished effeminate behavior and the "injection" of attention and affection from his father?

Mother: Yes, very much so. It's almost magical. You can't explain it to someone unless they live in your home.

More Comfortable with His Masculinity: "Ricky"

Nine-year-old Ricky appears to have made significant progress in the past few years. His father has stayed involved, he has a fairly good relationship with his brother, and he has a clear understanding of gender differences.

Dr. N.: Mrs. Smith, do you think Ricky's effeminacy has decreased from the way it used to be?

Mother: Absolutely. I would say we only have maybe 1 or 2 percent of the problem we used to have.

Dr. N.: Has the father been actively involved in Ricky's life?

Mother: Oh yes.

Dr. N.: He hasn't slacked off?

Mother: No. He's a lot more conscious about it. When he forgets, he remembers very fast. Or I give him a hint and he is immediately aware and will immediately change his behavior. It used to be that he waffled back and forth in the response that he might give. But now my husband will self-cue whenever he forgets about Ricky, or he will accept my cues without a problem.

Dr. N.: That's very, very important. You know, of all the parents I work with, it's always the mothers who are more enthusiastically involved. Most of the fathers have to be prompted. And the sons that do better are always the ones whose fathers really do get involved.

How is his self-esteem? Does Ricky seem to feel better about himself?

Mother: It's hard to tell because we haven't encountered any problems. I can only tell you that his acting up with the mannerisms of effeminacy is something of the past. We have introduced masculine activities, and now we're taking him to swimming practice. He's very much into that, and his older brother is now in swimming too. This is interesting, because I don't like swimming, I don't like baseball. As a matter of fact, I hate baseball! But he watches it with his brother on TV and they're both very enthusiastic about it.

Dr. N.: And is his father interested in baseball?

Mother: Not very much.

Dr. N.: So you've got the two brothers watching baseball together.

Mother: The boys watch baseball and somehow they manage to do their math homework between plays on the TV. I don't know how they do it. They're reading together; they will sit at the kitchen table, and my husband's reading his stuff and Ricky's there reading his stuff, too.

Dr. N.: Would you say his general maturity has developed?

Mother: I think so. He used to act more babyish. A lot of that has changed. This morning I was at school observing, because they had open house today. He didn't strike me as any different from any other kid there. He didn't act immature like some of the kids, and he has a curiosity he didn't have before. He wants to know, he wants to understand. So I think yes, he has matured. But I wish I saw more close male friendships.

Dr. N.: What about anxiety or depression? Have you seen any of that?

Mother: He still gets, I would say, sullen sometimes. But not that totally-giving-up attitude, throwing himself on the bed and sobbing like he used to. That kind of exaggeration. No. We don't tolerate that anymore.

Dr. N.: Does he get depressed like he used to? Sad or withdrawn?

Mother: No, not like he used to. But if he does, it usually has to do with something. It is more because of some one specific thing. But now he's willing to talk about it.

Dr. N.: So he gets along pretty well with his older brother?

Mother: Their relationship has gotten better. They're in swimming together and they spend more time together. Each day, they practice in our pool together. John can be a little mean and pick on Ricky sometimes. But John's mature enough now that I can tell him exactly what he's doing and he'll understand he has to treat Ricky differently.

Dr. N.: Does Ricky ever talk about being a boy? Does he ever make references to the difference between boys and girls?

Mother: Yes; in fact, he does. Take, for example, swimming. Just yesterday somebody walked up to me at the club and asked if I was going to try to get my daughter Sue on the swim team too. Ricky piped up and said, "No, swimming is not for her." I asked, "Why, Ricky?" He said, "Well, she's a girl. I don't want her at the swim club practicing with us."

Growing in Self-Understanding, Dad Stays Involved: "Felipe"

Felipe's father, Julio, is a popular high school soccer coach in a small town. The family has four boys and has strong traditional Catholic values. Felipe was always the gentler boy, and when he was quite young, he became quiet and withdrawn from his brothers. By the time he was eleven, he had no real male friends at school and had developed a strong interest in theater and acting.

When Felipe entered junior high, he became very depressed and uncommunicative. Then his mother discovered him downloading gay pornography from the Internet, so she made an appointment to see me.

Julio was a loving father to all his boys, but his job, which involved soccer competitions and practices many evenings and weekends, had often kept him away from home. Julio's other three sons all shared their father's athletic ability, so they saw a lot of their father, but because of Felipe's different interests, he got lost in the shuffle. The father's local success as a high school coach also created a high standard, within their large extended family of many uncles and cousins, that his sons, including Felipe, were expected to live up to.

After three years of occasional therapy, but mostly of intervention by his then concerned and aware dad, Felipe had improved greatly. At eighteen, he's now in college. He spoke to me in a follow-up interview.

Dr. N.: Felipe, how are your male friendships now?

Felipe: Much better.

Dr. N.: Why the change?

Felipe: I guess you could say that I came to realize that I *did* have male friendships all along, but I was blocking myself from believing it.

Dr. N.: Blocking yourself?

Felipe: Back then, I didn't really understand how friendships work on a male level. I was thinking they would be more emotional. And I know I had really low self-esteem. I now see that I always had male friendships, but I wouldn't let myself believe it.

Because of his neediness and isolation, Felipe had developed unrealistic expectations of male friendship. He wanted an all-or-nothing intimacy that would compensate for his feelings of not measuring up to the expectations that the world seemed to have of him as a young man. He has since come to recognize that good friends have, indeed, been there and available for him but that healthy male friendship is not characterized by deep emotional dependency and romanticism and especially not eroticism.

Felipe: Looking back, I see that there were guys in my life that would have been there for me, but I was blocking myself from taking advantage of what they had to offer me. But at that time, I never saw the potential. I really wasn't of an age to see those things clearly.

Dr. N.: You were lonely, because you were always thinking, *That guy would never be friends with me.*

Fear of rejection and feelings of unworthiness caused him to develop a defensive detachment.

Felipe: I felt like I was different. I don't know. . . The way I talked, my humor—so many things seemed different about me.

Dr. N.: Do you feel like one of the guys now?

Felipe: Definitely.

Dr. N.: So where do you see yourself in, say, ten years? Do you ever see yourself being part of the gay world?

Felipe: I never felt identified with the gay community. I know I wasn't born that way. I see them as hurting individuals who really believe they have no choice. And that makes me feel sorry for them.

Dr. N.: So you're saying you have decided that's not for you?

Felipe: Definitely. And my morals would never allow that, anyway.

Dr. N.: How would you describe your outlook on life?

Felipe: Much better. I know I have a goal to reach, a challenge ahead of me. There's much more optimism, even though I know the road ahead will still be a long one.

Dr. N.: How are you and your father doing?

Felipe: My dad and I have been much closer for the past five years.

Guidelines for Parents

By now, perhaps you have begun to see your child's need, and you have made some decisions about intervening and redirecting the child's behavior in a more gender-appropriate way. To sum up our overview of the healing process, here are four basic guidelines that may be helpful to you:

1. To advance and strengthen your child's gender-appropriate behavior, always remember that positive encouragement is more effective than punishment. When you want to extinguish exaggerated feminine (or in a girl, exaggerated tomboy) behavior, use clear, consistent, and nonpunitive disapproval in order to be most effective. In other words, gently redirect the child, but don't punish. On the other hand, ignoring or merely randomly disapproving of gender-inappropriate behavior will send your child the wrong message—that it's okay.

2. If you sense that you may be putting too much pressure on the child in order to initiate change, diminish your demands. Be patient. Offer posi-

tive affirmation for lesser efforts. It is far better to apply *less* stress n __ consistently than to apply *more* stress off and on.

3. If possible, work with a psychotherapist you trust. This professional should share your philosophy about gender as well as your treatment goals, and he or she should offer objective evaluation and specific advice regarding your intervention efforts.

4. Remember that your son or daughter will not feel safe giving up cross-gender behaviors if the child has no close, positive, same-sex role models to draw him or her into an appropriate gender identification. The child needs to see that being a man or woman is attractive and desirable.

I think you will agree that significant progress has been made in the lives of each of the fairly typical gender-confused boys described in the above transcripts. While improvement is still needed in some areas, the parents I've followed since their termination continue to remain committed to affirming the masculine development of their sons.

In the next chapter, you will read about other boys whose parents have persevered to build their children's gender esteem. You will see for yourself what they experienced, how they confronted challenges, and how the process helped them.

10

A MOTHER'S JOURNAL

It is a very difficult thing to teach maleness.

It takes a lot of consistent mindfulness.

But seeing him now, accepted by his friends, happy at school,

unafraid of being around other boys. . . .

I believe with all my heart that I have done the right thing.

MOTHER OF A GENDER-DISTURBED BOY

In this chapter we'll be sharing some excerpts from a mother's journal, written during the time she was making interventions with her son "Trevor" to help him feel happier and more secure about being a boy.

Trevor's gender-identity problem was more obvious than that of most pre-homosexual children. In fact, he would easily have qualified for the diagnosis of gender-identity disorder of childhood. Although your own son may be showing more subtle signs of the same problem of weak masculine identity, you may recognize warning signs here that will encourage you to take some action to support and affirm your son's growth into heterosexual maturity.

As you read these entries, you will see this mother's confusion—with times of certainty and confidence alternating with doubt as to whether she is making the best choices for her son. She offers an insightful record of the ups and downs, the hopes and disappointments that parents feel during the process.

Trevor's mother has a highly acute sensitivity to her son's emotional life, and she and her son are extremely close. She has kindly permitted us to reprint her private journal.

Her efforts involve not only changing the effeminate behaviors but also supporting and affirming the boy's internal sense of masculine identification. At first, she gives us a little background about her son.

*   *   *

I hate Valentine's Day, Cinderella, and the color pink. I dread them and fear that they could ruin my son. I used to adore all three until I started having problems with Trevor.

Trevor was always a happy and pleasant child. He always amused himself, so that you never thought there was a child in the house. He never did anything wrong or touched anything he wasn't supposed to. He was a joy and, to us, a genius. He knew all the letters of the alphabet when he was eighteen months old.

When he was only six months old, I had to go back to work, so his Aunt Lucy, who's single, offered to baby-sit him during the day. Then our daughter was born.

I remember coming home from work when Trevor was about three, and he would be playing with his sister and wearing my sister Lucy's shoes. My sister thought it was cute, but I never remember thinking so. I used to make him take them off after a little while, but I never gave it much thought after that.

When Trevor was almost three, I took him to the movies to see Disney's version of Cinderella. I loved the movie, but apparently he loved it even more. I don't remember if he started to pretend he was wearing a dress before or after he saw that movie, but around that time he started putting on his sister's nightgown and making believe it was a dress. Again, my mother and my sister Lucy saw no harm in this and never stopped him from doing it.

I used to pull it away and tell him that dresses are for girls and to stop it. However, the behavior continued. Each time I saw him pretending to wear a dress, I became more furious until, finally, when he knew I was around, he would quietly drop the nightgown.

Also around this time, he started to talk about the color pink. His chewable vitamins were pink, orange, and purple. He always chose the pink one. His favorite color was pink. If he could have anything pink, he wanted it. I used to tell him my favorite color was blue, hoping that might change his mind. I never thought that he associated the color pink with femininity at that young age. Although I dressed my daughter in pink, I never gave Trevor anything that was pink or feminine.

Then he started drawing a lot. That was fine, but he always drew pictures of a girl in a beautiful gown with a bow on her head. He loved Minnie Mouse but never bothered with Mickey. If he watched the Muppets, it was Miss Piggy that made him smile. I honestly worried that he was going to be a homosexual even back then, but I quickly dismissed the thought. How could a three-year-old be a homosexual? When I did say anything like that, my mother and sister laughed at me. "You're such a jerk," they told me repeatedly.

There was only one other child about Trevor's age at that time in the neighborhood. Joey lived across the street. During the summer when my son was four years old, Trevor and his sister would play with this little boy. Joey was a little tough, and perhaps he hit the other kids more than he should have, but my daughter could handle him. Trevor, however, couldn't. He used to come inside to get away from Joey. In fact, it soon ended up that Trevor never wanted to go out anymore—he just enjoyed staying with me and watching TV. At the time, I just considered him gentle, intellectual, and unwilling to fight. If that was his nature, well, that was okay; some boys are like that.

I've got to say that my relationship with my son was a beautiful one. Although I can honestly say I do not favor any one of my children, I felt like Trevor was my "soul mate," and I said as much to my husband, Jim.

Jim and I have had some communication problems for quite a few years. My husband is a very quiet, very nonverbal man. Figuratively and literally, Jim is a man of few words who believes every question can be answered with a "Yes" or "No." Never having known his biological parents, Jim (and his adoptive family) always seemed to me somewhat unexpressive. Believe it or not, during our early years together, I had actually found those qualities about Jim endearing! I thought of Jim as the strong, silent type. (In recent years, I have come to see his entire family as actually somewhat cold.)

Trevor loved me and always wanted to be near me. My ego soared when he preferred to be with me instead of his daddy, which was all the time. I continued to notice that he would pretend to wear a dress or talk about the color pink, and I always discouraged it. We were so perfectly in tune with one another that I could tell him anything. He and I were truly soul mates.

I remember him playing with tissues, pretending they were beautiful dresses. And I remember him playing with his sister's Minnie Mouse purse and the two of them playing with her dolls. By then, I was really becoming concerned, and one night I prayed to God for an answer. I knew that my mother-in-law and sister thought I was ridiculous. "He'll outgrow it," they assured me. And since I hadn't been exposed to many other children, I honestly wasn't sure if his behavior was abnormal or normal.

Two months before he was five, I noticed that Trevor was much more feminine than either my daughter or me. He and his sister caught strep throat that year and were home for almost a month by the time they were through with it. They spent their time watching TV. I remember that as soon as Trevor woke up, he turned the TV on and became so mesmerized with the fantasy characters that he never wanted to move away from it for the entire day—not even to eat. He was always watching those cartoons, mostly cartoons with feminine characters. He would never watch anything like *He-Man*. I didn't see any harm in *Star Wars*, until I saw Trevor in the dining room putting a triangular toy on his head trying to pretend he was Princess Leia.

By now his voice was high-pitched—a singsong kind of voice, a forced feminine voice. And he had begun to cry a lot.

Something else happened to him during this time. Suddenly, Trevor was afraid to go out of the house at all. When I tried to take him to library class or gymnastics, he was terrified to go in unless either his sister or I were holding his hand and staying there with him the entire time. There were three other boys in his library class, and when he saw them, he would go rigid. At first I thought the boys were picking on him, until I sat in the class and helped the librarian in order to watch what was going on. I noticed that although the boys tried to be nice to Trevor, he was still frightened of them. One day, when I didn't stay in the room with him, he ran outside. This class, which he had always enjoyed, was now his biggest fear.

His gymnastics class was similar. When it was Trevor's turn to perform, he did what the instructor told him to do. But unlike the other boys, he was extremely careful not to hurt himself. After he performed, he always tried to sit with the girls. Another mother sitting next to me said, "Your son is so good with little children. He's always very good with my daughter."

I noticed that he liked to play with the little girls before class started. He'd say, "Look at us, two girls and one boy!" I breathed a sigh of relief. At least he still knew he was a boy!

I knew in my heart that Trevor's excessive crying and his fear of going into these classes and being with other children, particularly boys, was because he was uncomfortable with himself. I was sure of this because he was my soul mate. Nonetheless, the phone call I made to the psychologist that had been recommended to me was a difficult one. It is hard to talk about a physical impairment that your child has, but an emotional impairment suggesting homosexuality is even more difficult.

I explained to Dr. N. that my son liked to pretend he was wearing a dress and that he loved the color pink. I described how he was behaving in the classes that I was taking him to, that he was feminine in both voice and actions. My son had also, by now, begun to sit down on the toilet when urinating, even though he had previously stood up.

Dr. N. was very supportive, but he agreed that we had a serious problem. What amazed me was that he was able to describe Trevor's personality before I did. He knew from experience with other clients that Trevor was afraid of getting hurt physically and therefore did not like rough play, that he was not very coordinated in sports, and that he absolutely loved fantasy.

The first question he asked was what type of pictures Trevor drew. My son only drew pictures of girls in beautiful dresses—he never drew males. That was a problem. Dr. N. informed me that at this age a child usually draws his own interpretation of himself and how he feels about himself. I felt myself sinking. The only inanimate things he drew were houses. That was also bad. A house represents security, which is more a typically feminine concern than a masculine one.

The next question Dr. N. asked me was about Trevor's relationship with his father. Did he run to him when he came home from work? Jim does spend time with the children, even though he is driving around much of the time with his job as a salesman and he is really exhausted when he gets home. But as far as what he does with the kids, the problem is, Jim's idea of spending time with our children is watching what he wants to watch on TV while the kids are in the same room. Like his own father, Jim does not like sports and he never plays ball with the children.

I have often heard Jim angrily say that the children never say hello to him or stop what they are doing to greet him when he arrives home. He has to go after them. But maybe if he would play with them on a more personal level, not just watch TV, they would show more of an interest in being with him.

Dr. N. explained to me that during what is a child's crucial gender-identity phase (about one and a half to two years old), my son had evidently not bonded with his father. This usually occurs when a boy who was born particularly sensitive and gentle perceives his father as critical, distant, and unavailable. Therefore, the boy thinks, Dad's not like me—this is not who I am. This causes this temperamentally vulnerable type of boy to build a defensive detachment against his father and identify with his mother. But the reality remains, of course, that Trevor is a boy, and no amount of wishful thinking on his part can ever change that!

Dr. N. told me that Trevor's treatment must primarily focus on improving the relationship between Trevor and his father. He indicated that my husband would have to break down his son's "defensive detachment" by being especially loving with Trevor. At every opportunity he had to work with our son, pointing out male/female differences and gently discouraging the feminine behavior. It was very important that he never yell at Trevor, because our son was so easily hurt. He should be especially patient with him, more so than with our other kids, and whenever he did become really angry, rather than letting him see that he was angry or frustrated with him, Jim should simply walk away.

We were both supposed to reinforce Trevor's maleness and masculine behavior, explain the anatomical differences between boys and girls, and basically puncture Trevor's feminine fantasies with love, bringing him back to reality. Trevor simply couldn't go on pretending to be a girl. He's a boy, no matter what illusions he held on to about himself.

My husband was to wrestle with him every night, to help overcome his fears of rough-and-tumble play with other males. It was also important that my husband make it appear that Trevor was having some success at outwrestling his father. Part of the problem was that Trevor did not feel he measured up, that he wasn't as good as other boys. Also, Trevor was not to spend his day playing with girls.

Since the basic objective of the treatment was to repair the relationship between my husband and my son, where was I to fit into all of this? After praying and crying alternately, and finally coming to grips with the situation, I had to face many things.

First, I would have to stand my ground with my mother-in-law and my sister Lucy. No matter what they thought or how opposed they were to what Jim and I were doing to help Trevor, they must respect my wishes when I asked them not to baby him or encourage his girlishness. Whether they called me "silly" or not, I would have to persevere.

My mother had continued to insist that there was nothing wrong with Trevor. Yes, when she visited, she had seen him cross-dressing, she had seen him playing with dolls, she had seen him drawing elaborate pictures of girls in gowns, yet she continued to deny that anything was wrong. I almost wondered if they enjoyed indulging my son's fantasies. There's a lot of satisfaction in mothering a soft, gentle boy who you can cuddle and who's so affectionate back to you. Of course, I had to tell both of them about Trevor's problem, because he spent so much time with them.

I had to get my husband more emotionally connected with his son. I began to suggest weekend activities for the two of them, which included hiking, roller-skating, and bowling. I bought toys for my son, but I asked my husband to give them to him. I stuck a reminder list into Jim's briefcase, which is akin to the "rules of the road" about to how to behave with his son: (1) Love him so much that you attract him into the masculine sphere. (2) Be gentle; don't yell at him. (3) Take him to work with you. And so on.

Sometimes I felt like I was the director of the entire production, while my son and husband were merely the passive players. I was always looking for ways to point out the similarities between them. I even bought them matching shirts whenever possible.

Finding other boys Trevor's age for him to play with and making friends with their mothers was also critical. I needed to observe the behavior of these other boys while they played with Trevor. I often casually ask him questions about what they did together. I am lucky that my son will tell me what's happening. Now he will refuse to play girls' games, because he understands that boys have different games.

Trying to get Trevor to be unafraid of playing with the "real" boys was my goal. I picked out boys who I thought were the most masculine boys at his birthday party and, based on what he told me about them, made friends with their moms and invited the boys over. Trevor did not feel especially comfortable with them in the beginning, but each day their play time got better. He is now active on the school playground with these boys, and I encourage him every time he plays with them.

This is a great step forward! Not long ago, he hated going to school. He would cry the night before and beg me, "Please don't make me go!" He would also tell me that he didn't have any friends. Many times when I picked him up, I would watch him through the window playing on the playground—Trevor was always by himself, watching the other boys. I felt so bad for him. I wished he had a real good boy friend, but he wouldn't let himself approach any boy at school. I knew he wanted to be friendly, but he just didn't have the courage to do it. He was always, I think, intimidated by the kids.

I have also signed Trevor up for swimming and gymnastics, but always in a class where some of his buddies are, so that he is more enthusiastic about going. At nighttime I tell him stories about boys, substituting his and his friends' names for the characters. I have even made up adventure stories at bedtime about him and his buddies, so that he could hear his name included along with the rest of the guys.

Although my husband is supposed to be the key player in all of this, in reality, I have been the one who runs myself ragged. It's me who arranges to have all the boys over to the house and who ensures that their behavior is a positive influence on Trevor. It's always me who drives him to his sports classes. My sister Lucy criticizes me for making all this effort, but I have to ignore her.

I have no guarantees that this will all turn out the way I pray every night that it will. I do believe with all my heart that I have done the right thing and that my son is more comfortable with himself than he would have been had I let the situation continue as it was.

It is not easy, and I can understand why parents don't follow through with this treatment. It was especially hard in the beginning, because that's when I really did feel that I might be hurting his feelings. But seeing him now, accepted by his friends, happy at school and eager to go there, unafraid of being around other boys and eager to play with them, receiving invitations to so many of the other boys' birthday parties, I have no regrets. He still confides in me, and every day I hug and kiss him and tell him I love him, and he does the same to me, so it really hasn't hurt our relationship.

After all is said and done, I have no regrets. I am confident I did the right thing. I will always be close to my son however this turns out—I know this boy's heart almost like my own, and I love him dearly. But because I love him, I want the best for him, and so I still pray for him to grow up strong and confident in being a man.

That is my hope and my prayer for Trevor.

After providing us with background about Trevor's gender confusion, his mother now allows us to see the journal she kept almost ten years ago, during the family's year and a half of therapy. You will notice that the encouraging progress Trevor makes is often followed by regression into old habits: two steps forward, one step back. It is a time-consuming and demanding battle. But as you will see, little by little she has been rewarded.

February 10. A week ago we saw Dr. N. at his office. Even though he has clearly explained to us what needs to be done, it is a very difficult thing to teach maleness. With steady pressure, I've been getting Jim to get into play "fights" with Trevor every night—holding him and hugging him, kissing him, and saying fatherly words of affection to him. He brings Trevor gifts—anything to begin to build a trust between them.

If we see Trevor doing anything female, we're to gently tell him that boys don't do those things and try to point out what boys are supposed to do. For example, I told him that boys have "pee-pees" that stick out and that's what makes him a boy, and that boys can never be girls and girls can never be boys.

The first few days have been extremely tough. In the beginning Trevor rebelled a little, but not as much as Dr. N. indicated he might. Since my husband isn't home that much, I have to deal with it most of the time. A couple of days ago, I spoke to him about the feminine things he had done and then, I went my room and just cried. There are times Jim just cries too. We both feel overwhelmed at times by having to tell Trevor about so many things he's not supposed to do. Trevor has always been a good boy, and he's just not used to being told that he's doing so many things the wrong way. He looks at me with eyes so sad, asking if he's doing something wrong. And I notice that he's not coming to me as readily as he did before, because he's afraid of what behavior I might criticize.

February 16. There have been several times when Trevor has said, "I don't feel good. I want to go to bed." Then I'd notice that he was lying in front of the television with his sister's nightgown on top of him, the way he used to do when he was pretending to be a girl. I immediately told him to stop it.

I have also noticed that when Trevor kisses his father when he comes home from work, now it is more of a seductive kiss. Rather than a father/son kiss, it seems more like a husband/wife kiss. My husband probably doesn't see this, and I think he is clueless to this observation.

Since we've been going to see Dr. N., I've had to redirect my own son's behavior many times. It's just so painful, but Jim and I have persisted. But as for me, my life has taken on new meaning. I am going to do everything possible to fight this. And so perfect has been my relationship with Trevor that he trusts me. So as hard as it is for him, he believes what I am now trying to explain to him.

At this point, I had to intervene to tell these parents to back off. In their enthusiasm to change the feminine behaviors, they were going overboard in ways that would hurt the parent-child relationship. Positive reinforcement, that is, praise, is always the best way to change behavior. Don't overwhelm the child with new expectations all at once. And above all, no shaming!

February 26. For a long time, I've noticed that Trevor cannot look men in the eye when speaking with them, although this isn't a problem when he's around a woman. I can see that my son is nervous about talking to men.

He's not only nervous about talking to men; he's also uncomfortable about being nude in front of males. I've begun to notice the difference between Trevor's degree of comfort with his nudity when in my presence (which is not a problem for him) as opposed to being in the presence of his dad. Today, Jim happened to pee in front of him with the bathroom door open. Next, Trevor went in to pee, but he closed the door so his dad couldn't see him. Jim told him, "Guys don't need to be embarrassed in front of other guys."

But on the positive side, I don't see Trevor pretending to wear a dress anymore. I also don't hear him imitating a little girl's voice while he's playing, although his voice is still a forced, high-pitched one. He has stopped drawing recently. I can't help but wonder if we are only suppressing the behavior and that this will all resurface later on. However, Trevor has started playing that he is the doctor and his sister is the nurse. The patient was a Minnie Mouse doll, but I let it go because he was taking on a masculine identity. I've also noticed that he is no longer crying as much as he used to, which he did a lot prior to the start of treatment.

March 1. We're approximately three weeks into treatment. I see some encouraging signs. Yesterday, although he was afraid, Trevor made himself run into his library class alone. Since I had told him not to stay with just the girls, he sat next to the smallest boy he could find—but at least it was a boy! I felt the sweet sensation of some progress. A couple of days ago, he went to work with his father—something he would not have done before. He still rejects male images and prefers neuter-type animals like Daffy Duck, Dumbo, or Bambi. He is also rejecting the color blue. He now prefers red.

March 6. Trevor does not mention pink anymore. He and his sisters are fighting more. In a strange way, this may actually be a good sign. I am hoping it is, because he is now starting to have different interests than theirs.

Television causes him to regress back to fantasyland—yesterday I saw him acting like Tweety Bird again. I try to sit down with him when he watches it to make sure that there aren't too many feminine mannerisms for him to imitate, or at least I explain—again, gently—"Trevor, boys do not act like this." Dr. N. says Jim should be doing more of this reminding than I do.

March 11. A step backward today. Trevor tried pushing his penis back inside his body this morning, and he refuses to wear the shirt that is like his father's. This weekend he seemed to regress and become slightly more feminine in movements and he screamed a lot. I have a feeling that too much time with his father right now makes him regress. It amounts to overkill. We've got to learn to strike the right balance.

March 17. At his cousin Cathy's house, Trevor played with Lego blocks while my daughter and Cathy played with Barbie dolls. However, rather than making a building, he made the Lego blocks into a necklace and a crown, which he placed on his head. He said he was a prince. My husband gently explained that we only wear costumes on Halloween. This evening, while playing house, my daughter played "Mommy," and Trevor wanted to play "children." I told him he should play "Daddy" because he is a boy.

March 24. Maury's birthday party. There were six boys total. Trevor won third in the sack race and won the hot potato game. I hope this helps build confidence in himself.

March 26. Trevor really did well in his gymnastics class. Later, he picked out a baseball shirt and shorts at the store. While watching TV, he began playing with the VCR buttons when two things came on—the pink Care Bear and Cherry Merry Muffin. He made a big effort not to keep on staring at them. Then he went to have breakfast rather than finish watching the cartoon.

Trevor is also picking Mario or Luigi in addition to Toad (the neuter) when playing Mario 2 on Nintendo. He is also definitely more assertive when speaking, and his fighting technique is much better.

March 28. Jim and I were playing Nintendo, and Trevor urged his father to beat me at the game! This is a first, although Jim missed the significance of this. Before the start of treatment, Trevor would have always rooted for me to win against his father. I am so happy about this that it doesn't even hurt my ego! This afternoon, he drew pictures where the males and females were drawn to look exactly alike. I pointed out the differences for him.

April 5. Trevor is still afraid to talk with boys in his library class, but at least he does sit with them. He is catching a ball much better and has lost a few pounds because he is more active and spends less time transfixed in front of the VCR.

April 13. Last weekend he was playing Duck Hunt on the Nintendo, which is a boy's game that his friend Joey lent him. He will sometimes ask to play kickball or catch, and at night he has been asking to watch baseball games on TV. Thank goodness, now he always is asking for his dad to be home! Lucy notices that his voice is deeper and he is more aggressive.

April 22. We got a small, child's wiffle ball set for Trevor and have encouraged him to play. His batting form is pretty masculine. (You'd be surprised, by watching different boys, how there is a definite masculine way to throw or hit a ball.) Also, he doesn't shy away from playing with Tommy anymore (Tommy's the really boyish new kid down the block).

Today Trevor wanted to go with his dad to pick up Jim's new truck, and now he prefers his daddy over me all the time. My son and I are not as close as we were. I feel like I am saying good-bye to my little boy; we are not so similar anymore. It is a tough feeling since we were so close, but I honestly believe that I am doing the right thing by him.

His voice is deeper sometimes. Last Sunday he hit his cousin Eddie, who is eight years older than him, because Eddie had hit his cousin Cathy. Yesterday he picked a pair of socks to wear because he wanted to look like Daddy.

April 28. I think Trevor no longer has doubts about the fact that he's a boy. He says that someday he is going to marry a nice girl and have lots of children. Although Trevor never said he would marry a boy, there seemed to be reluctance in the beginning when he heard he was expected to marry a girl. He couldn't seem to imagine himself as a daddy.

April 29. Today Trevor played wiffle ball with Daddy. He really loves Daddy now. Tonight he said that on Wednesday he would wear his black and red shirt and on Thursday he would wear his Nintendo shirt (I gave Jim the shirt so he could give it to Trevor). They are playing Duck Hunt together right now.

It's amazing how his voice sounds so deep and grown up (with no singsong to it) when he speaks about Nintendo. He has excelled at it. He is also picking more Nintendo games involving sports now, rather than his previous choices of all games involving castles and fantasy.

October 2. I met with Trevor's teacher to see how he is doing in class. Dr. N. said I should tell her about Trevor's problem without giving her too much detail as to what the problem is. He is always with the boys, so I am confident that Trevor is working at it with me.

I always explain to parents that they can gain the cooperation of a child's teachers and coaches by explaining to them that their son feels insecure about being a boy. "We need to work together," the parent should tell the teacher, "to build this child up in his self-esteem regarding his gender—to help him be confident and happy about the fact that he's a male."

October 7. Problems. Lately, I haven't seen as much closeness between Trevor and his father. Jim just got a promotion, so he has been very busy at his job and is often short-tempered with the kids after doing so much driving all day long. Right now Trevor is not showing an interest in sports and his father has not been watching any TV with him.

October 16. Trevor started his swimming class at the club today. Initially he was afraid to go in and wanted me to stay with him, which none of the parents were allowed to do. I watched him, however, from another door (always afraid I was sending the lamb to the slaughter), and he did quite well. He was shown how to dive and how to turn underwater. He was so excited after class that he said he wanted to come here every day, not just one day a week. When he got home, he was actually playing with his wiffle ball, and then he asked me if we could get him a basketball hoop.

Trevor has been drawing a lot this past week. He draws boys and girls, usually the same size, and neither sex is dominant. He and his father are closer again, and Jim has once again started watching sports with him. I think the swim class really gave Trevor some much-needed male confidence.

November 9. Today he was playing with his sister and my niece. I noticed that Trevor pretended to be the king and the other two girls were the queen and princess. It is rewarding to see him take the male role, even in a fantasy scenario.

February 5. Now it's one full year into treatment. Trevor still lacks confidence in himself, although he does accept the male role—he'll play Daddy, the king, etc. He now also can handle being tackled by Alan and playing in the playground school.

March 26. I noticed more drawing of girls, hearts, etc., around Valentine's Day. This is a problem, because that's what the teacher told them to draw. I had to talk to Trevor about the fact that boys don't draw just pictures of girls. Later I saw him crayoning over a picture of a girl in a coloring book—not coloring her but trying to block her out.

The important thing here is not to discourage Trevor's creative abilities, which are his natural gifts, but to discourage him from using fantasy to support the pretension that he is a girl.

For his birthday party I invited every boy from his class, plus three boys from another class, and also his buddy from swim class—fifteen boys, no girls. Anything to help solidify the male picture. I have made it my business to become friends with the mother of any boy his age, and I am constantly inviting these boys over to play after school. It runs me ragged sometimes, but I feel it is a small price to pay to avoid a far bigger price, if Trevor becomes a homosexual.

There was a girl from his kindergarten class who kept kissing Trevor at a party he attended. Now he's talking about marrying her! I drew the family tree for him and told him that when he marries someday, I will place the girl's name in the box next to his and draw the branches for each of the children they have together. I talk to him and say that when he is a daddy, his wife will be the mommy, and I will be the grandma, and Daddy will be the grandpa. This he accepts without reservation or doubt.

This is very important for Trevor to sort out. Androgynous fantasies—the myth that he can be both male and female, mother and father, husband and wife—can become lifelong distortions of reality.

April 2. I notice lately that the relationship between my husband and son runs hot and cold. Right now, Trevor and Jim are at a cool-down. My husband has told him that he will build him a tree house in a few weeks. I am sure that will heat up the relationship again. Trevor can't wait until they start, and he keeps asking me when Daddy will do it.

April 5. Problems today. We went to the club and watched a men's swim meet where Trevor's cousins were competing. Trevor sat close to the pool and crossed his legs and posed these feminine poses as he watched the boys compete in the pool. We couldn't believe that he would act like that, almost like he was flirting. It's like he was doing the exact opposite of what most boys would do if they were showing off to try to impress bigger boys. We called him over and told him—privately, of course—to uncross his legs and act like a boy so that the bigger boys wouldn't think that he was a baby or a sissy. It was like he really wanted the older boys' attention, but he did not know how to get it in a real way—as an equal and as a boy.

May 12. Better today! At the club, all the boys (who are all older than Trevor) went into the pool, and the water was freezing, but Trevor still made himself jump in too! It was a macho thing to do. All day, he was on what I would call a "masculine high."

What pleased me the most was that the teacher gave the kids back two pictures that they had made of themselves. One was done in September, and I remember dreading seeing it hanging in the classroom, because my son made the clothes in the picture look like he was wearing a dress! The other picture was drawn in April, and to my relief, he drew himself as a boy— no doubt about it. He was wearing pants and short hair and wasn't the least bit girlish.

July 15. Yesterday he followed his father around with his baseball glove on (they were going to have a practice). I was very touched by this scene. At that moment, I wanted to cry for him and what he has had to deal with in his young life. I doubt he will ever be an athlete, but still, I can see that he really wants to do well.

The gender-confused boy does not need to be a "macho man." If nature hasn't gifted him with athletic ability but has given him artistic ability, that's not a problem. However, it's helpful for him to be able to at least throw the ball acceptably and play some sports adequately. Otherwise, the feeling of being shamed, of not measuring up with the other boys will reinforce his sense of differentness.

September 6. Toward the end of the summer, I sensed a slight regression— nothing feminine. It was a shying away from Father, leaning toward Mother with his voice in an artificial, slightly higher pitch. But then the last two weeks of August, Dad took him along on a fishing trip in his new truck, and I noticed a complete change—a masculine change. Since then he has been playing with Matchbox cars. He made a parking lot out of the top of his sneaker box and plays with these cars.

I know a lot of his interests will always be more on the artistic side. But I do want him to understand guy things and not to be intimidated by them.

September 20. Trevor is showing an interest in the piano. I asked Dr. N. if piano lessons would be appropriate at this point. He said, "Yes, of course, if that's his natural gift. But get him a male teacher, preferably a masculine teacher who is married."

Tonight Trevor was playing cards with my sister Lucy and she began singing "Cinderelly, Cinderelly" from Disney's Cinderella, and my son was getting off on that. Really, my sister is no help at all!

October 16. Since the beginning of school there has been a distancing between father and son that we are having trouble repairing. Since this distancing, Trevor is no longer playing with Matchbox cars or Duck Hunt.

There is a second-grade young male teacher, and I am going to request that Trevor gets him next year so that he sees that teaching is not just for women. Every day I ask him casually and in an offhand way that isn't really snooping who he sits with on the bus to and from school. He always sits with boys. However, it is amazing to me how his behavior changes to coincide with the current relationship he has with his father! When he and his father are not close, he goes back to some of the girl stuff. And their relationship still seesaws regularly.

Trevor's mother is correctly observing her son's gender-identity ambivalence. One year ago, Trevor was identified with her and with the femininity she represents; today, he is ambivalent about whether to identify with the masculine or the feminine. That ambivalence centers around two things: first, Trevor's own uncertainty that he is capable of doing boy things and measuring up to a male role; and second, his father's shifting attractiveness to Trevor as a masculine identification object.

November 24. The father-son relationship is currently back on track. Trevor and I went to Sea World in San Diego with just the kids and my mom and

Lucy, and Trevor cried for his father because he missed him!

On November 4 and November 21, I saw Trevor wrestling with Alan and doing well. He also received a swim trophy last Sunday at the country club, which was another big boost to his male ego. He seems to be genuinely liked by the other boys in school. When he catches a ball, he is so happy and amazed at himself. He's learning that he can do it. Tonight he is going bowling with Jim.

January 2, 1992. Early in December, Trevor's relationship with his father went slightly off. Trevor wanted his dad to "jump" whenever he wanted him to do something, and if Dad didn't jump, Trevor got very angry. He had a Christmas play at church, and he chose to play the role of one of the lambs in the stable rather than Joseph or a shepherd or a wise man. That disappointed me.

Then on December 11th his class went to see a Tchaikovsky ballet and his teacher (who I have spoken to before about this) put him in a group with five girls. I was annoyed that this happened, but I let it go without comment.

December 31. Several things have happened between Christmas and today that somehow make me feel—do I dare say it?—that my son is truly on the right path and making certain progress.

First, Trevor and Dad did a lot of drawing together during Christmas week, and he even dedicated a book he wrote in school to Dad. (Usually he dedicates his books to "My Mom.")

On December 31st we had a party and Alan was there. I am always afraid of what Alan can do to Trevor's ego, but on New Year's Day there was a different Trevor—a more masculine Trevor—and he wasn't intimidated by Alan.

Today when Dad came home from work, Trevor grabbed his dad's hat and put it on his own head and left it there. He had always rejected wearing any of Dad's clothes in the past, and if he did put them on, he was quick to remove them. My daughter tried to take the hat from him, but he wouldn't let her have it. Then he began making fun of her in the teasing way little boys do to little girls.

Tonight Trevor and his father were in bed talking about the solar system for about a half hour and I noticed his voice was real—not an artificial and forced feminine one. It was as if he'd gone through puberty. Tonight I feel like a major breakthrough occurred.

Another friend called and asked Trevor to go over tomorrow. Trevor told me he did not feel like going but wants to spend time at home with his family. A very assertive Trevor today! Usually he just wants to be accommodating, and he doesn't stand up for himself and express what it is he wants. He said he would not mind if his friend came over here, but he wants to stay home. I feel tonight as if he has finally found himself, and he is becoming complete and whole.

January 3. Trevor drew a picture in school today of himself and his father going over the bridge in Dad's new truck. I pray to God that this is the end of this nightmare.

January 5. Last night Trevor made a race car track by taping many sheets of paper together and raced his Matchbox cars on it. Right now he is again playing with it. The other kids kept calling him "Daddy" (he's playing that role!), and he is making his voice really adult-deep to play the part of a grown-up.

He wanted to stay up all night last night with his father. They played Duck Hunt on the Nintendo, which they hadn't played in a very long time. They are playing it again now. I feel like the "defensive detachment" against his father is truly breaking down and he's feeling more and more like he belongs with the guys.

January 17. On January 13, Trevor wrote on the computer, with some help in the spelling from his sisters, "My Dad is special. I want to be a sales manager some day and go to work with him. I love him." I also noticed that when his father makes a critical comment that would have made him walk away feeling rejected, Trevor now stays and fights back. I am very happy to see that assertion. He has been drawing pictures of himself winning the Olympics. I am so happy that these are fantasies of himself as a male.

But the struggle is not over. The next entry in this diary illustrates the special vulnerability of the sensitive child. Where the thicker-skinned child might be temporarily hurt by such a blowup but quickly move on, the sensitive boy is dealt a setback that causes him to regress to the feminine fantasies.

February 20. How sad I am to write this, when I thought the worst of the battle might be all over! Last Sunday my husband was in a foul mood, and I heard him yelling at the kids harshly. Jim seems to forget—or I sometimes wonder if he doesn't care enough to remember—that Trevor is very sensitive to any scolding. My two girls can take it, but not Trevor.

Prior to the blowup, Trevor had said he wanted to stay home this summer and work with his dad taking care of our vegetable garden. Now, since Jim's blowup, I have seen serious regression. I saw him lying under his old Minnie Mouse blanket with his sister's nightgown like he used to do when he pretended to be wearing a dress. I am sure this is what he was doing. Trevor hasn't wanted to sleep with his father much since then, which is a strong indication that something has gone awry.

Tomorrow is Trevor's birthday party. He will be six, and fifteen boys are invited, along with his sisters. He drew a picture of his party, and his two sisters were the largest and most dominant, central figures. I know that all of this is bad, but my husband just does not see it.

Jim resents my coaching him. Yet if I don't remind him of what our son needs, nothing gets done. He never plays rough-and-tumble with Trevor unless I tell him what to do, and now he only sits and watches TV with him. Obviously, that won't help our son.

I am tired and frustrated and feel like I am so alone in this battle. Yet I love my son and I want the best for him, and I can never throw in the towel. I pray that this turns around again. Time is running out as Trevor gets older. He still wants to be a judge. And when I ask him who he will marry when he grows up, he still says, "A nice girl, and I'm going to be a daddy and have lots of kids."

Still, this much regression causes me much heartache. The "defensive detachment" against his own masculinity is back up again, and I can see that he's feeling weak and vulnerable.

February 23. It is amazing what a couple of days of kindness and camaraderie with his father can do. Yesterday I took my son shopping, and he asked me to buy him Matchbox cars. Yesterday I gave him boys' brown fuzzy slippers and he didn't find them repulsive. He also followed Jim around yesterday and then fell asleep next to him on the couch. They played games together all night and today he keeps calling for Daddy to play with him. I am reminded that a mother can't do this alone—everything depends on and revolves around how the relationship with his dad is going.

May 28. Trevor was sick three times this spring with stomach flu and hay fever. And as always when he is sick, I see regression and more babyish and effeminate behavior. The thing that sticks out in my mind is his covering up with his sister's nightgown. With him, it always seems to be taking that nightgown that indicates his regressive or feminine behavior. Also turning on the VCR and watching those Disney films with female characters.

Again, Jim is of little help. I can preach what he should do until I am blue in the face, but he is simply not capable of doing everything that needs to be done, and he does not know how to effectively communicate on a regular basis with his son. I fear that it is really not his top priority, at least not the way that healing Trevor is mine. There hasn't been any physical play between them lately. That never happens unless I get after Jim and remind him. Then he resents me for taking charge and telling him what to do. This puts me in such a bind.

On the flip side, Trevor has started playing soccer, and his coach is fantastic, really nurturing and confidence-boosting, especially when a player doesn't perform well. Trevor has no confidence on the field right now, but with the help of his teacher, he's persevering. But he did qualify for the Most Improved Player award last week, of which I am extremely proud.

I am fighting hard with the school administration for him to get a male second-grade teacher. It's not easy, because no one seems to understand. I spoke to his first-grade teacher today about it, and she assures me that he is an absolutely healthy boy and is well respected by his classmates and that basically I am nuts for thinking he needs a male influence. Then in her next statement she asks me if he is completely recovered from his stomach flu, because he has been acting very shy around the other kids lately! Why doesn't she get it? The woman is so out of touch with the children's personalities. Doesn't she see how quickly he can regress when he is hurt? I wish she was more attuned to him. I can't wait for this school year to be over!

August 8. Trevor is really doing great in gymnastics. His teacher sings his praises. But what impresses me most is that when he speaks to other boys in his class that he hardly knows, he now looks them in the eye and speaks to them confidently as an equal. This is a major development.

His relationship with his father has improved now that Jim has taken him to work a few times and told him about what he does all day when he's driving around seeing the company's customers. Trevor told me two days ago that he wants to go to the Coast Guard Academy, knowing that it means going away to sea. He thinks working for the government will help him toward his goal of becoming a judge on the Supreme Court!

If I had to describe this whole experience, I'd say it reminds me of my pot of azaleas. I was given a beautiful pot of bright-red azaleas for Easter, and unfortunately I forgot to water them. One day I looked at them and they were wilted so bad that I just about threw them out. Thinking it was hopeless, I watered them anyway and went to bed. The next morning those pathetic wilted flowers had sprung back to life! There sat a beautiful red azalea plant, the same one I had almost given up on. Trevor reminds me of the azalea, because the results are immediate. Pay attention to him and he flourishes; ignore him and he wilts. When Jim is too busy to spend time with him, then Trevor becomes dependent on me. But when Jim gives his son the attention he needs, he's all over him.

It takes a lot of consistent mindfulness.

*   *   *

Follow-Up Interview: The Teen Years

Ten years after Trevor first started therapy, I called his mother for a follow-up interview. Trevor had just turned sixteen years old, and she reported that although "he's not super macho like his cousins are," the effeminacy is, much to her relief, "now gone." Continuing with her story, she told me, "When he was very young, he was extremely insecure. He still has his insecurities, but I would say that today, he has a sense of a male self. I would predict now that someday he'll marry and have kids."

I asked her how he was getting along with his schoolmates.

"He's extremely well respected by his schoolmates because of his intelligence and because he's a really nice kid," she explained. "He is still insecure about team sports, though. If he had to pick what he would participate in, I think it would be a noncontact sport like golf or swimming."

Happily, Trevor suffers from none of the social ostracism and depression so characteristic of effeminate boys. He "will talk to anybody," his mother says, and except for a rare incident with a bully who takes advantage of his sensitive nature, he is happy, well liked, and well adjusted in school. He remains close to his extended family.

Trevor is still a dreamer who is fascinated with drawing comic strips or scenes from Hollywood action films. His mother knows this is an asset and a gift, but she encourages him not to use fantasy as a way of avoiding the risk taking and self-assertion that's required to call up another guy to make plans. He still needs support and encouragement when he experiences rejection.

She remains somewhat resentful, though, that the improvement in Trevor's gender identity has come largely through her own efforts. Trevor has improved, she says, "in *spite* of my husband, not because of him. Not that Jim doesn't *love* the kids, but he just doesn't know how to connect with them. I can understand that this is hard for him because he didn't get the emotional connection from his own family, but when he became a parent himself, he should have pushed himself past that emotional block. Over the years, my husband didn't consistently put himself out to the extent Trevor needed it, and that's been a source of friction between us." As she explains:

> So at every opportunity in our home, I, myself, do what I can to quietly reinforce the male image. I will call Trevor "fellah" and "young man," "my boy." I have always referred to him with a male emphasis. I have to. I hate to sound like I'm back in the "old times," but with my son's gender confusion, I had an obligation to enforce clear gender-role differences.
>
> My two daughters will help me in the kitchen; my sons will take out the garbage. My daughters will not be asked to take out the garbage, but they will straighten up the laundry room and put away the grocery shopping. My son will shovel the driveway and change the oil in Jim's truck; my daughters do not have to do that. I've had to delineate the family's roles by gender. And I've done all this for the sake of my son, so Trevor will have a clear sense of himself as the young man he has become.

Growth into Manhood Is a Journey

Over and over we hear from ex-gay men, such as Alan Medinger, that a heterosexual identity can still be established in adulthood after years of doubt and insecurity. Medinger's *Growth into Manhood: Resuming the Journey* offers the wise and insightful counsel of a Christian ministry leader who describes his own decades of "going AWOL" on the journey to manhood—a journey that he actively resumed after giving up his double life as a gay man.

Echoing the advice of Medinger, Richard Wyler (<www.peoplecanchange .com>) explains, "Our homosexual feelings were not the problem—but were actually symptoms of deeper, underlying problems and long-buried pain that usually had little or nothing to do with erotic desire. Rather, they had to do with our self-identity, self-esteem (especially our "gender esteem"), our relationships and spiritual life. Once we discovered and healed the underlying pain, the symptoms of homosexuality took care of themselves."

Why Persevere? A Look at the Hard Realities

Let's say your son is approaching the teenage years, and you suspect he tends to detach himself from and romanticize other males. There's a point at which you might say, "My son obviously has some intense emotional needs for other guys. Why not just forget about encouraging him to work on his heterosexual potential? Wouldn't it be much more compassionate if I just gave him my blessing? Then my son would have peace, and there'd be peace in our family."

In the short term, there probably would be peace. It's true that the struggle to develop one's heterosexual potential will, for some people, be a long and difficult one. And it's also true that your ongoing, loving relationship with your son must never be sacrificed.

But there are reasons to continue to encourage your child's gender development. First, the risk of death from AIDS must be realistically considered. In fact, a group of medical researchers who assessed the data in a major city concluded recently that—if the current death rate persists—about half of gay and bisexual men will not reach their sixty-fifth birthday.[1]

Besides the risk of AIDS and other serious sexually transmitted diseases, and besides the enormously important issue of your family's moral convictions, your son should be aware of the characteristics of same-sex relationships. In spite of his deep yearning for a stable same-sex love relationship, it is highly unlikely he will find both sex and faithful love in a long-term male partnership.

Is this just our biased opinion? To answer, I will let several gay advocates speak for themselves. The first is Andrew Sullivan.

In his book *Love Undetectable,* Sullivan admits that gay men tend to be addicted to endless cycles of infatuation. He says he now realizes that romantic infatuation will inevitably be short-term, unpredictable, and untrustworthy as a pathway leading to enduring love. So in the final analysis, Sullivan says, it is friends—not lovers—who will actually be a gay man's most reliable source of support and affection. It is friends who will give him "what love promises, but fails to provide."[2] In other words, a gay man can't count on an intimate partner.

If Sullivan's observation is right—and he has long been an astute observer of the gay world—then the young man who dreams of having an emotionally intimate, lifelong, faithful relationship with one person will not—after all he has hoped for—be likely to find it.

Sullivan, it should be emphasized, is not a radical but is a part of the conservative faction within the gay community. Yet as a Catholic and a conservative (of sorts), he still defends "the beauty and mystery and spirituality of sex, even anonymous sex." As for gay marriage, Sullivan says gay men have "a greater understanding of the need for extramarital outlets"![3]

Infidelity as a Fact of Life

Another well-known gay advocate, psychologist Eli Coleman, also advises young gay men that mature, long-term relationships must be realistic—meaning, he says, they must offer "freedom."[4] Dr. Coleman helped draft the 2001 Surgeon General's report on the nation's sexual health, and he is considered an expert on gay health issues.

Why should the gay world be so promiscuous? We believe this is due to the deficit-driven nature of homosexual attraction, which limits two men to constant cycles of infatuation that do not ripen into mature love. Loyal friendship, yes, but not mature, enduring, and sexually faithful love such as a man and a woman experience in a lifelong marriage.

There is also the inherent and unresolvable problem of two men coming together, when both are driven by masculine sexuality, which is by its very nature promiscuous. This is in contrast with the bond a man can form with a woman, who, by her feminine nature, grounds him and stabilizes him. At the same time, the married couple's biological children seal the union through blood.

And there is also a disturbing, "schizophrenic" inconsistency within male homosexuality, in which many gay men present two faces to the world—hanging on to the "good little boy" personality of childhood when in the straight world, then morphing into the sexual outlaw when in the company of other gay men. This phenomenon makes mature personality integration very difficult.

Researchers Mattison and McWhirter (a gay couple themselves—one a psychiatrist, the other a psychologist) confirm the observation that infidelity is characteristic of gay life. In their 1984 book *The Male Couple,* they describe their in-depth study of the quality and stability of long-term homosexual couplings. They studied 156 male couples in relationships that had lasted from one to thirty-seven years. Two-thirds of the respondents had entered the relationship with the expectation of fidelity. Of those 156 couples, not one was able to maintain sexual fidelity for more than five years.

The authors admit that sexual activity outside the relationship "often raises associated issues of trust, self esteem and dependency." However, they believe that "the capacity for mature intimacy does not preclude the possibility of sexual activity outside the couple's relationship as being psychologically healthy in the context of the gay subculture."[5] They conclude: "We believe that the single most important factor that keeps couples together past the ten-year mark is the lack of possessiveness they feel. Many couples learn very early in their relationship that ownership of each other sexually can become the greatest internal threat to their staying together."[6] In other words, a gay couple is likely doomed to split up if they expect faithfulness from their partner.

A study published in the *Journal of Sex Research* surveyed 2,585 homosexually active men. The study painted a dismal picture, especially for older gay men. Fully half of the men age forty and up were engaging in casual sex only. Half of the men age fifty and up were living alone, even though 62 percent of them had, at one time, been married. Very few of the men (14.7 percent) in the age group of forty to forty-nine were currently involved in a monogamous relationship. The average range of lifetime sexual partners for men over age fifty was between 101 and 500.[7]

Words of Advice: That "Quick Fix" Makes It Hard to Leave Gay Life

Gordon Opp, an ex-gay man who has been married for many years, has some words of advice from his own experience:

> I will look at a man who is attractive to me and I just can't proceed with pursuing that, because, as you might say, I "know the trick." That is, I know what the fan-

tasy is. I know what's behind the illusion. And I have the logical understanding that it's not going to satisfy—if I did pursue any type of sexual encounter, I know it would have nothing but negative effect on me.

But it's more than that, though. . . . It's recognizing that the whole experience is counterfeit. It's knowing this, based on my own repeated attempts for four years, to make it work.

The problem . . . is when you've already gotten into a habit pattern. The sexual experience is like taking an opium drug. It's soothing, it's anesthetizing, and it's a "quick fix." This can make it very difficult to leave homosexuality.

When we have sexualized those emotional needs—when we have already learned to get those needs temporarily met in a sexual way—we've taken a normal, legitimate, God-given need [same-sex intimacy] and met it with a "drug."

Then when you're getting your needs met through a straight relationship with a nice-looking guy, in a very wholesome relationship, it won't have the "zing" that the homosexual encounter does.

That's one of the things that I've had to recognize and admit to myself; it wasn't meant to have that kind of zing. The "zing" is artificial, but it is very compelling, and it is what keeps a lot of men in the gay life.[8]

Prevention Is Easier Than Healing

It is our conviction that, to live well, humankind must live in conformity with the natural order. Gender complementarity and heterosexuality are, we believe, foundational to that natural order. When we deny the importance of gender differences, we fail to respect an integral part of what makes us human.

No intervention can guarantee heterosexuality, of course. Nor can any parent—even the most dedicated—control every influence that contributes to his or her child's sexuality. But there remains much that *can* be done, and we believe it is the wise parent who listens to the stories that so many men tell us, over and over, about what was missing in their young lives.

Richard Wyler captures these men's experience—the feeling of reconnecting with the masculine self that leads to life-transforming change:

> Where once we felt sexual lust, today we feel brotherly love. Where once we felt fear of heterosexual men and estrangement from them, today we feel trust and authentic connection.
>
> Where once we felt self-hate and a feeling of never being "man enough," today we feel self acceptance and a strong and confident masculine identity.
>
> We experienced this profound change by uncovering and healing the under-

lying pain and alienation from men, masculinity and God that, we found, had caused so much of our homosexual symptoms. . . .

We can only speak for ourselves—about our own experience, about what was right for us, about what brought about change in our lives.

And what brought us joy. (<www.peoplecanchange.com>)

NOTES

Introduction

[1]Unless otherwise noted, references to "I" and "me" indicate Joseph Nicolosi.

[2]Charles W. Socarides, *Homosexuality: A Freedom Too Far* (Phoenix: Adam Margrave, 1995).

[3]Simon LeVay, *Queer Science* (Cambridge, Mass.: MIT Press, 1996), p. 224.

[4]Clinton Anderson, Office of Lesbian, Gay, and Bisexual Concerns, American Psychological Association, letter to NARTH, August 8, 2001.

[5]Ronald V. Bayer, *Homosexuality and American Psychiatry: The Politics of Diagnosis* (New York: BasicBooks, 1981), pp. 3-4.

[6]G. Rekers and M. Kilgus, "Differential Diagnosis and Rationale for Treatment of Gender Identity Disorders and Transvestism," in *Handbook of Child and Adolescent Sexual Problems,* ed. G. Rekers (New York: Lexington, 1995), pp. 267-68.

[7]Robert Redding, "Socio-Political Diversity in Psychology: A Case for Pluralism," *American Psychologist,* March 2001, p. 205-15.

Chapter 1: Masculinity Is an Achievement

[1]I have been interviewed by many TV interviewers over the past ten years, including Oprah Winfrey, Larry King, and Montel Williams, and my opinion has been sought by television newsmagazines such as ABC's *20/20* and the *CNN Medical Report.* I have also had an opportunity to speak with a wide spectrum of radio hosts and their callers on hundreds of talk shows.

[2]L. Newman, "Treatment for Parents of Feminine Boys," *American Journal of Psychiatry* 133, no. 6 (1976): 683.

[3]Charles W. Socarides, *Homosexuality: A Freedom Too Far* (Phoenix: Adam Margrave, 1995), p. 52; Joseph Nicolosi, *Reparative Therapy of Male Homosexuality: A New Clinical Approach* (Jason Aronson, 1991), xv-xvi.

[4]E. Abelin, "Some Further Observations and Comments on the Earliest Role of the Father," *International Journal of Psychoanalysis* 56 (1975): 293-302.; R. Greenson, "Dis-Identifying from Mother: Its Special Importance for the Boy," *International Journal of Psychoanalysis* 49 (1968): 370-74; I. Bieber et al., *Homosexuality: A Psychoanalytic Study of Male Homosexuals* (New York: BasicBooks, 1962); R. J. Stoller, "Boyhood Gender Aberrations: Treatment Issues," *Journal of the American Psychoanalytic Association* 27 (1979): 837-866; C. W. Socarides, "Abdicating Fathers, Homosexual Sons: Psychoanalytic Observations on the Contribution of the Father to the Development of Male Homosexuality," in *Father and Child: Developmental and Clinical Perspectives,* ed. S. H. Cath (Boston: Little, Brown, 1982), pp. 509-21; S. M. Wolfe, "Psychopathology and Psychodynamics of Parents of Boys with a Gender Identity Disorder of Childhood" (Ph.D. diss., City University of New York, 1990); Richard Green, *The "Sissy Boy Syndrome" and the Development of Homosexuality* (New Haven, Conn.: Yale University Press, 1987); Lawrence Hatterer, *Changing Homosexuality in the Male* (New York: McGraw-Hill, 1960); J. Fischhoff, "Preoedipal Influences in a Boy's Determination to Be 'Feminine' During the Oedipal Period," *Journal of the American Academy of Child Psychiatry* 3 (1964): 273-86.

[5]Not all gender-disturbed boys are remarkably good-looking, but Richard Green saw a connection and concluded that the more beautiful the boy, the more parents permitted and encouraged his effeminacy (Green, *"Sissy Boy Syndrome,"* pp. 64-68).

[6]See also G. A. Rekers et al., "Family Correlates of Male Childhood Gender Disturbance," *Journal of Genetic Psychology* 142 (1983): 31-42.

[7]P. A. Tyson, "Developmental Line of Gender Identity, Gender Role, and Choice of Love Object," *Journal of the American Psychoanalytic Association* 30 (1982): 61-68.

[8]Robert Stoller, *Presentations of Gender* (New Haven, Conn.: Yale University Press, 1985), p. 183.

[9]Richard Green, letter to author. During my research, I met Dr. Green at his office at UCLA. We disagreed on one important point: the disordered nature of the homosexual condition. But at one point I asked Dr. Green if he would want his son, then three years old, to grow up as a homosexual. "Oh, no," he said quickly. "His life would be too difficult."

[10]Socarides, *Homosexuality.*

[11]R. J. Stoller, *The Transsexual Experiment,* vol. 2 of *Sex and Gender* (London: Hogarth, 1975), p. 24.

[12]S. Coates, "Extreme Boyhood Femininity: Overview and New Research Findings," in *Sexuality: New Perspectives,* ed. Z. DeFries, R. C. Friedman, and R. Corn (Westport, Conn.: Greenwood, 1985), pp. 101-24; S. Coates, "Ontogenesis of Boyhood Gender Identity Disorder," *Journal of the American Academy of Psychoanalysis* 18 (1990): 414-38; S. Coates, "The Etiology of Boyhood Gender Identity Disorder: An Integrative Model," in *Interface of Psychoanalysis and Psychology,* eds. J. W. Barron, M. N. Eagle, and D. L. Wolitzky (Washington, D.C.: American Psychological Association, 1992), pp. 245-65; S. Coates, R. C. Friedman, and S. Wolfe, "The Etiology of Boyhood Gender Identity Disorder: A Model for Integrating Temperament, Development, and Psychodynamics," *Psychoanalytic Dialogues* 1 (1991): 481-523; S. Coates and E. S. Person, "Extreme Boyhood Femininity: Isolated Behavior or Pervasive Disorder?" *Journal of the American Academy of Child Psychiatry* 24 (1985): 702-9; S. Coates and S. M. Wolfe, "Gender Identity Disorder in Boys: The Interface of Constitution and Early Experience," *Psychoanalytic Inquiry* 15 (1995): 6-38; S. Marantz and S. Coates, "Mothers of Boys with Gender Identity Disorder: A Comparison of Matched Controls," *Journal of the American Academy of Child and Adolescent Psychiatry* 30 (1991): 310-15; B. Thacher, "A Mother's Role in the Evolution of Gender Dysphoria: The Initial Phase of Joint Treatment in the Psychotherapy of a Four-Year-Old Boy Who Wanted to Be a Girl" (paper presented at the meeting of the Division of Psychoanalysis, American Psychological Association, New York, April 1985); Green, *"Sissy Boy Syndrome."*

[13]Abelin, "Some Further Observations," 293-302; R. Greenspan, "The 'Second Other': The Role of the Father in Early Personality Formation and the Dyadic-Phallic Phase of Development," in *Father and Child;* Greenson, "Dis-identifying from Mother," pp. 370-74; A. J. Horner, "The Role of the Female Therapist in the Affirmation of Gender in Male Patients," *Journal of the American Academy of Psychoanalysis* 20 (winter 1992): 599-610; Socarides, *Homosexuality;* J. Snortum et al., "Family Dynamics and Homosexuality," *Psychological Reports* 24 (1969): 763-70.

[14]G. van den Aardweg, *On the Origins and Treatment of Homosexuality: A Psychoanalytic Reinterpretation* (Westport, Conn.: Praeger, 1986).

[15]A. P. Bell, N. S. Weinberg, and S. K. Hammersmith, *Sexual Preference: Its Development in Men and Women* (Bloomington: Indiana University Press, 1981).

[16]Ibid., p. 76.

[17]Snortum et al., "Family Dynamics and Homosexuality," pp. 763-70.

[18]Finkelhor found that half of the college men in his study who were currently involved in homosexual activity reported a childhood sexual experience with an older man. He hypothesized that boys molested by older men may label the event as a homosexual experience and therefore label themselves as homosexual. These boys will then reinforce the homosexual label through further homosexual behav-

ior (D. Finkelhor, *Sexually Victimized Children* [New York: Free Press, 1979]).

[19]See also D. J. West, "Parental Figures in the Genesis of Male Homosexuality," *International Journal of Social Psychiatry* 5 (1959): 85-97.

[20]For examples of the poor father-son relationship, some in the clinical literature, some autobiographical, see W. Aaron, *Straight* (New York: Bantam, 1972); J. R. Ackerly, *My Father and Myself* (New York: Poseidon, 1968); M. Boyd, *Take Off the Masks* (Philadelphia: New Society, 1984); Greg Louganis, *Breaking the Surface* (New York: Plume, 1996); G. A. Rekers et al., "Family Correlates of Male Childhood Gender Disturbance," *Journal of Genetic Psychology* 142 (1985): 31-42; Andrew Sullivan, *Virtually Normal* (New York: Vintage, 1996); Fischhoff, "Preoedipal Influences," pp. 273-86.

Chapter 2: The Prehomosexual Boy

[1]Daryl Bem cites a study by Bell et al.(*Sexual Preference: Its Development in Men and Women* [Bloomington: Indiana University Press, 1981]) describing path analyses that show "gender non-conformity in childhood was a causal antecedent of later sexual orientation for both men and women"—with the usual caveat that even path analysis cannot "prove" causality. Bem writes that "prospective studies have come to the same conclusion. The largest of these (Green, Richard, 1987, *The Sissy Boy Syndrome*) involved a sample of 66 gender-nonconforming and 56 gender-conforming boys with a mean age of 7.1 years. The researchers were able to assess about two-thirds of each group in late adolescence or early adulthood, finding that about 75% of the previously gender-nonconforming boys were either bisexual or homosexual compared to only one (4%) of the gender-conforming boys. This body of data may be the most consistent, well-documented and significant finding in the entire field of sexual-orientation research and perhaps in all of human psychology. . . . It is difficult to think of other individual differences (besides IQ or sex itself) that so strongly predict socially significant outcomes across the life span." Daryl J. Bem, "Exotic Becomes Erotic: A Developmental Theory of Sexual Orientation," *Psychological Review* 103, no. 2 (1995): 322-323.

[2]K. Zucker and S. Bradley, *Gender Identity Disorder and Psychosexual Problems in Children and Adolescents* (New York: Guilford, 1995), p. 282.

[3]See "Gay Genes Revisited: Doubts Arise over Research on the Biology of Homosexuality," *Scientific American,* November 1995, p. 26, a kind of apology from the editors for having trumpeted "discoveries" of gay genes and gay brains in previous issues. In this short piece the editors of *Scientific American* say that, so far, there is no scientific evidence of a gay gene or a gay brain. Ruth Hubbard—a board member of the Council for Responsible Genetics, professor emeritus of biology at Harvard, and the author of *Exploding the Gene Myth*—told a Boston writer, Matthew Brelis, that searching for a gay gene is not even a worthwhile pursuit. "Let me be very clear: I don't think any single gene governs any complex human behavior. There are genetic components in everything we do, and it is foolish to say genes are not involved, but I don't think they are decisive" (Matthew Brelis, "The Fading Gay Gene," *Boston Globe,* February 7, 1999).

[4]Alan Medinger, *Growth into Manhood: Resuming the Journey* (Colorado Springs, Colo.: WaterBrook, 2000), pp. 1-9.

[5]Richard Fitzgibbons and Joseph Nicolosi, "When Boys Won't Be Boys: Gender Identity Disorder in Children," *Lay Witness,* June 2001, p. 21.

[6]Kenneth Zucker and Susan Bradley, *Gender Identity Disorder and Psychosexual Problems in Children and Adolescents* (New York: Guilford, 1995). While not conceding homosexuality to be a problem in itself, Zucker believes treatment of the GID child is justified.

[7]M. L. Lalumière, R. Blanchard, and K. L. Zucker, "Sexual Orientation and Handedness in Men and Women: A Meta-Analysis," *Psychological Bulletin* 126, no. 4 (2000): 575-92.

[8]N. E. Whitehead, "Is There a Link Between Left-Handedness and Homosexuality?" *NARTH Bulletin,*

December 2000, p. 10.

[9]G. Rekers, O. Lovaas, and B. Low, "Behavioral Treatment of Deviant Sex Role Behaviors in a Male Child," *Journal of Applied Behavioral Analysis* 7 (1974): 134-51.

[10]Lawrence E. Newman, "Treatment for the Parents of Effeminate Boys," *American Journal of Psychiatry* 133, no. 6 (1996): 687.

[11]K. Zucker, "Gender Identity Disorder in the DSM-IV," *Journal of Sex and Marital Therapy* 25 (1999): 5-9.

[12]J. Bailey, M. Dunne, and N. Martin, "Genetic and Environmental Influences on Sexual Orientation and Its Correlates in an Australian Twin Sample," *Journal of Personality and Social Psychology* 78, no. 3 (1997): 524-36.

[13]This initiation is played out rather dramatically in cultures such as that of the Sambia tribe of New Guinea. This tribe places great value on masculinity. Its men believe that their young men's masculinity is threatened by too much intimacy with their mothers. During their rites of passage into manhood, they are taken away from their mothers and sisters and initiated in rituals that are sometimes brutal and frightening to outsiders—until they achieve their goal, that the young men learn to become brave and manly and, ultimately, good husbands and fathers. The Sambian rite of initiation illustrates these points: (1) prolonged identification with their mother is a threat to the boys' masculinity; (2) masculinity can only be transmitted by other men; and (3) masculinity is a prized commodity that can be achieved only with effort, not something simply endowed on the young men when they reach puberty. Robert Stoller and George Herdt, "Development of Masculinity: A Cross-Cultural Contribution," *Journal of the American Psychology Association* 30 (1981): 29-59.

[14]Linda Ames Nicolosi, "Some Psychologists Say Bisexuality Opens Up New Possibilities for Creative Expression," *NARTH Bulletin,* August 2001, p. 8.

[15]Brian Camenker, *The Homosexual Agenda in Massachusetts Schools* (Newton, Mass.: Parents' Rights Coalition), audiocassette. This tape is available by calling (781) 433-7106.

[16]Charles W. Socarides, *Homosexuality: A Freedom Too Far* (Phoenix: Adam Margrave, 1995), pp. 34-35, reports that "there was a real run on transsexual operations in the 1960s and 1970s. But those operations have come under a cloud. Not many of Dr. [John] Money's associates [at Johns Hopkins University] are advocating them any more . . . because they cannot have failed to notice that many of these operations failed to help people."

[17]Elaine Siegel, *Middle Class Waifs: The Psychodynamic Treatment of Affectively Disturbed Children* (Hillsdale, N.J.: Analytic, 1991), p. 69.

[18]Daryl Bem, "Exotic Becomes Erotic: A Developmental Theory of Sexual Orientation," *Psychological Review* 103, no. 2 (1996): 320-35.

[19]American Psychiatric Association, *Diagnostic and Statistical Manual,* 4th ed. (Washington, D.C.: American Psychiatric Association, 1994), p. 532; see also Newman, "Treatment for the Parents of Effeminate Boys," *American Journal of Psychiatry* 133, no. 6 (1976): 683.

By the way, it may seem ironic to you (it does to us) that the APA still acknowledges gender-identity disorder of *childhood* as a problem but then considers its *adult* manifestation (homosexuality) perfectly normal. Gay activists recognize that logical inconsistency too. And so they have made increasingly vocal efforts in recent years to force the removal of GID from the psychiatric manual.

[20]Richard Green, *The "Sissy Boy Syndrome" and the Development of Homosexuality* (New Haven, Conn.: Yale University Press, 1987).

[21]Melissa Healy, "Pieces of the Puzzle," *Los Angeles Times,* May 21, 2001, p. S1.

[22]Green, *"Sissy Boy Syndrome,"* pp. 15-16.

[23]I. Bieber and T. B. Bieber, "Male Homosexuality," *Canadian Journal of Psychiatry* 24 (1979): 409-21. Also, S. Hadden speaks of social and physical inadequacy and fear of physical injury in "Group Psycho-

therapy of Male Homosexuals," *Current Psychiatric Theories* 6 (1966): 177-86. I. Sipova and A. Brzek write about gays as "perpetual outsiders" in "Parental and Interpersonal Relationship of Transsexual and Masculine and Feminine Homosexual Men," *Journal of Homosexuality* 9 (1983): 75-84. N. Thompson et al. write about male rejection in "Parent-Child Relationships and Sexual Identity in Male and Female Homosexuals and Heterosexuals," *Journal of Consulting and Clinical Psychology* 4 (1973): 120-27. Similarly, G. van den Aardweg writes about poor self-esteem and the common feeling among GID boys that they are not virile like other boys in *Homosexuality and Hope: A Psychologist Talks About Treatment and Change* (Ann Arbor, Mich.: Servant, 1985).

[24]Joseph Nicolosi, *Reparative Therapy of Male Homosexuality: A New Clinical Approach* (Northvale, N.J.: Jason Aronson, 1991), pp. 58, 63.

[25]S. Coates, R. C. Friedman, and S. Wolfe, "The Etiology of Boyhood Gender Identity Disorder: A Model for Integrating Temperament, Development, and Psychodynamics," *Psychoanalytic Dialogues* 1 (1991): 483.

[26]K. Zucker and S. Bradley, *Gender Identity Disorder and Psychosexual Problems in Children and Adolescents* (New York: Guilford, 1995), p. 22.

[27]Richard Fitzgibbons, "The Origins and Therapy of Same-Sex Attraction Disorder," in *Homosexuality and American Public Life*, ed. Christopher Wolfe (Dallas: Spence, 1999).

[28]Zucker and Bradley, *Gender Identity Disorder*, p. 22, state that although a number of studies find poor coordination, they themselves more consistently observe a fear and aversion toward rough-and-tumble play but not necessarily poor coordination, as some such boys do quite well in noncontact sports, such as swimming.

[29]A. D. Pellegrini, "What Is a Category? The Case of Rough-and-Tumble Play," *Ethology and Sociobiology* 10 (1989): 331-41; P. K. Smith and M. Boulton, "Rough-and-Tumble Play, Aggression, and Dominance: Perception and Behaviour in Children's Encounters," *Human Development* 33 (1990): 271-82; A. Costabile et al., "Cross-national Comparison of How Children Distinguish Serious and Playful Fighting," *Developmental Psychology* 27 (1991): 881-87.

[30]G. van den Aardweg, *On the Origins and Treatment of Homosexuality: A Psychoanalytic Reinterpretation* (New York: Praeger, 1986).

[31]R. G. Slaby and K. S. Frey, "Development of Gender Constancy and Selective Attention to Same-Sex Models," *Child Development* 46 (1975): 849-56.

[32]Daryl Bem, "Exotic Becomes Erotic: A Developmental Theory of Sexual Orientation," *Psychological Review* 103, no. 2 (1996): 320-35.

[33]G. van den Aardweg, "Parents of Homosexuals—Not Guilty? Interpretation of Childhood Psychological Data," *American Journal of Psychotherapy* 38 (1984): 180-89.

[34]Justin Richardson, "Setting Limits on Gender Health," *Harvard Review of Psychiatry* 4 (1996): 49-53.

Chapter 3: Born This Way?

[1]Linda Ames Nicolosi, "NARTH Member Answers Ann Landers," *NARTH Bulletin,* December 1996, p. 5.

[2]Neil Whitehead, "The Importance of Twin Studies," *NARTH Bulletin,* April 2001, p. 26.

[3]S. LeVay, "A Difference in Hypothalamic Structure Between Heterosexual and Homosexual Men," *Science* 258 (1991): 1034-37.

[4]Quoted in David Nimmons, "Sex and the Brain," *Discover,* March 1994, pp. 64-71.

[5]Mubarak Dahir, "Why Are We Gay?" *The Advocate,* July 17, 2001, p. 38.

[6]D. H. Hamer et al., "A Linkage Between DNA Markers on the X Chromosome and Male Sexual Orientation," *Science* 261 (1993): 321-27.

[7]G. Rice et al., "Male Homosexuality: Absence of Linkage to Microsatellite Markers at Xq28," *Science* 284 (1999): 665-67.

[8]John Horgan, "Gay Genes, Revisited: Doubts Arise over Research on the Biology of Homosexuality," *Scientific American*, November 1995, p. 26.

[9]D. Hamer and P. Copeland, *Living with Our Genes: Why They Matter More Than You Think* (New York: Bantam Doubleday Dell, 1998), p. 188.

[10]J. M. Bailey and R. C. Pillard, "A Genetic Study of Male Sexual Orientation," *Archives of General Psychiatry* 48 (1991):1081-96.

[11]Whitehead, "Importance of Twin Studies," p. 26, emphasis added.

[12]Neil Whitehead, "What Is the Genetic Contribution to Homosexuality?" *NARTH Bulletin*, December 1999, p. 22.

[13]Ibid., p. 26.

[14]R. Lerner and Althea Nagai, *No Basis: What the Studies Don't Tell Us About Same-Sex Parenting* (Washington, D.C.: The Marriage Law Project, 2001).

[15]Quoted in "Preventing Parenting: A Florida Judge Upholds Florida's Ban on Adoption by Gays," *The Advocate*, October 9, 2001, p. 15.

[16]Christopher Rosik, "Conversion Therapy Revisited: Parameters and Rationale for Ethical Care," *Journal of Pastoral Care* 55, no. 1 (2001): 47-67.

[17]Association for Clinical Pastoral Education, summary report of the actions of the Board of Representatives meeting, spring 2001.

[18]W. Byne and B. Parsons, "Human Sexual Orientation: The Biologic Theories Reappraised," *Archives of General Psychiatry* 50 (March 1993): 228-39; theory is paraphrased here.

[19]Judd Marmor, "Overview: The Multiple Roots of Homosexual Behavior," in *Homosexual Behavior: A Modern Reappraisal*, ed. J. Marmor (New York: BasicBooks, 1980), p. 9.

[20]For further information, see NARTH's fact sheet titled "Is There a Gay Gene?" Online, go to the NARTH website <www.narth.com>.

[21]American Psychological Association, "Answers to Your Questions About Sexual Orientation and Homosexuality" (pamphlet).

[22]Parents and Friends of Lesbians and Gays, "Why Ask Why? Addressing the Research on Homosexuality and Biology" (booklet, 1995), prepared with the assistance of the American Psychological Association's Clinton Anderson.

[23]Steven Goldberg, *When Wish Replaces Thought: Why So Much of What You Believe Is False* (Buffalo, N.Y.: Prometheus, 1994), p. 63.

[24]J. Satinover, "Reflections from Jeffrey Satinover," *NARTH Bulletin*, April 1995, p. 3.

[25]S. LeVay, "Sexual Orientation: The Science and Its Social Impact," forthcoming in *Reverso*. The article is also available online <http://members.aol.com/_ht_a/slevay/page12.html.> LeVay's article provides an in-depth summary of the current scientific evidence for a biological (prenatal hormonal as well as genetic) influence on gender nonconformity—and subsequent homosexuality—in some people. We believe it overstates the case for the effect of biological influence and for the inevitability of a homosexual outcome.

[26]Jeffrey Satinover, "The Gay Gene?" *Journal of Human Sexuality*, ed. G. Rekers (Addison, Tex.: Lewis & Stanley, 1996), p. 3.

[27]Ann Landers, "Lesbian Daughter Needs to Know She Is Accepted," syndicated newspaper column, September 28, 2001.

Chapter 4: All in the Family

[1]Richard Green, *The "Sissy Boy Syndrome" and the Development of Homosexuality* (New Haven, Conn.: Yale University Press, 1987).

[2]"Child Psychiatrist Encourages Gender Blending," *NARTH Bulletin*, August 1998, p. 11.

[3]I. Bieber et al., *Homosexuality: A Psychoanalytic Study of Male Homosexuals* (New York: BasicBooks, 1962). See chap. 6, "The Triangular System."

[4]Jack Nichols, *The Gay Agenda: Talking Back to the Fundamentalists* (New York: Prometheus, 1996), p. 112.

[5]Richard Fitzgibbons, "The Power of Peer Rejection," *NARTH Bulletin,* August 1997, p. 3.

[6]Bieber et al., *Homosexuality*; R. Evans, "Childhood Parental Relationships of Homosexual Men," *Journal of Consulting and Clinical Psychology* 33 (1969):129-135; Judd Marmor, "Overview: The Multiple Roots of Homosexual Behavior," in *Homosexual Behavior: A Modern Reappraisal,* ed. J. Marmor (New York: BasicBooks, 1980), pp. 20-21; C. Socarides, *The Overt Homosexual* (New York: Grune & Stratton, 1968).

[7]Anita Worthen and Bob Davies, *Someone I Love Is Gay* (Downers Grove, Ill.: InterVarsity Press, 1996), p. 119.

[8]R. Stoller, "Healthy Parental Influences on the Earliest Development of Masculinity in Baby Boys," *Psychoanalytic Forum* 5 (1975): 232-62.

[9]J. E. Bates et al., "Gender Abnormalities in Boys: An Analysis of Clinical Ratings," *Journal of Abnormal Child Psychology* 2 (1974): 1-16.

[10]S. Coates and E. S. Person, "Extreme Boyhood Femininity: Isolated Behavior or Pervasive Disorder?" *Journal of the American Academy of Child Psychiatry* 24, no. 6 (1985): 702-9; G. A. Rekers and J. J. Swihart, "The Association of Identity Disorder with Parental Separation," *Psychological Reports* 65 (1989): 1272-74; Bieber et al., *Homosexuality*; M. Saghir and E. Robins, *Male and Female Homosexuality* (Baltimore: Williams & Wilkins, 1973).

[11]G. A. Rekers et al., "Family Correlates of Male Childhood Gender Disturbance," *Journal of Genetic Psychology* 142 (1983): 31-42.

[12]Gregory Dickson, "Environmental Factors and the Development of Male Homosexuality" (doctoral thesis, Fuller Theological Seminary, 1997).

[13]S. Fisher and G. Greenberg, *Freud Scientifically Reappraised: Testing the Theories and Therapy* (New York: Wiley, 1996), p. 135; see pages 135-39 for discussion of mothers and fathers.

[14]Rock Hudson and Sara Davidson, *Rock Hudson: His Story* (New York: William Morrow, 1986), p. 130.

[15]Andrew Sullivan, *Virtually Normal* (New York: Alfred A. Knopf, 1995), p. 9.

[16]Judy Shepard in a fund-raising letter sent out on behalf of P-FLAG, 2000.

[17]Bieber et al., *Homosexuality,* corroborates this observation.

[18]Kenneth Zucker and Susan Bradley, *Gender Identity Disorder and Psychosexual Problems in Children and Adolescents* (New York: Guilford, 1995).

[19]R. Green, *Sexual Identity Conflict in Children and Adults* (New York: BasicBooks, 1974); Green, *"Sissy Boy Syndrome"*; C. W. Roberts et al., "Boyhood Gender Identity Development: A Statistical Contrast of Two Family Groups," *Psychology* 23 (1987): 544-57.

[20]J. Money and A. Russo, "Homosexual Outcome of Discordant Gender Identity/Role in Childhood: Longitudinal Follow-up," *Journal of Pediatric Psychology* 4 (1979): 29-41.

[21]P. R. Miller, "The Effeminate, Passive, Obligatory Homosexual," *AMA Archives of Neurology and Psychiatry* 80 (1958): 612-18.

[22]Green, *"Sissy Boy Syndrome"*; Zucker and Bradley, *Gender Identity Disorder.*

[23]Green, *Sexual Identity Conflict.*

[24]Fitzgibbons, "Power of Peer Rejection," p. 3.

[25]Joseph Nicolosi, "Fathers of Male Homosexuals: A Collective Clinical Profile," *NARTH Bulletin,* April 1997, p. 7.

[26]Philip Gambone, "Not Crying for Dad," *James White Review,* spring 2000, p. 5.

[27]Kenneth Zucker and Susan Bradley, *Gender Identity Disorder and Psychosexual Problems in Children and*

Adolescents (New York: Guilford, 1995).

[28]Ibid., p. 263.

Chapter 5: Friends and Feelings

[1]Andrew Sullivan, *Virtually Normal* (New York: Knopf, 1995).

[2]B. I. Fagot, "Beyond the Reinforcement Principle: Another Step Toward Understanding Sex Role Development," *Developmental Psychology* 21 (1985): 1097-104.

[3]R. C. Friedman, *Male Homosexuality: A Contemporary Psychoanalytic Perspective* (New Haven, Conn.: Yale University Press, 1988), esp. chap. 5.

[4]Ibid.; see also A. P. Bell, N. S. Weinberg, and S. K. Hammersmith, *Sexual Preference: Its Development in Men and Women* (Bloomington: Indiana University Press, 1981).

[5]R. Fitzgibbons, "The Power of Peer Rejection: Interview with Richard Fitzgibbons," *NARTH Bulletin,* August 1997, p. 3; Gerald van den Aardweg, *Homosexuality and Hope* (Ann Arbor, Mich.: Servant, 1995).

[6]Tom Hess, "It's a Gay World After All?" *Citizen,* July 2001, p. 14.

[7]James Saslow, in Mark Thompson, *Gay Soul: Finding the Heart of Gay Spirit and Nature, with Sixteen Writers, Healers, Teachers and Visionaries* (San Francisco: Harper, 1994), pp. 133-47.

[8]Camille Paglia, "The Biological Nature of Homosexuality and the Psychological Development of Gay Men and Lesbians" (symposium at the Harvard Medical School, Cambridge, Mass., March 1993), reprinted in *Harvard Gay and Lesbian Review* 4, no. 3 (1997): 3.

[9]Daryl Bem, "Exotic Becomes Erotic: A Developmental Theory of Sexual Orientation," *Psychological Review* 103, no. 2 (1996): 332.

[10]Andrew Harvey, in Thompson, *Gay Soul,* p. 56.

[11]James Broughton, in Thompson, *Gay Soul,* p. 13.

[12]Andrew Harvey, in Thompson, *Gay Soul,* p. 71.

[13]Dale O'Leary, "Destabilizing the Categories of Sex and Gender," *NARTH Bulletin,* December 2000, p. 22.

[14]Ibid.

[15]Richard Fitzgibbons and J. Nicolosi, "When Boys Won't Be Boys: Gender Identity Disorder in Children," *Lay Witness,* June 2001, p. 21.

[16]Bem, "Exotic Becomes Erotic."

[17]Joseph Nicolosi, *Reparative Therapy of Male Homosexuality: A New Clinical Approach* (Northvale, N.J.: Jason Aronson, 1991), p. 94.

[18]William Aaron, *Straight* (New York: Bantam, 1972), pp. 21-22, 29.

[19]Malcolm Boyd, *Take Off the Masks* (Philadelphia: New Society, 1984), p. 34.

[20]Linda Nicolosi, "A Mother's Letter to NARTH," *NARTH Bulletin,* December 1998, p. 11.

[21]Linda Nicolosi, "Planned Parenthood Encourages Valuing of Homosexuality," *NARTH Bulletin,* April 1999, p. 11.

[22]G. A. Rekers, *Handbook of Child and Adolescent Sexual Problems* (New York: Lexington, 1995).

Chapter 6: Confronting Adolescence

[1]This psychologist's observations are corroborated by similar accounts from school counselors in "Teens Ponder: Gay, Bi, Straight?" *Washington Post,* July 15, 1993.

[2]Amy C. Butler, "Trends in Same-Gender Sexual Partnering, 1988-1989," *Journal of Sex Research* 37 (2000): 333-43.

[3]"Psychiatrist 'Reassures' Parents About Lesbian Experimentation," *NARTH Bulletin,* December 1997, p. 12, reporting from "Elite Schools Face the Gay Issue," *New York Times,* June 13, 1997, p. B7-8.

[4]R. F. C. Kourany, "Suicide Among Homosexual Adolescents," *Journal of Homosexuality* 13 (1987): 111-17; K. Erwin, "Interpreting the Evidence: Competing Paradigms and the Emergence of Lesbian and Gay Suicide as a 'Social Fact,'" *International Journal of Health Services* 23 (1993): 437-53; S. Prenzlauer, J. Drescher, and R. Winchel, "Suicide Among Homosexual Youth," letter to the editor, *American Journal of Psychiatry* 149 (1992): 1416; G. Remafedi, "Adolescent Homosexuality: Psychosocial and Medical Implications," *Pediatrics* 79 (1987): 331-37; G. Remafedi et al., "Demography of Sexual Orientation in Adolescents," *Pediatrics* 89 (1992): 714-21; S. G. Schneider, N. L. Farberow, and G. Kruks, "Suicidal Behavior in Adolescent and Adult Gay Men," *Suicide and Life-Threatening Behavior* 19 (1989): 381-94; C. L. Rich et al., "San Diego Suicide Study: Comparison of Gay to Straight Males," *Suicide and Life-Threatening Behavior* 16 (1986): 448-57.

[5]D. Fergusson et al., "Is Sexual Orientation Related to Mental Health Problems and Suicidality in Young People?" *Archives of General Psychiatry* 56, no. 10 (1999): 875-80.

[6]Peter LaBarbera, "Gay Youth Suicide: Myth Is Used to Promote Homosexual Agenda" (Washington, D.C.: Family Research Council, pamphlet).

[7]G. Remafedi, J. Farrow, and R. Deisher, "Risk Factors for Attempted Suicide in Gay and Bisexual Youth," *Pediatrics* 87 (1991): 869-75.

[8]A. Bell, M. Weinberg and S. Hammersmith, *Sexual Preference* (Bloomington: Indiana University Press, 1981).

[9]Dale O'Leary, "Gay Teens and Attempted Suicide," *NARTH Bulletin,* December 1999, p. 11.

[10]J. Satinover, "Reflections from Jeffrey Satinover," *NARTH Bulletin,* April 1995, p. 3.

[11]J. Nicolosi, *Reparative Therapy of Male Homosexuality* (Northvale, N.J.: Jason Aronson, 1991), pp. 68-70.

[12]E. O. Laumann et al., *The Social Organization of Sexuality: Sexual Practices in the U.S.* (Chicago: University of Chicago Press, 1994).

[13]G. Remafedi et al., "Demography of Sexual Orientation," pp. 714-21.

[14]"The Adolescent Brain: A Perilous Renovation," *Family Therapy Networker,* January–February 2001, p. 15.

[15]"L.A. Studies Show Increase in Risky Sex by Gay Men," *Los Angeles Times,* February 17, 2001, p. 11.

[16]D. Haney, "Young Gay Black Men Suffer High HIV Rates," Associated Press, February 6, 2001.

[17]Ibid.

[18]"HIV Rate Rising Among Gay Men in San Francisco," *Los Angeles Times,* January 25, 2001, p. A3.

[19]Anita Worthen and Bob Davies, *Someone I Love Is Gay* (Downers Grove, Ill.: InterVarsity Press, 1996), chap. 6.

[20]Laumann et al., *Social Organization of Sexuality,* p. 344.

[21]Martin Mansovitz, "Early Sexual Behavior in Adult Homosexual and Heterosexual Males," *Journal of Abnormal Psychology* 76 (1970): 396-402.

[22]M. Tomeo, "Comparative Data of Childhood and Adolescence Molestation in Heterosexual and Homosexual Persons," *Archives of Sexual Behavior* 30, no. 5 (2001): 535-41.

[23]Bruce Rind, "Gay and Bisexual Adolescent Boys' Sexual Experiences with Men: An Empirical Examination of Psychological Correlates in a Nonclinical Sample," *Archives of Sexual Behavior* 30, no. 4 (2001): 345-67.

[24]Los Angeles Unified School District, *Project 10 Manual,* 1987.

[25]Linda Nicolosi, "Pamphlet to Schools Discourages Reorientation Therapy," *NARTH Bulletin,* April 1999, p. 1.

[26]Richard Friedman and Lenore Stern, "Juvenile Aggressivity and Sissiness in Homosexual and Heterosexual Males," *Journal of the American Academy of Psychoanalysis* 8, no. 3 (1980): 433.

[27]Ibid., p. 437.

[28]Joseph Nicolosi, A. Dean Byrd, and Richard W. Potts, "Retrospective Self-Reports of Changes in Ho-

mosexual Orientation: A Consumer Survey of Conversion Therapy Clients," *Psychological Reports* 86 (June 2000): 1071-88.

[29]Joseph Nicolosi, A. Dean Byrd, and Richard W. Potts, "Beliefs and Practices of Therapists Who Practice Sexual Reorientation Psychotherapy," *Psychological Reports* 86 (April 2000): 689-702.

[30]Other famous personalities described as gay without definitive evidence include Leonardo da Vinci, Michelangelo, James Dean, George Frederick Handel, Marlon Brando, Henry James, William Shakespeare, Sigmund Freud, Marilyn Monroe, Gustav Mahler, Greta Garbo, Henry David Thoreau, Leo Tolstoy, Napoleon Bonaparte, Johann Wolfgang von Goethe, Amelia Earhart, Claude Debussy, and Robert Louis Stevenson.

[31]D. McWhirter and A. Mattison, *The Male Couple: How Relationships Develop* (Englewood Cliffs, N.J.: Prentice-Hall, 1984).

[32]For a critique of the book *Biological Exuberance: A Study of Diversity*, which uses animal same-sex behavior as a model for the normality of human homosexuality, see James Phelan, "Is Homosexuality Normal for Some Animals?" *NARTH Bulletin,* August 1999, p. 19.

[33]John and Anne Paulk, *Love Won Out* (Wheaton, Ill.: Tyndale House, 1999).

[34]T. Sandfort et al., "Same-Sex Sexual Behavior and Psychiatric Disorders: Findings from the Netherlands Mental Health Survey and Incidence Study (NEMESIS)," *Archives of General Psychiatry* 58 (2001): 85-91.

[35]Thomas Gregory, "The Power of Peer Rejection: Interview with Richard Fitzgibbons, M.D.," <www.narth.com>.

[36]Dr. Robert Spitzer, interview by Reichenberg Fellowship, videotape, New York City, February 29, 2000.

[37]Warren Smith, "In This Life We Struggle," *Charlotte (N.C.) World,* August 31, 2001, p. 3.

[38]Alan Medinger, *Growth into Manhood: Resuming the Journey* (Colorado Springs, Colo.: WaterBrook, 2000), p. 240.

Chapter 7: From Tomboys to Lesbians

[1]Linda Ames Nicolosi, "One Woman's Struggle: Interview with Jane Boyer," *NARTH Bulletin,* August 1999, p. 3.

[2]Linda Ames Nicolosi, "Interview: Diane Eller-Boyko," *NARTH Bulletin,* April 1998, p. 3.

[3]Elaine Siegel, *Female Homosexuality, Choice Without Volition: A Psychoanalytic Study* (Hillsdale, N.J.: Analytic, 1988).

[4]Linda Ames Nicolosi, "Elaine Siegel on Lesbianism," *NARTH Bulletin,* December 1996, p. 3.

[5]Siegel, *Female Homosexuality,* p. 537.

[6]Gerald Schoenewolf, "Gender Narcissism and Its Manifestations," *NARTH Collected Papers,* 1996 <www.narth.com>.

[7]Ibid.

[8]Richard Fitzgibbons, "The Origins of Same-Sex Attraction Disorder," in *Homosexuality and American Public Life,* ed. Christopher Wolfe (Dallas: Spence, 1999), pp. 85-97.

[9]C. Socarides, *Homosexuality: A Freedom Too Far* (Phoenix: Adam Margrave, 1995), p. 279.

[10]G. A. Rekers and S. Mead, "Early Intervention for Female Sexual Identity Disturbance: Self-Monitoring of Play Behavior," *Journal of Abnormal Child Psychology* 7 (1979): 405-23.

[11]M. Saghir and E. Robins, *Male and Female Homosexuality* (Baltimore: Williams & Wilkins, 1973).

[12]Selma Fraiberg, *The Magic Years: Understanding and Handling the Problems of Early Childhood* (New York: Scribner, 1959), pp. 231-32.

[13]Saghir and Robins, *Male and Female Homosexuality.*

[14]Rekers and Mead, "Early Intervention," pp. 405-23.

[15]Robert Stoller, "The Sense of Femaleness," *Psychoanalytic Quarterly* 37 (1968): 42-55.

[16]Kenneth Zucker and Susan Bradley, *Gender Identity Disorder and Psychosexual Problems in Children and Adolescents* (New York: Guilford, 1995), p. 252.

[17]Ibid., p. 253.

[18]Ibid.

[19]Carol Brockmon, "A Feminist View of Sado-Masochism in the Nineties," *In the Family* 3, no. 4 (1998): 11.

[20]Ibid.

[21]Anita Worthen and Bob Davies, *Someone I Love Is Gay* (Downers Grove, Ill.: InterVarsity Press, 1996), p. 83. See pages 82-94 for a chapter on sexual abuse.

[22]Andria Sigler-Smalz, "Understanding the Lesbian Client," *NARTH Bulletin,* April 2001, p. 12.

[23]A. P. Bell, N. S. Weinberg, and S. K. Hammersmith, *Sexual Preference: Its Development in Men and Women* (Bloomington: Indiana University Press, 1981).

[24]Linda Nicolosi, "Interview: Diane Eller-Boyko," p. 3.

[25]Chastity Bono, *Family Outing* (New York: Little, Brown, 1999), p. 7.

[26]Richard Fitzgibbons, "The Origins and Therapy of Same-Sex Attraction Disorder," *NARTH Bulletin,* December 2000, p. 3.

[27]Linda Nicolosi, "Interview: Diane Eller-Boyko," p. 3.

Chapter 8: The Politics of Treatment

[1]In an article in the "Notes and Comment" section of *American University Law Review,* editor Karolyn Ann Hicks argued against the parental right to influence a child's sexual orientation. Karolyn Ann Hicks, "Reparative Therapy: Whether Parental Attempts to Change a Child's Sexual Orientation Can Legally Constitute Child Abuse," *American University Law Review* 49 (December 1999): 505-47.

[2]"Breast Is Best—for Adoptive Moms and Dads, Too!" *Alternative Family,* March-April 2000, p. 11. The nature-defying device allows a man to "nurse" an adoptive infant through a tube extended from the infant's mouth to the man's nipple via a baby bottle.

[3]C. D. King, "The Meaning of Normal," *Yale Journal of Biology and Medicine* 18 (1945): 493-501.

[4]Gary Greenberg, "Right Answers, Wrong Reasons: Revisiting the Deletion of Homosexuality from the DSM," *Review of General Psychology* 1, no. 3 (1997): 256-70.

[5]J. Satinover, "Reflections from Jeffrey Satinover," *NARTH Bulletin,* April 1995, p. 3.

[6]G. A. Rekers, *Handbook of Child and Adolescent Sexual Problems* (New York: Lexington, 1995); Kenneth Zucker and Susan Bradley, *Gender Identity Disorder and Psychosexual Problems in Children and Adolescents* (New York: Guilford, 1995).

[7]Judd Marmor, *Homosexual Behavior: A Modern Reappraisal* (New York: BasicBooks, 1980), p. 274.

[8]Ibid.

[9]Ibid., p. 19.

[10]Ibid., p. 274.

[11]Zucker and Bradley, *Gender Identity Disorder,* p. 270.

[12]T. Sandfort et al., "Same-Sex Sexual Behavior and Psychiatric Disorders: Findings from the Netherlands Mental Health Survey and Incidence Study (NEMESIS)," *Archives of General Psychiatry* 58 (2001): 85-91.

[13]Ibid.

[14]J. M. Bailey, "Commentary: Homosexuality and Mental Illness," *Archives of General Psychiatry* 56 (1999): 876-80.

[15]Peter LaBarbera, "Gay Activists Target Dr. Laura," *NARTH Bulletin,* December 1999, p. 25.

[16]Joseph Nicolosi, "On the Right to Self-Determination," *NARTH Bulletin,* August 2000, p. 1.

[17]Norine Johnson, "President's Column," *Monitor in Psychology,* July-August 2001, p. 3.

[18]Richard Isay, "Remove Gender Identity Disorder in DSM," *Psychiatric News* 32, no. 22 (1997): 9; M. Coleman, "Nontraditional Boys: A Minority in Need of Reassessment," *Child Welfare* 65 (1986): 252-69.

[19]S. Kirk and H. Kutchins, *Making Us Crazy* (New York: Free Press, 1977), chap. 4.

[20]Ibid.

[21]S. Kirk and H. Kutchins, "Standards Higher, Success Assured, But DSM-IV Book 'A Travesty,' " *The National Psychologist,* September-October 1994, p. 12.

[22]Stuart Kirk and Herb Kutchins, *The Selling of DSM: The Rhetoric of Science in Psychiatry* (New York: De-Gruyter, 1992).

[23]Jeffrey Satinover, *Homosexuality and the Politics of Truth* (Grand Rapids, Mich.: Baker/Hamewith, 1996), p. 146.

[24]M. Weinberg and C. Williams, *Male Homosexuals: Their Problems and Adaptations* (New York: Oxford University Press, 1974).

[25]Linda Ames Nicolosi, "Gay Activists Describe Their Values," *NARTH Bulletin,* April 1999, p. 12, quoting from *The Gay and Lesbian Review* 5, no. 2 (1998): 24 (Gabriel Rotello, "This Is Sexual Ecology") and 27 (Michelangelo Signorile, "Nostalgia Trip").

[26]D. McWhirter and A. Mattison, *The Male Couple* (Englewood Cliffs, N.J.: Prentice-Hall, 1984).

[27]Daryl Bem, "Exotic Becomes Erotic: A Developmental Theory of Sexual Orientation," *Psychological Review* 103 (1996): 332.

[28]K. J. Zucker et al., "A Gender Identity Interview for Children," *Journal of Personality Assessment* 61 (1993): 443-56.

[29]M. Hoffman, *The Gay World: Male Homosexuality and the Social Creation of Evil,* (New York: BasicBooks, 1968), p. 17.

[30]Barry Dank, "The Homosexual," in *Sexual Deviance and Sexual Deviants,* eds. E. Goode and R. Troiden (New York: William Morrow, 1974), p. 191.

[31]A. Bell and M. Weinberg, *Homosexualities: A Study of Diversity Among Men and Women* (New York: Simon & Schuster, 1978), p. 92.

[32]Joe Dallas, *A Strong Delusion: Confronting the "Gay Christian" Movement* (Eugene, Ore.: Harvest House, 1996), p. 48.

[33]Ibid., p. 49.

[34]Charles Socarides, *A Freedom Too Far* (Phoenix: Adam Margrave, 1995), p. 66.

[35]S. Jones and M. Yarhouse, *Homosexuality: The Use of Scientific Research in the Church's Moral Debate* (Downers Grove, Ill.: InterVarsity Press, 2000), pp. 43-44.

[36]Peter LaBarbera, "Gay Task Force Conference Includes 'Public Sex' Activists," *Lambda Report,* January-February 1999, pp. 1-2.

[37]Michael Shernoff, "Monogamy and Gay Men: When Are Open Relationships a Therapeutic Option?" *Family Therapy Networker,* March-April 1999, pp. 63-71.

Chapter 9: The Healing Process

[1]Dr. Rekers, letter to Dr. Nicolosi, October 26, 2001.

[2]G. Remafedi, J. Farrow and R. Deisher, "Risk Factors for Attempted Suicide in Gay and Bisexual Youth," *Pediatrics* 87, no. 6 (1991): 869-75.

[3]George Rekers, ed., *Handbook of Child and Adolescent Sexual Problems* (New York: Lexington, 1995).

[4]Kenneth Zucker and Susan Bradley, *Gender Identity Disorder and Psychosexual Problems in Children and Adolescents* (New York: Guilford, 1995), p. 282.

Chapter 10: A Mother's Journal

[1]R. S. Hogg et al., "Modelling the Impact of HIV Disease on Mortality in Gay and Bisexual Men," *In-*

ternational Journal of Epidemiology 26, no. 3 (1997): 657-61.

[2]Andrew Sullivan, Love Undetectable: Notes on Friendship, Sex and Survival (New York: Knopf, 1998), p. 202.

[3]Andrew Sullivan, Virtually Normal: An Argument About Homosexuality (New York: Knopf, 1995).

[4]E. Coleman, "Developmental Stages of the Coming-out Process," in Homosexuality: Social, Psychological, and Biological Issues, W. Paul et al. (Beverly Hills: Sage, 1982), pp. 149-57.

[5]David McWhirter and Andrew Mattison, The Male Couple: How Relationships Develop (Englewood Cliffs, N.J.: Prentice-Hall, 1984), p. 256.

[6]Ibid., p. 256.

[7]Paul Van de Ven et al., "A Comparative Demographic and Sexual Profile of Older Homosexually Active Men," Journal of Sex Research 34, no. 4 (1997): 349-60.

[8]Linda Ames Nicolosi, "Interview with Gordon Opp," NARTH Bulletin, April 1999, p. 3.